ABC

OF TYPOGRAPHY

First published in English in 2019
by SelfMadeHero
139–141 Pancras Road
London NW1 1UN
www.selfmadehero.com

English translation © 2019 SelfMadeHero

Written by David Rault
Illustrated by Seyhan Argun, Aseyn, François Ayroles,
Hervé Bourhis, Alexandre Clérisse, Olivier Deloye
Libon, Delphine Panique, Jake Raynal, Anne Simon, Singeon
Original layout design by Jean-Christophe Menu

Translated by Edward Gauvin

Publishing Director: Emma Hayley
Sales & Marketing Manager: Sam Humphrey
Editorial & Production Manager: Guillaume Rater
English edition layout design: Txabi Jones
UK Publicist: Paul Smith
With thanks to: Nick de Somogyi

© Gallimard, 2018

A CIP record for this book is available from the British Library

ISBN: 978-1-910593-71-4

10 9 8 7 6 5 4 3 2 1

Printed and bound in Slovenia

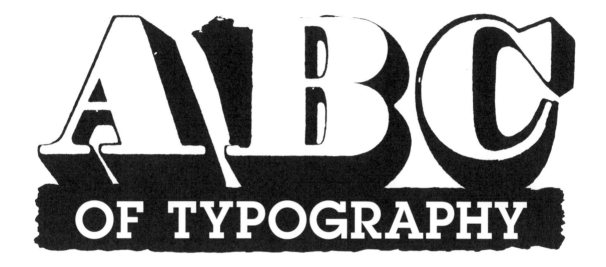

ABC
OF TYPOGRAPHY

Written by
DAVID RAULT

Illustrated by
SEYHAN ARGUN, ASEYN, FRANÇOIS AYROLES,
HERVÉ BOURHIS, ALEXANDRE CLÉRISSE,
OLIVIER DELOYE, LIBON, DELPHINE PANIQUE,
JAKE RAYNAL, ANNE SIMON, SINGEON

Translated by
EDWARD GAUVIN

SELF MADE HERO

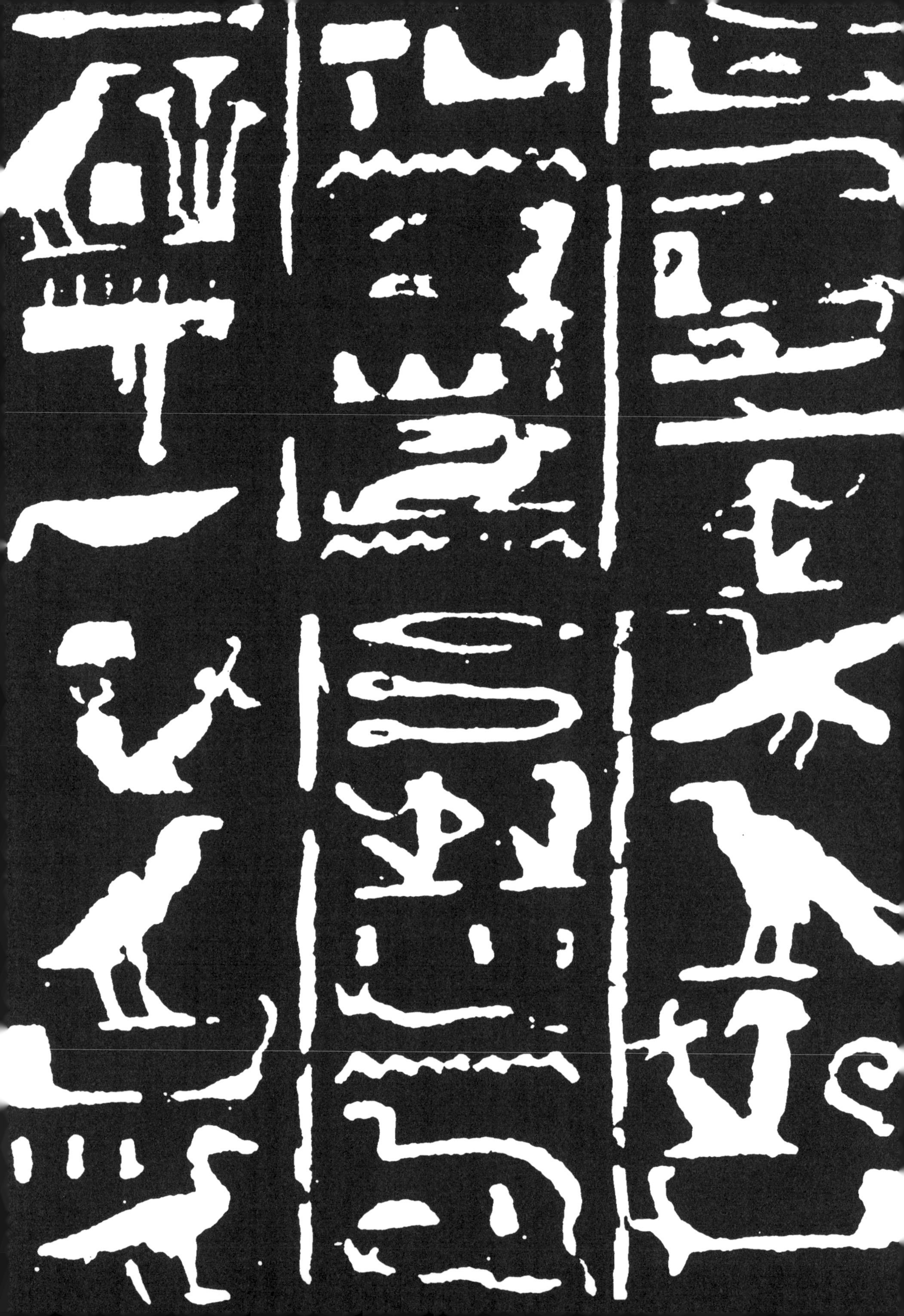

CONTENTS

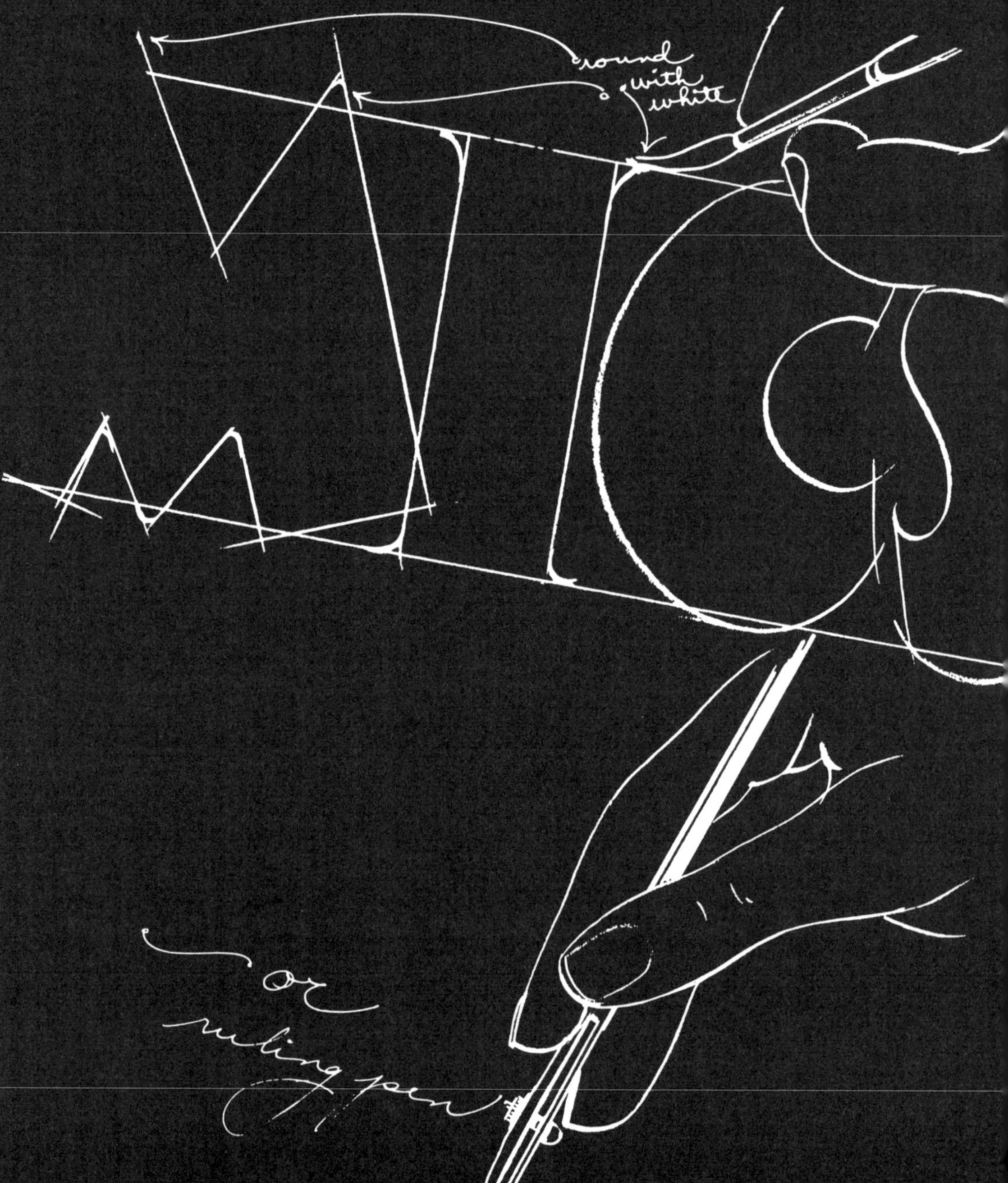
round with white
or ruling pen

PREFACE

Typography, comics... they were destined to meet. Better still that such a meeting should entail one telling the other's story, as is the case here.

A mass medium by its very nature, comics as a pop cultural phenomenon found a home in early 20th century America, only to be disdained for its very popularity and ability to reach audiences. That is, until the 1960s, when in one of those sudden reversals that lend cultural life its charm, public opinion changed overnight, and comics found themselves literally praised to the skies, promoted to the rank of the "ninth art".

But in the end, whether the medium is disdained or idolized matters little. What's important is that it gratify us now and then with unforgettable works: for starters, Winsor McCay's fabulous and unsurpassable *Little Nemo in Slumberland*, which began appearing in the Sunday comics section of the *New York Herald* in 1905.

Over the course of more than five centuries of existence, typography has never exactly known disdain — but has its fate in terms of broader recognition really been more enviable? Nothing could be less certain. Its fifty-two letters (twenty-six capital, twenty-six lower-case) — its letters patent, so to speak — belong to that silent domain of things made so commonplace by daily use that we look right past them: unseen, unsung, and quite forgotten.

All things being equal, it must be admitted that typography played its own little part in maintaining this cordial neglect, for it is true indeed that convolutions never make a subject easier to understand, especially for the general public. And if ever a subject seemed to delight in its own convolutedness, it was typography!

Indeed, until recently considered an almost universal part of the printing and reproduction process, typography nevertheless sank without trace into the mists of oblivion when the age of film gradually replaced the age of lead halfway through the last century. However, this eventuality did not prevent typography from rising again under the same name, this time referring to an activity indirectly tied to what it previously specified: namely, *typeface design*.

For herein lies typography's fundamental ambiguity today: is it a technique that, with its close, long-standing ties to printing, now denotes only a late if major chapter in the history of the written word? Or is it an applied art that, with its fifty-two letters constantly revised to meet fashions and variations in style, dreams of being legitimized as an art unto itself — the tenth?

Whatever the answers to these questions (if they even require definitive answers), we can at least note that typography has this much in common with comics: it, too, gave us a timeless masterpiece early on — Garamond, a typeface that splendidly balanced audacity of design with the constraints of legibility, and which since 1544 has been transforming every page of text set in its admirable italic into a true visual symphony.

Tracing the course of eras from the present back to the dawn of civilization, should it be any surprise to find that ancient peoples, fumbling their way along through trial and error, with little notion of posterity, proved no less industrious or innovative than their distant descendants?

The Sumerians, for instance: did they suspect, when carving their cuneiform into clay tablets for purely utilitarian ends 3,500 years before our time, that they were in fact inventing a *system* of writing? And the Egyptians, driven by their perfectionist concern for all things sacred: did they suspect that by painstakingly slaving away over their hieroglyphic drawings seven centuries later, they'd invent the *aesthetics* of writing? Putting the finishing touches in 1000 BCE to what would become our alphabet, did the Phoenicians realize they were endowing humanity with the ideal instrument for expressing and communicating ideas and knowledge for the next thirty centuries (and more, if things work out)? Likewise, from atop his imperial throne, could Charlemagne have known that by forcing his Carolingian minuscule on monks, he was setting in motion a genuine cultural revolution — the *Admonitio generalis* of 789? By lining up and inking his little movable letters, and working his rudimentary manual press, did Gutenberg imagine... et cetera.

So many remarkable events and picturesque anecdotes speckle a history informed, for once, more by exhilarating discoveries rather than blood-spattered feats of arms. A history that the book you now hold proposes to reconstruct, as convoluted as a Möbius strip.

Or as sequential as a comic.

Jean Alessandrini
Strasbourg, August 2018

INTRODUCTION

Typography is everywhere.

The Internet is 95% typography. As our primary medium of communication, typography is of fundamental importance. But how much do we really know about this astonishing tool? Why does our letter "A" look the way it does, and not otherwise? Why does a poster set in Comic Sans seem less serious than one that uses Trajan?

Books about the history of typography abound, of course, as do online instructional videos and websites. But until now, those looking for a different way of tackling the material had few if any alternatives. I know for a fact that there were no comics about typography.

So I had an idea: to write the first-ever graphic history of Latin type, and in so doing make fundamental knowledge about a humongous swath of Western culture available to new audiences. I pitched my idea to some of our generation's most talented artists, and, lucky me — they decided to take up the challenge.

That is how the book you now hold in your hands came into being, and what it is trying to accomplish. It is aimed at amateurs and enthusiasts who want to find out more about the typefaces that have become so familiar to us, from their presence on street signs, newspapers, movie titles, websites, ads, packaging, and smartphone screens — and about which, in the end, we know almost nothing at all.

David Rault

THE BIRTH
OF WRITING

ASEYN

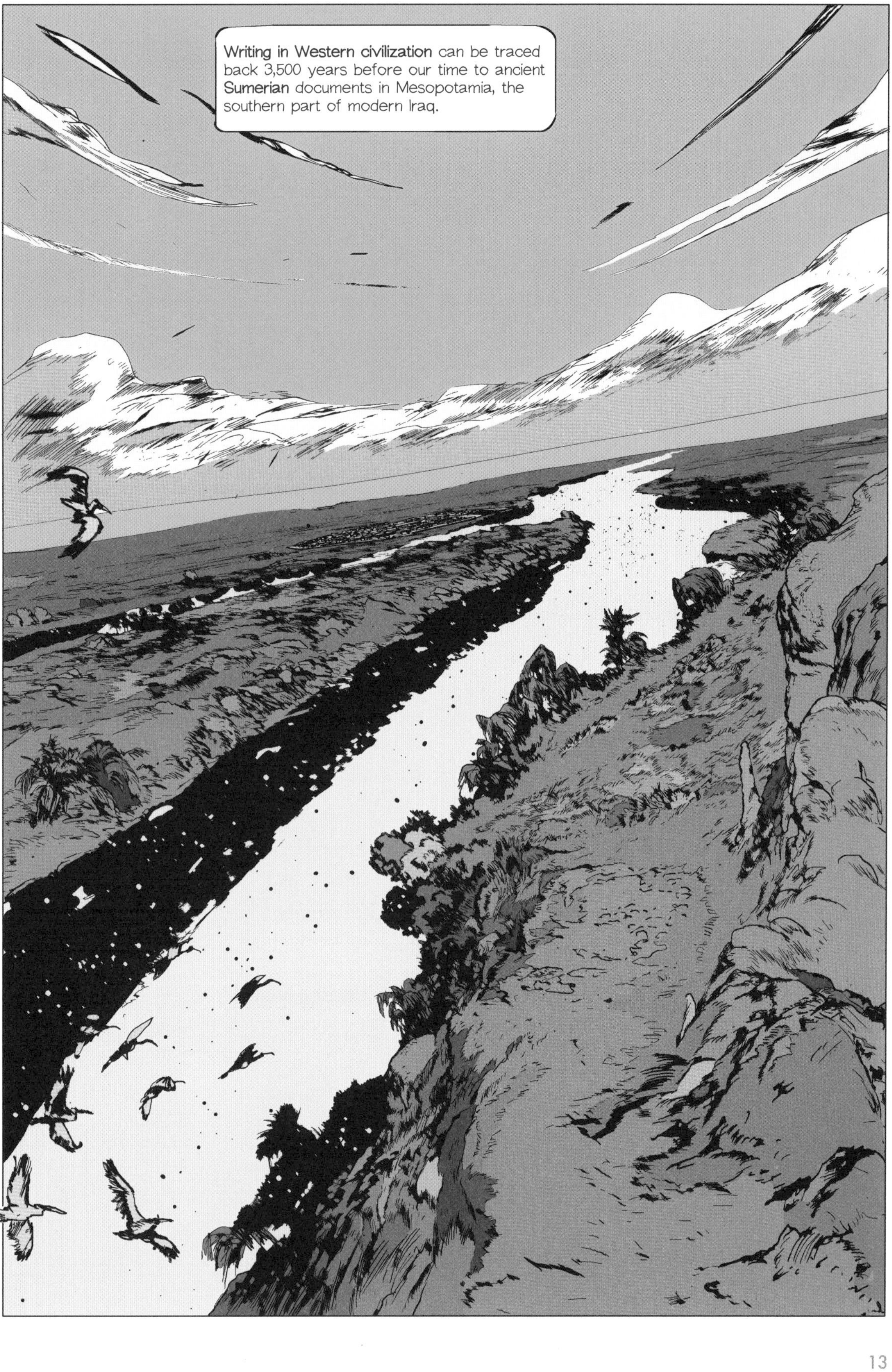
Writing in Western civilization can be traced back 3,500 years before our time to ancient **Sumerian** documents in Mesopotamia, the southern part of modern Iraq.

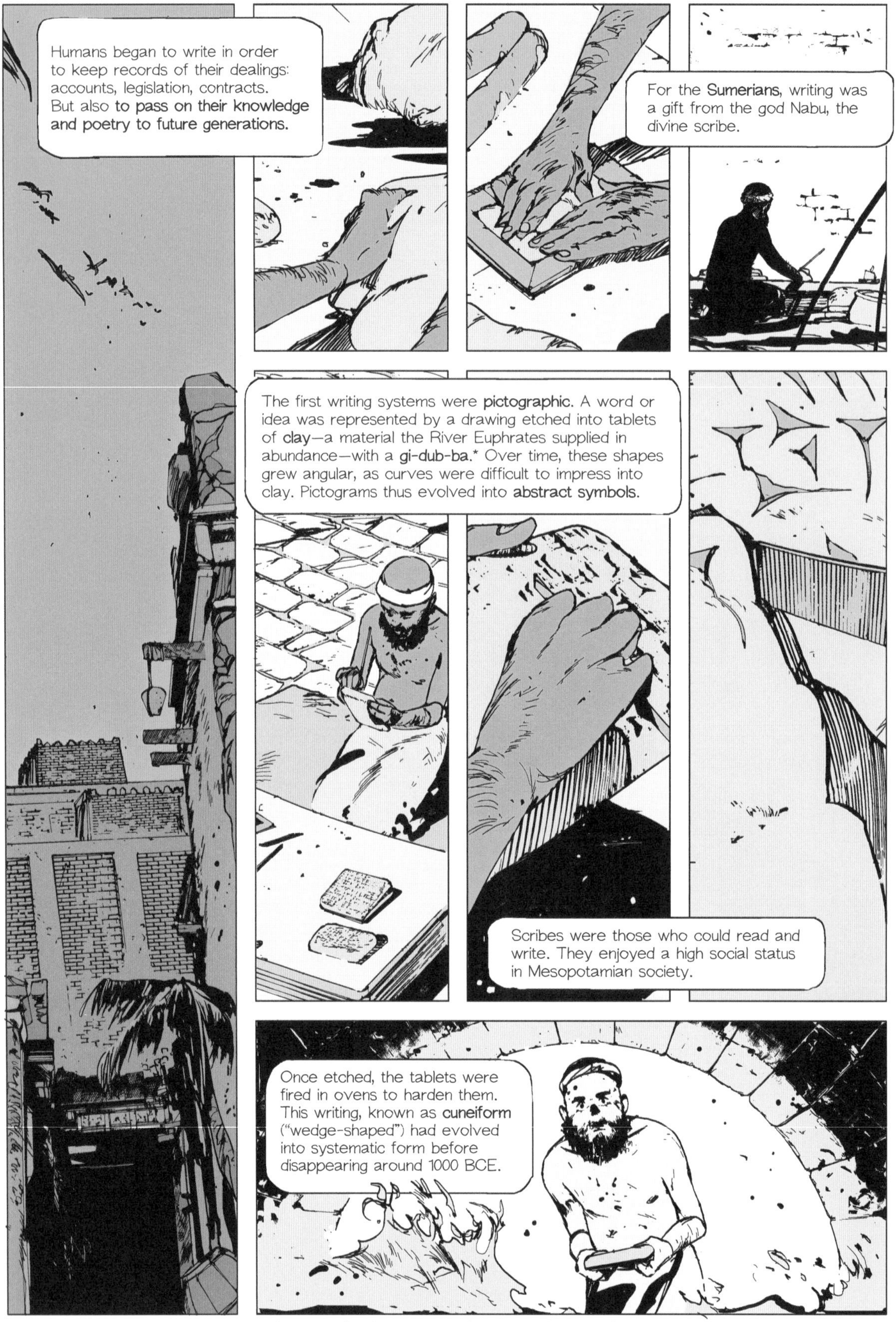
Humans began to write in order to keep records of their dealings: accounts, legislation, contracts. But also to pass on their knowledge and poetry to future generations.
For the Sumerians, writing was a gift from the god Nabu, the divine scribe.
The first writing systems were pictographic. A word or idea was represented by a drawing etched into tablets of clay—a material the River Euphrates supplied in abundance—with a gi-dub-ba.* Over time, these shapes grew angular, as curves were difficult to impress into clay. Pictograms thus evolved into abstract symbols.
Scribes were those who could read and write. They enjoyed a high social status in Mesopotamian society.
Once etched, the tablets were fired in ovens to harden them. This writing, known as cuneiform ("wedge-shaped") had evolved into systematic form before disappearing around 1000 BCE.

* Sumerian (lit. "tablet reed") for *stylus*. See the Glossary at end of this book.

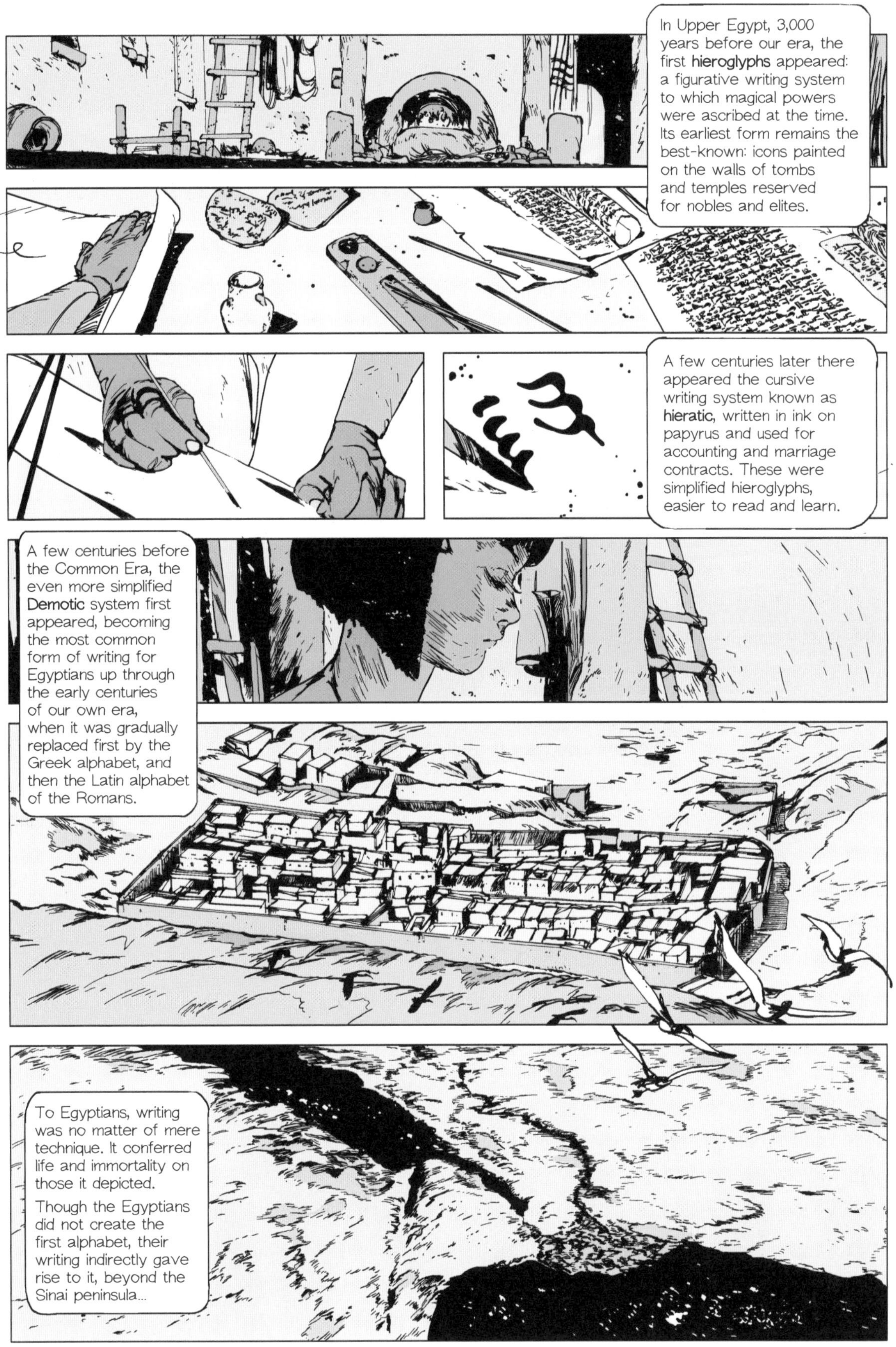
In Upper Egypt, 3,000 years before our era, the first hieroglyphs appeared: a figurative writing system to which magical powers were ascribed at the time. Its earliest form remains the best-known: icons painted on the walls of tombs and temples reserved for nobles and elites.
A few centuries later there appeared the cursive writing system known as hieratic, written in ink on papyrus and used for accounting and marriage contracts. These were simplified hieroglyphs, easier to read and learn.
A few centuries before the Common Era, the even more simplified Demotic system first appeared, becoming the most common form of writing for Egyptians up through the early centuries of our own era, when it was gradually replaced first by the Greek alphabet, and then the Latin alphabet of the Romans.
To Egyptians, writing was no matter of mere technique. It conferred life and immortality on those it depicted.
Though the Egyptians did not create the first alphabet, their writing indirectly gave rise to it, beyond the Sinai peninsula...

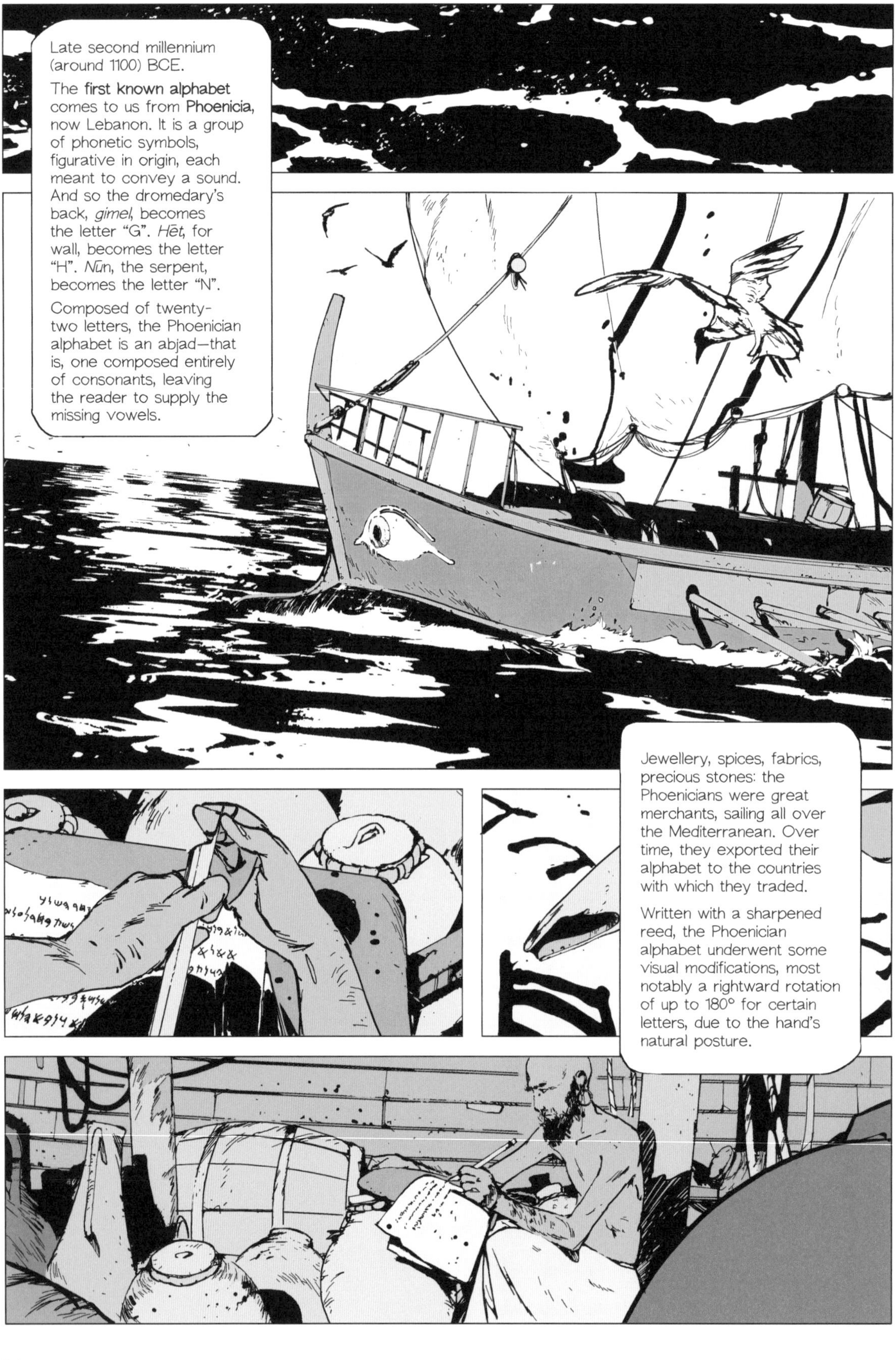
Late second millennium (around 1100) BCE.
The **first known alphabet** comes to us from **Phoenicia,** now Lebanon. It is a group of phonetic symbols, figurative in origin, each meant to convey a sound. And so the dromedary's back, *gimel*, becomes the letter "G". *Hēt*, for wall, becomes the letter "H". *Nūn*, the serpent, becomes the letter "N".
Composed of twenty-two letters, the Phoenician alphabet is an abjad—that is, one composed entirely of consonants, leaving the reader to supply the missing vowels.
Jewellery, spices, fabrics, precious stones: the Phoenicians were great merchants, sailing all over the Mediterranean. Over time, they exported their alphabet to the countries with which they traded.
Written with a sharpened reed, the Phoenician alphabet underwent some visual modifications, most notably a rightward rotation of up to 180° for certain letters, due to the hand's natural posture.

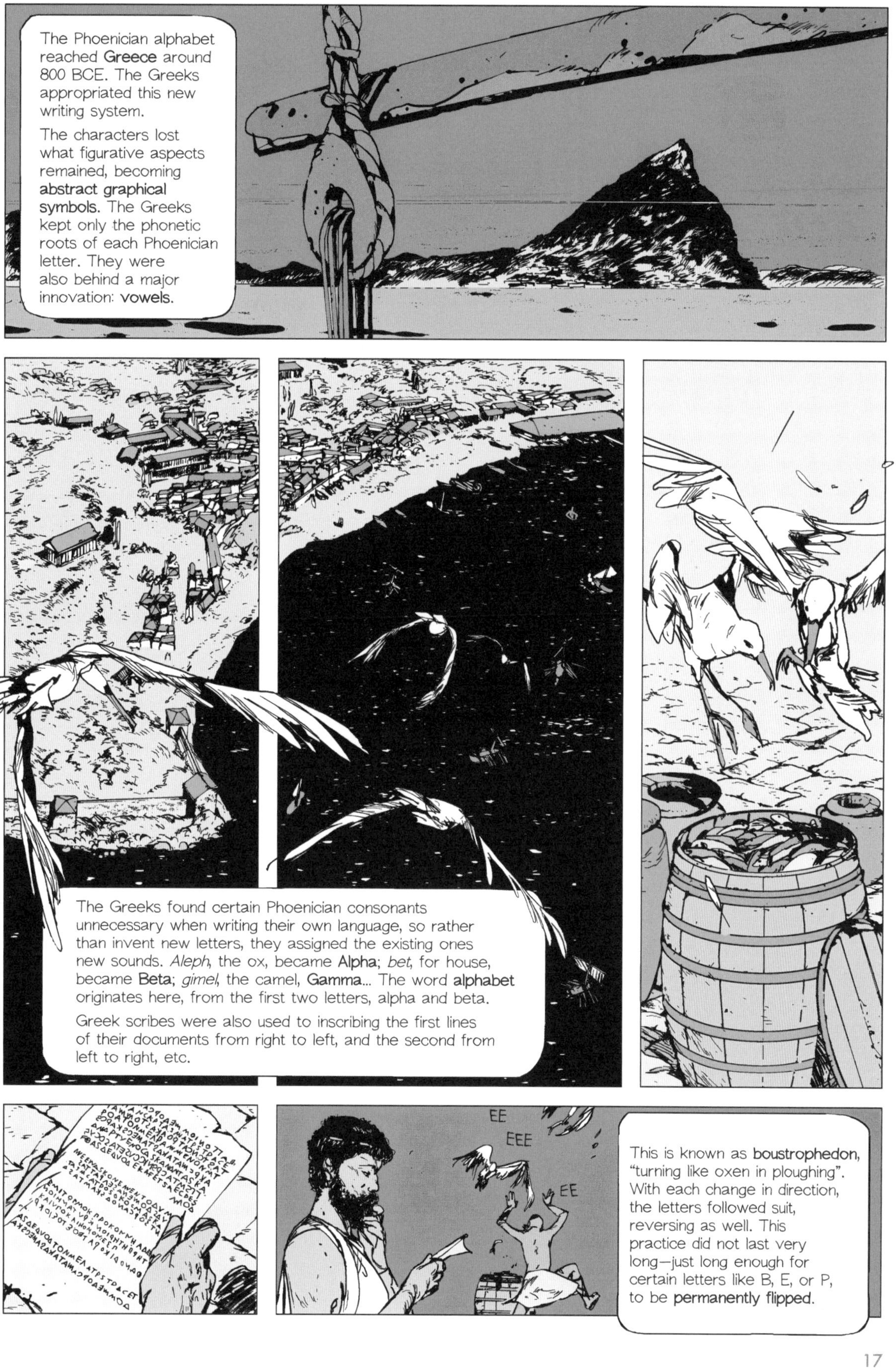
The Phoenician alphabet reached **Greece** around 800 BCE. The Greeks appropriated this new writing system.
The characters lost what figurative aspects remained, becoming **abstract graphical symbols.** The Greeks kept only the phonetic roots of each Phoenician letter. They were also behind a major innovation: **vowels.**
The Greeks found certain Phoenician consonants unnecessary when writing their own language, so rather than invent new letters, they assigned the existing ones new sounds. *Aleph*, the ox, became **Alpha**; *bet*, for house, became **Beta**; *gimel*, the camel, **Gamma**... The word **alphabet** originates here, from the first two letters, alpha and beta.
Greek scribes were also used to inscribing the first lines of their documents from right to left, and the second from left to right, etc.
EE
EEE
EE
This is known as **boustrophedon**, "turning like oxen in ploughing". With each change in direction, the letters followed suit, reversing as well. This practice did not last very long—just long enough for certain letters like B, E, or P, to be **permanently flipped**.

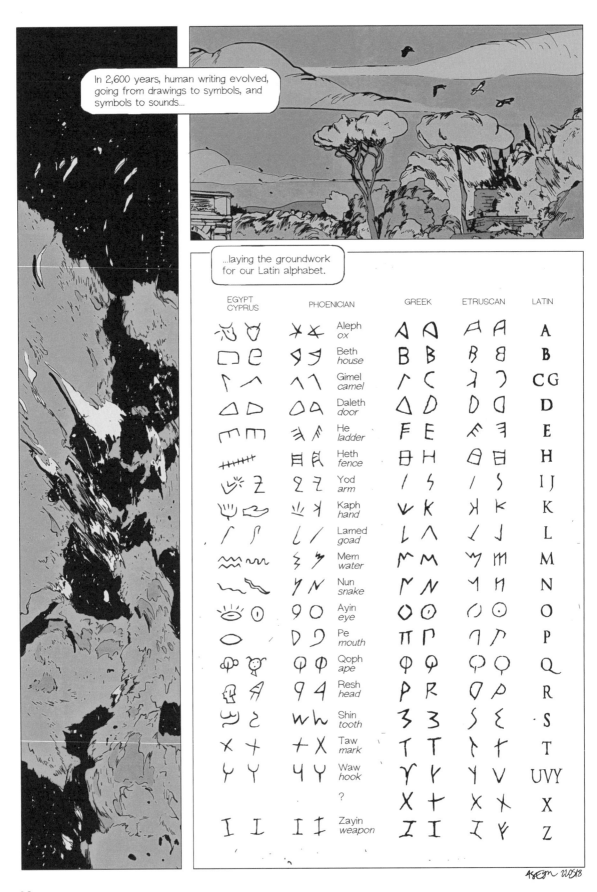

In 2,600 years, human writing evolved, going from drawings to symbols, and symbols to sounds...

...laying the groundwork for our Latin alphabet.

EGYPT CYPRUS		PHOENICIAN			GREEK		ETRUSCAN		LATIN
				Aleph *ox*					A
				Beth *house*					B
				Gimel *camel*					C G
				Daleth *door*					D
				He *ladder*					E
				Heth *fence*					H
				Yod *arm*					I J
				Kaph *hand*					K
				Lamed *goad*					L
				Mem *water*					M
				Nun *snake*					N
				Ayin *eye*					O
				Pe *mouth*					P
				Qoph *ape*					Q
				Resh *head*					R
				Shin *tooth*					S
				Taw *mark*					T
				Waw *hook*					UVY
				?					X
				Zayin *weapon*					Z

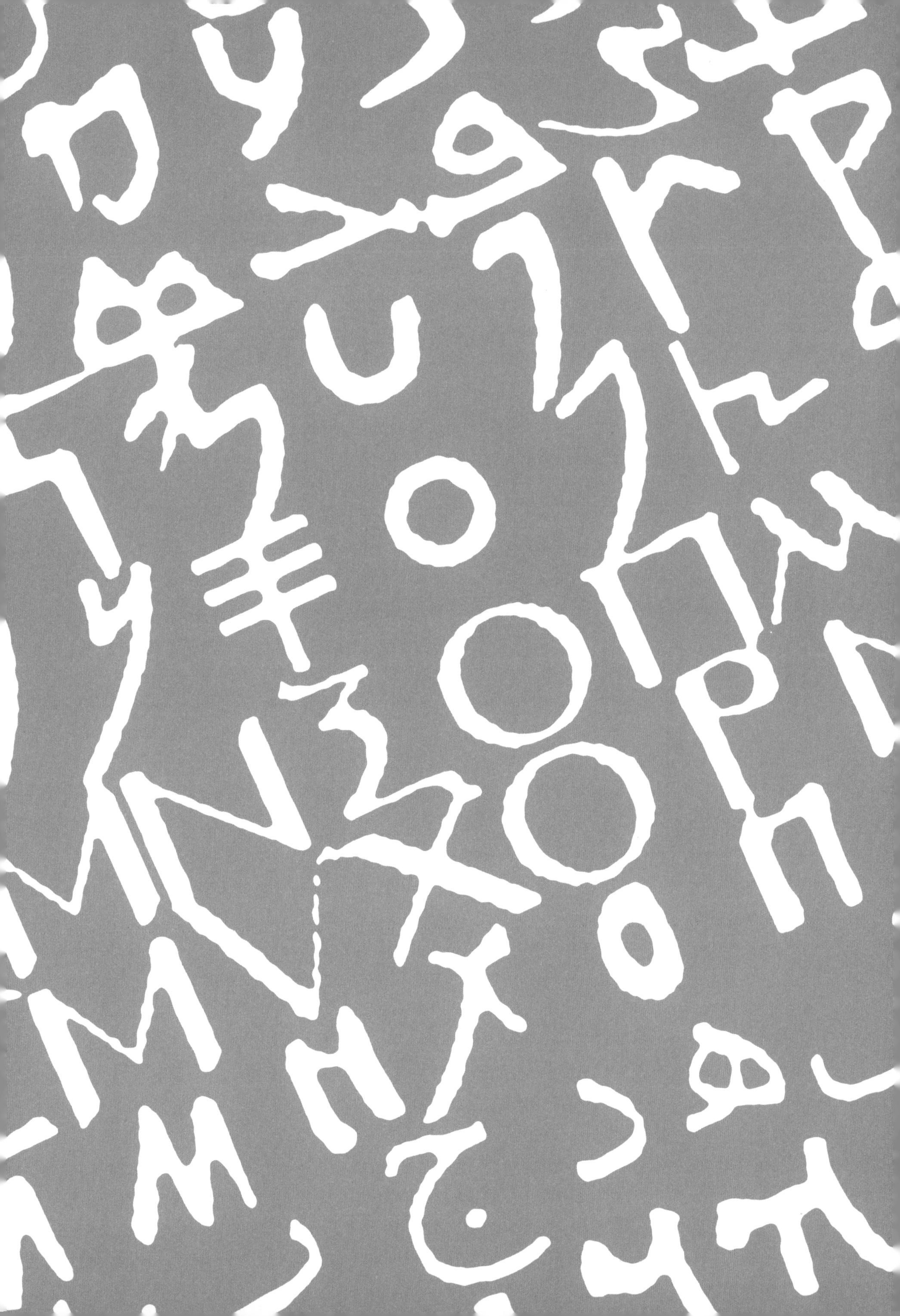

THE ROMANS
AND THEIR WRITING

SINGEON

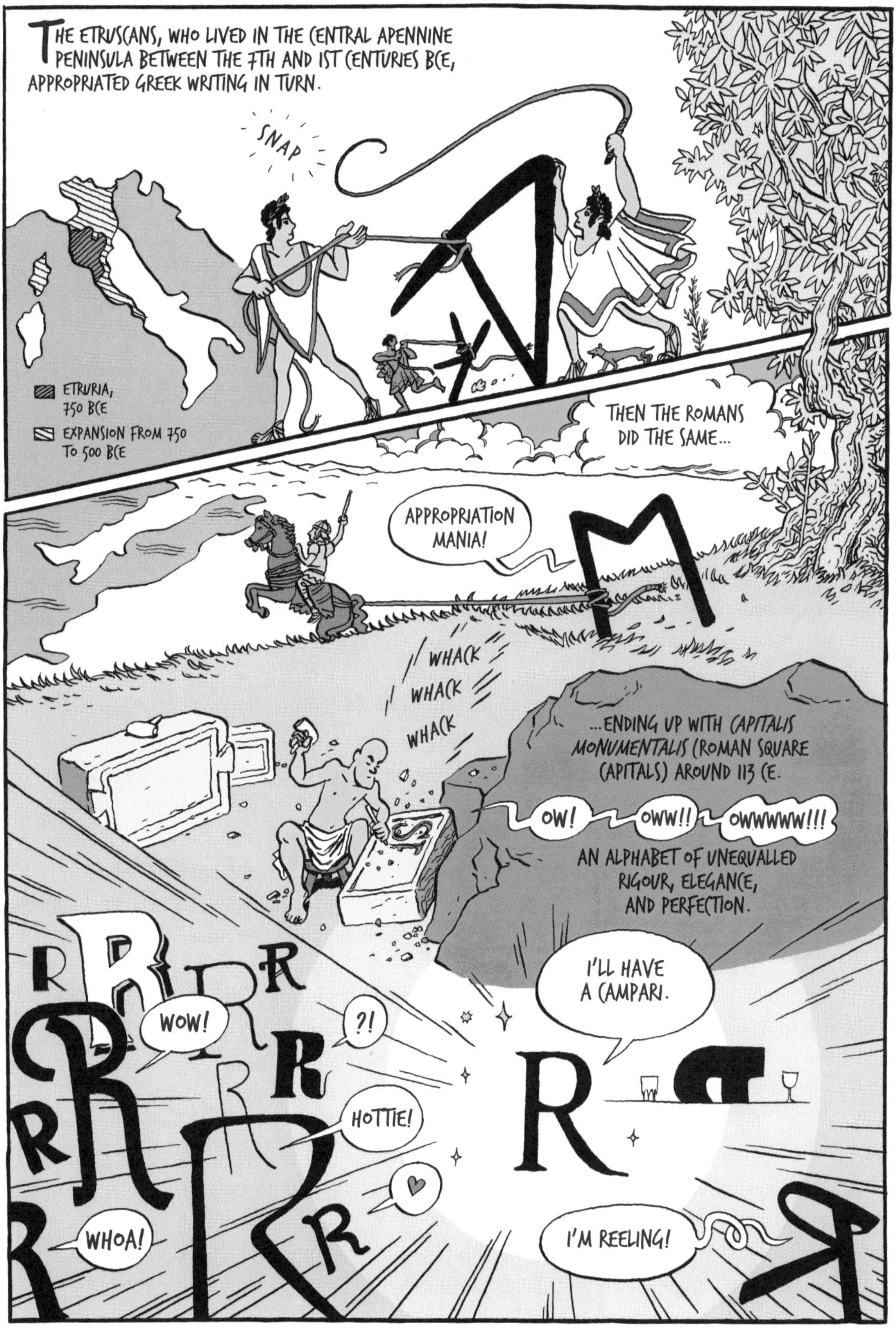
THE ETRUSCANS, WHO LIVED IN THE CENTRAL APENNINE PENINSULA BETWEEN THE 7TH AND 1ST CENTURIES BCE, APPROPRIATED GREEK WRITING IN TURN.
SNAP
ETRURIA, 750 BCE
EXPANSION FROM 750 TO 500 BCE
THEN THE ROMANS DID THE SAME...
APPROPRIATION MANIA!
WHACK
WHACK
WHACK
...ENDING UP WITH *CAPITALIS MONUMENTALIS* (ROMAN SQUARE CAPITALS) AROUND 113 CE.
OW!
OWW!!
OWWWWW!!!
AN ALPHABET OF UNEQUALLED RIGOUR, ELEGANCE, AND PERFECTION.
WOW!
?!
HOTTIE!
WHOA!
I'LL HAVE A CAMPARI.
I'M REELING!

THAT YEAR IN FACT SAW THE COMPLETION OF TRAJAN'S COLUMN,

RAISED IN ROME AS A TRIBUTE TO THE EMPEROR'S EXPLOITS.

MARCUS ULPIUS TRAIANUS A.K.A. **TRAJAN**

THE BASE OF THIS COLUMN FEATURES THE MOST ACCOMPLISHED, MOST BEAUTIFUL, AND MOST FAMOUS EXAMPLE OF THIS ALPHABET.

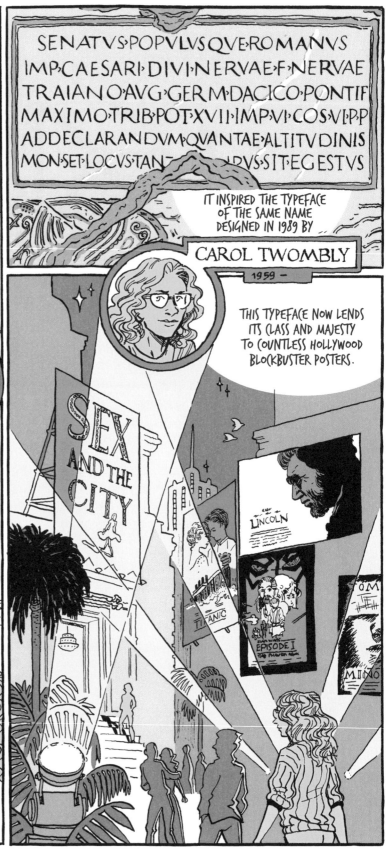

SENATVS·POPVLVSQVE·ROMANVS
IMP·CAESARI·DIVI·NERVAE·F·NERVAE
TRAIANO·AVG·GERM·DACICO·PONTIF
MAXIMO·TRIB·POT·XVII·IMP·VI·COS·VI·P·P
ADDECLARANDVM·QVANTAE·ALTITVDINIS
MONS·ET·LOCVS·TAN~   ~RVS·SIT·EGESTVS

IT INSPIRED THE TYPEFACE OF THE SAME NAME DESIGNED IN 1989 BY

CAROL TWOMBLY

1959 —

THIS TYPEFACE NOW LENDS ITS CLASS AND MAJESTY TO COUNTLESS HOLLYWOOD BLOCKBUSTER POSTERS.

SEX AND THE CITY

LINCOLN

TITANIC

EPISODE I

CLICK

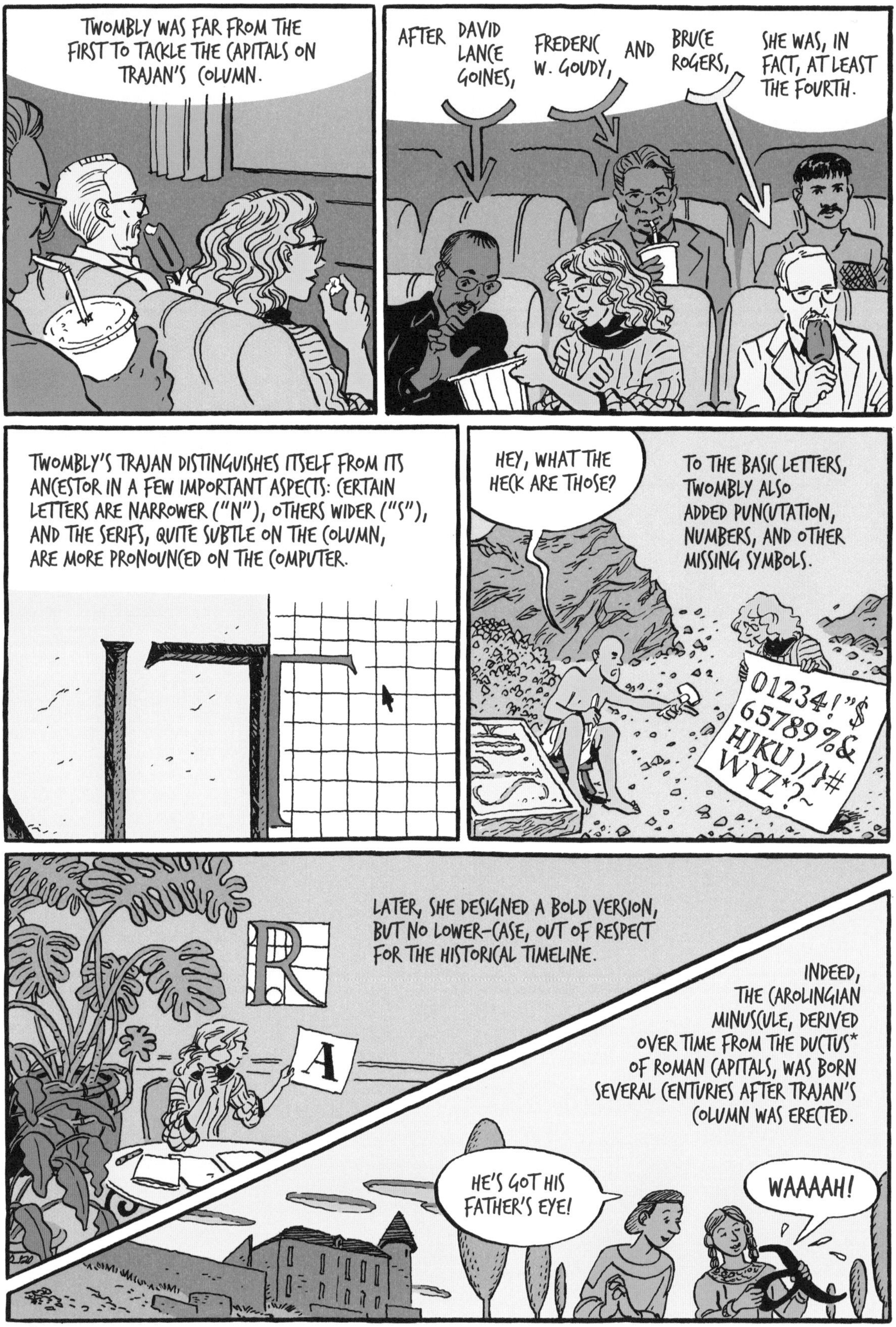
TWOMBLY WAS FAR FROM THE FIRST TO TACKLE THE CAPITALS ON TRAJAN'S COLUMN.
AFTER
DAVID LANCE GOINES,
FREDERIC W. GOUDY,
AND
BRUCE ROGERS,
SHE WAS, IN FACT, AT LEAST THE FOURTH.
TWOMBLY'S TRAJAN DISTINGUISHES ITSELF FROM ITS ANCESTOR IN A FEW IMPORTANT ASPECTS: CERTAIN LETTERS ARE NARROWER ("N"), OTHERS WIDER ("S"), AND THE SERIFS, QUITE SUBTLE ON THE COLUMN, ARE MORE PRONOUNCED ON THE COMPUTER.
HEY, WHAT THE HECK ARE THOSE?
TO THE BASIC LETTERS, TWOMBLY ALSO ADDED PUNCUTATION, NUMBERS, AND OTHER MISSING SYMBOLS.
01234!"$
65789%&
HJKU)/}#
WYZ*?~
LATER, SHE DESIGNED A BOLD VERSION, BUT NO LOWER-CASE, OUT OF RESPECT FOR THE HISTORICAL TIMELINE.
R
A
INDEED, THE CAROLINGIAN MINUSCULE, DERIVED OVER TIME FROM THE DUCTUS* OF ROMAN CAPITALS, WAS BORN SEVERAL CENTURIES AFTER TRAJAN'S COLUMN WAS ERECTED.
HE'S GOT HIS FATHER'S EYE!
WAAAAH!

*SEE THE GLOSSARY AT THE END OF THIS BOOK.

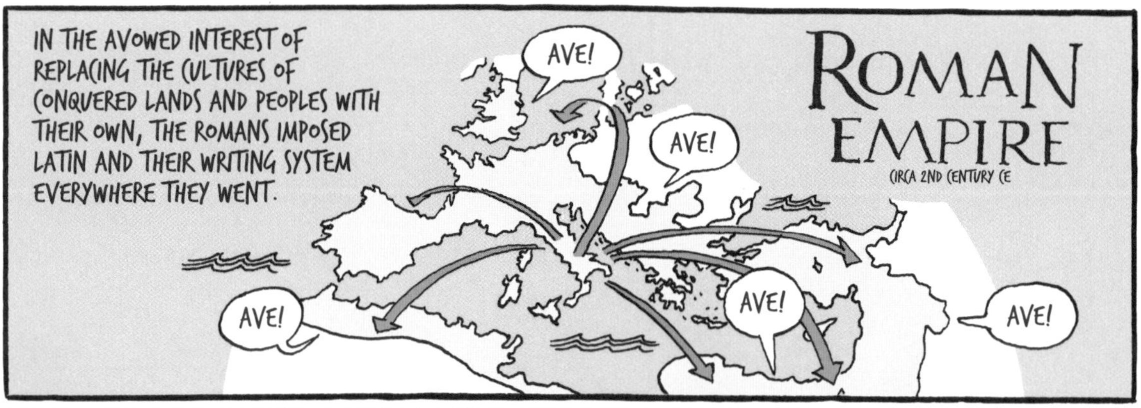
IN THE AVOWED INTEREST OF REPLACING THE CULTURES OF CONQUERED LANDS AND PEOPLES WITH THEIR OWN, THE ROMANS IMPOSED LATIN AND THEIR WRITING SYSTEM EVERYWHERE THEY WENT.
AVE!
ROMAN EMPIRE
CIRCA 2ND CENTURY CE
AVE!
AVE!
AVE!
AVE!

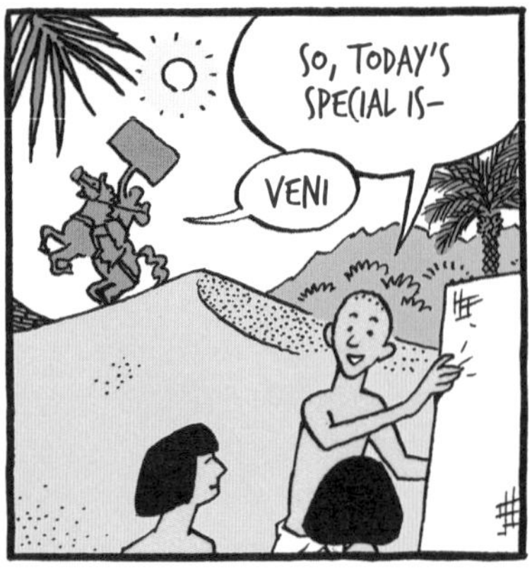
SO, TODAY'S SPECIAL IS–
VENI

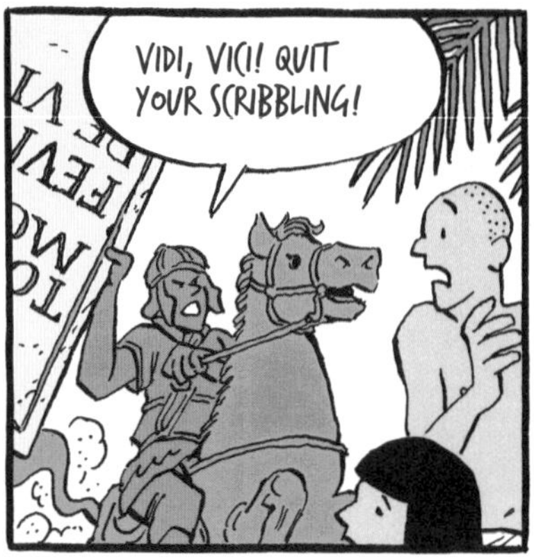
VIDI, VICI! QUIT YOUR SCRIBBLING!

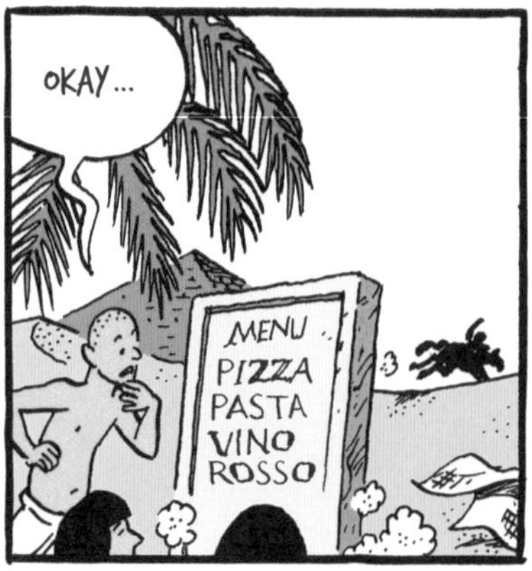
OKAY...
MENU
PIZZA
PASTA
VINO
ROSSO

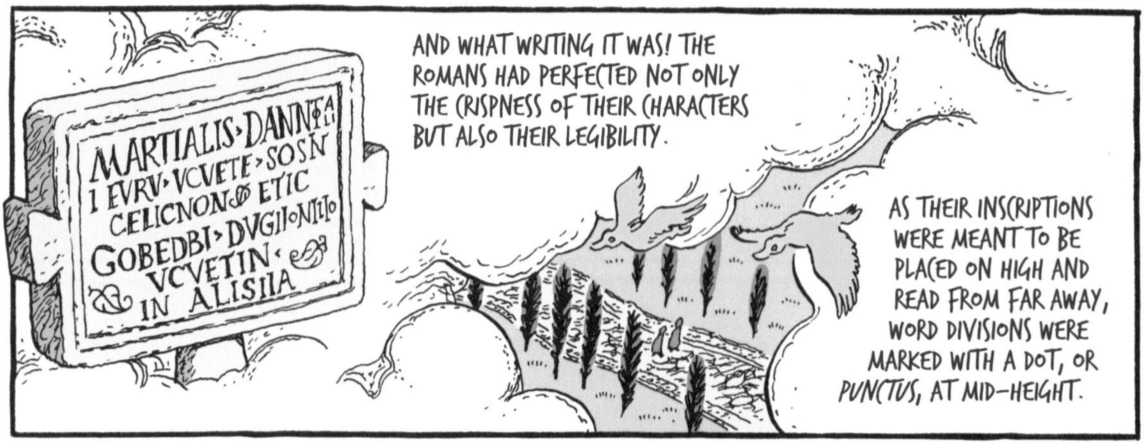
AND WHAT WRITING IT WAS! THE ROMANS HAD PERFECTED NOT ONLY THE CRISPNESS OF THEIR CHARACTERS BUT ALSO THEIR LEGIBILITY.
AS THEIR INSCRIPTIONS WERE MEANT TO BE PLACED ON HIGH AND READ FROM FAR AWAY, WORD DIVISIONS WERE MARKED WITH A DOT, OR *PUNCTUS*, AT MID-HEIGHT.

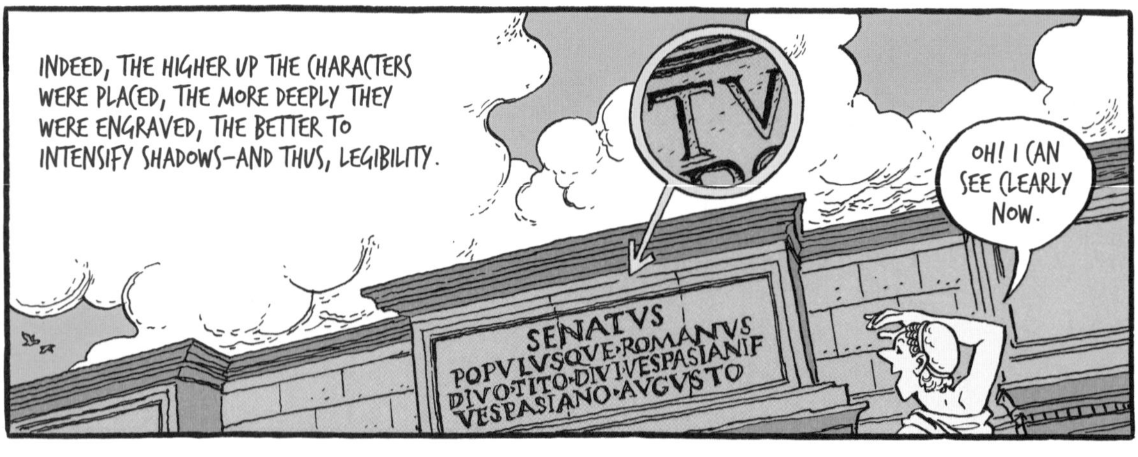
INDEED, THE HIGHER UP THE CHARACTERS WERE PLACED, THE MORE DEEPLY THEY WERE ENGRAVED, THE BETTER TO INTENSIFY SHADOWS–AND THUS, LEGIBILITY.
TV
OH! I CAN SEE CLEARLY NOW.
SENATVS
POPVLVSQVE·ROMANVS
DIVO·TITO·DIVI·VESPASIANI·F
VESPASIANO·AVGVSTO

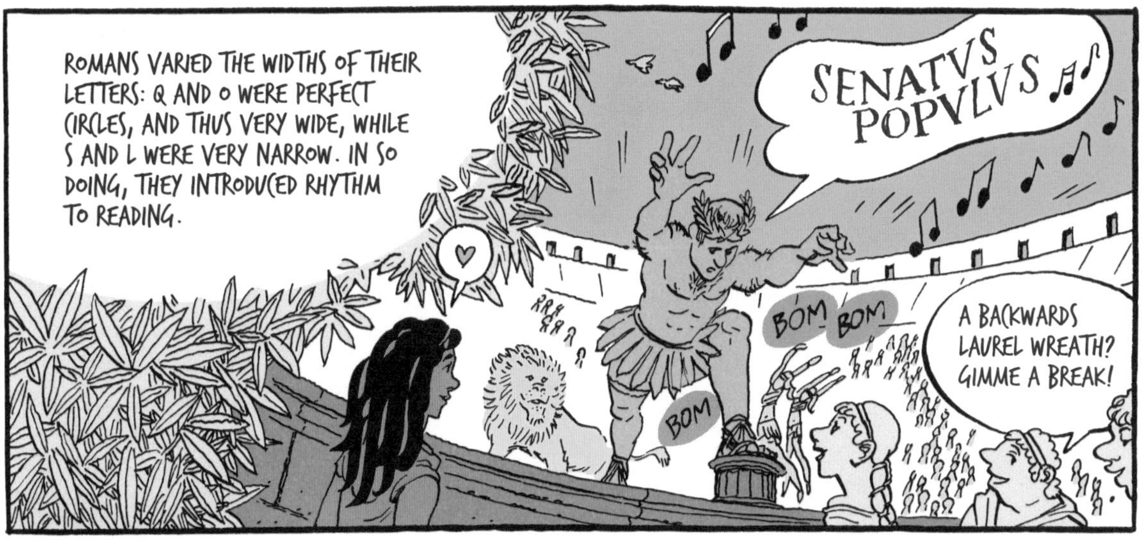
ROMANS VARIED THE WIDTHS OF THEIR LETTERS: Q AND O WERE PERFECT CIRCLES, AND THUS VERY WIDE, WHILE S AND L WERE VERY NARROW. IN SO DOING, THEY INTRODUCED RHYTHM TO READING.
SENATVS POPVLVS
BOM BOM
BOM
A BACKWARDS LAUREL WREATH? GIMME A BREAK!

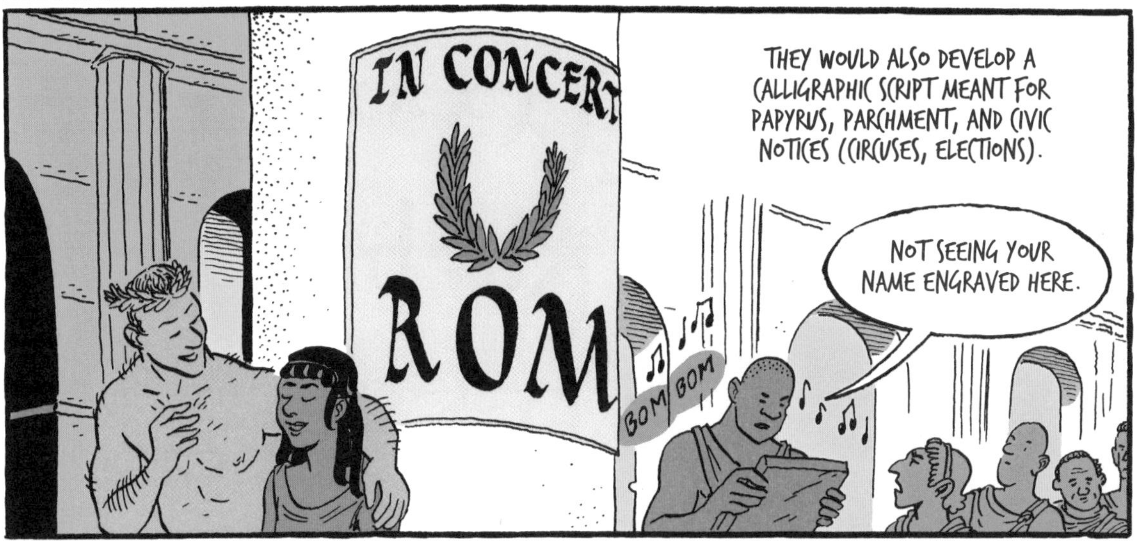
IN CONCERT
ROM
THEY WOULD ALSO DEVELOP A CALLIGRAPHIC SCRIPT MEANT FOR PAPYRUS, PARCHMENT, AND CIVIC NOTICES (CIRCUSES, ELECTIONS).
NOT SEEING YOUR NAME ENGRAVED HERE.
BOM BOM

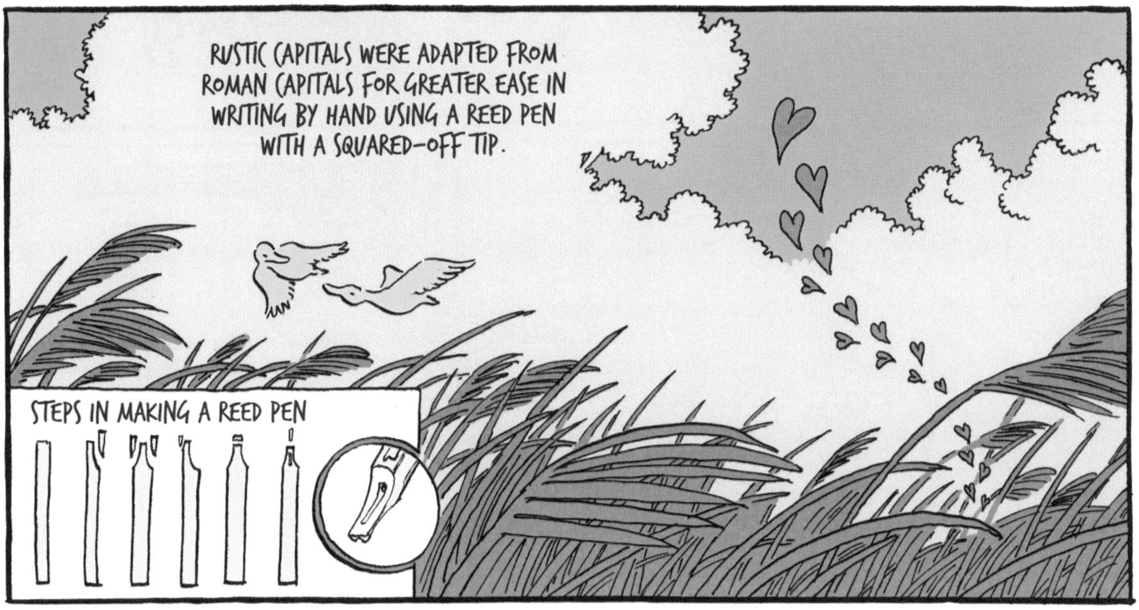
RUSTIC CAPITALS WERE ADAPTED FROM ROMAN CAPITALS FOR GREATER EASE IN WRITING BY HAND USING A REED PEN WITH A SQUARED-OFF TIP.
STEPS IN MAKING A REED PEN

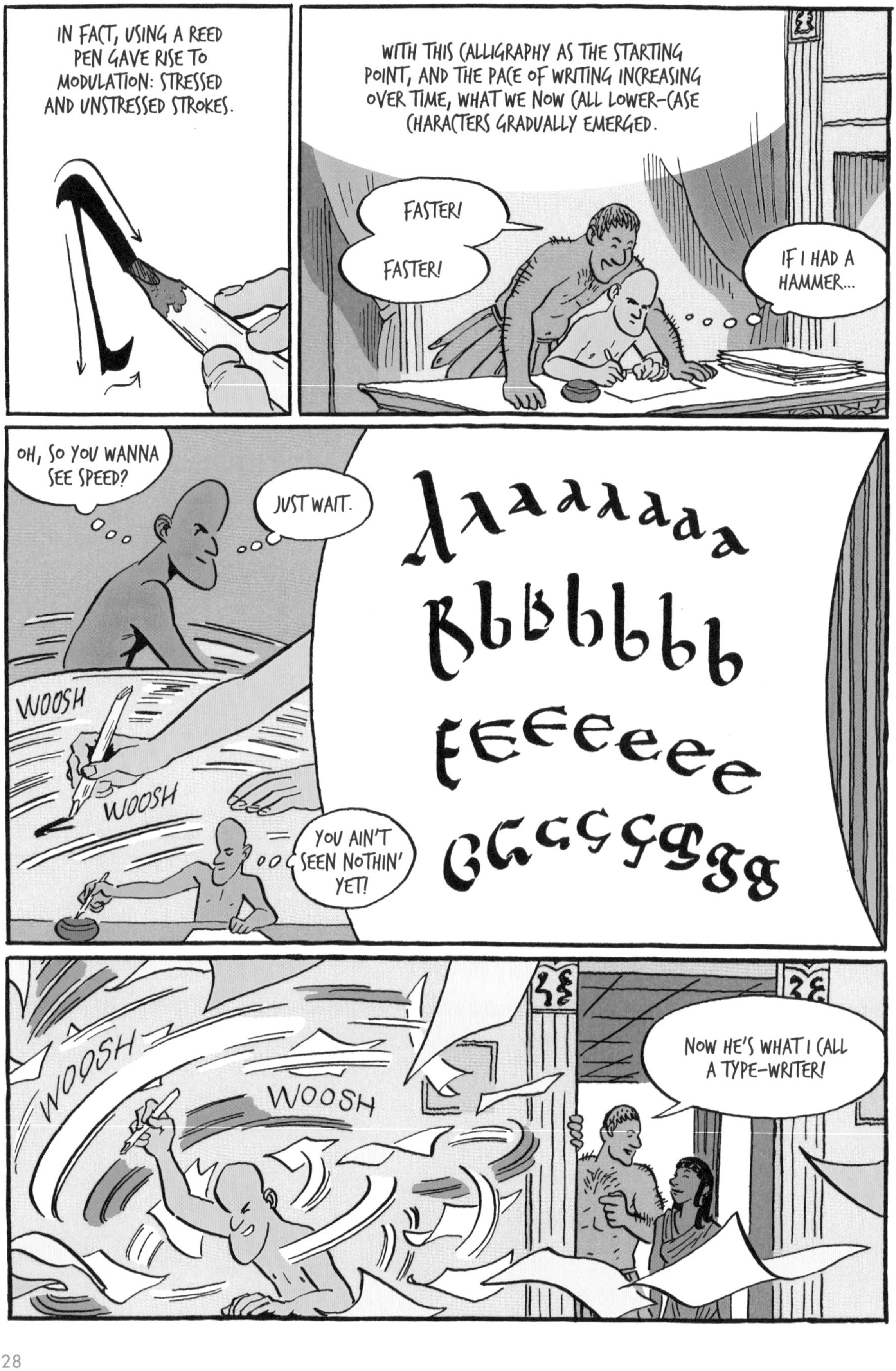
IN FACT, USING A REED PEN GAVE RISE TO MODULATION: STRESSED AND UNSTRESSED STROKES.
WITH THIS CALLIGRAPHY AS THE STARTING POINT, AND THE PACE OF WRITING INCREASING OVER TIME, WHAT WE NOW CALL LOWER-CASE CHARACTERS GRADUALLY EMERGED.
FASTER!
FASTER!
IF I HAD A HAMMER...
OH, SO YOU WANNA SEE SPEED?
JUST WAIT.
WOOSH
WOOSH
YOU AIN'T SEEN NOTHIN' YET!
WOOSH
WOOSH
NOW HE'S WHAT I CALL A TYPE-WRITER!

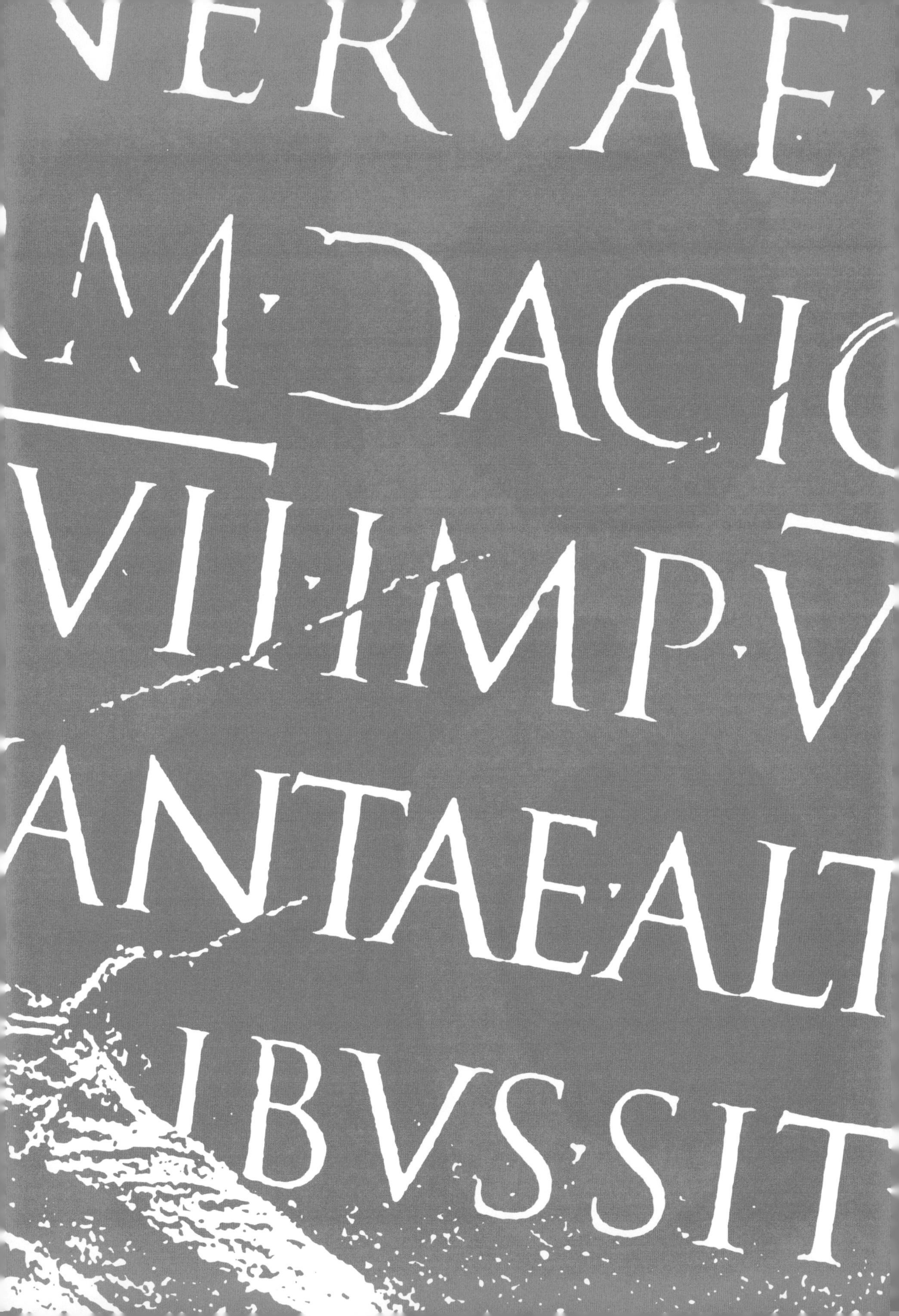
NERVAE
M·DACIC
VII·IMP·V
ANTAE·ALT
IBVS·SIT

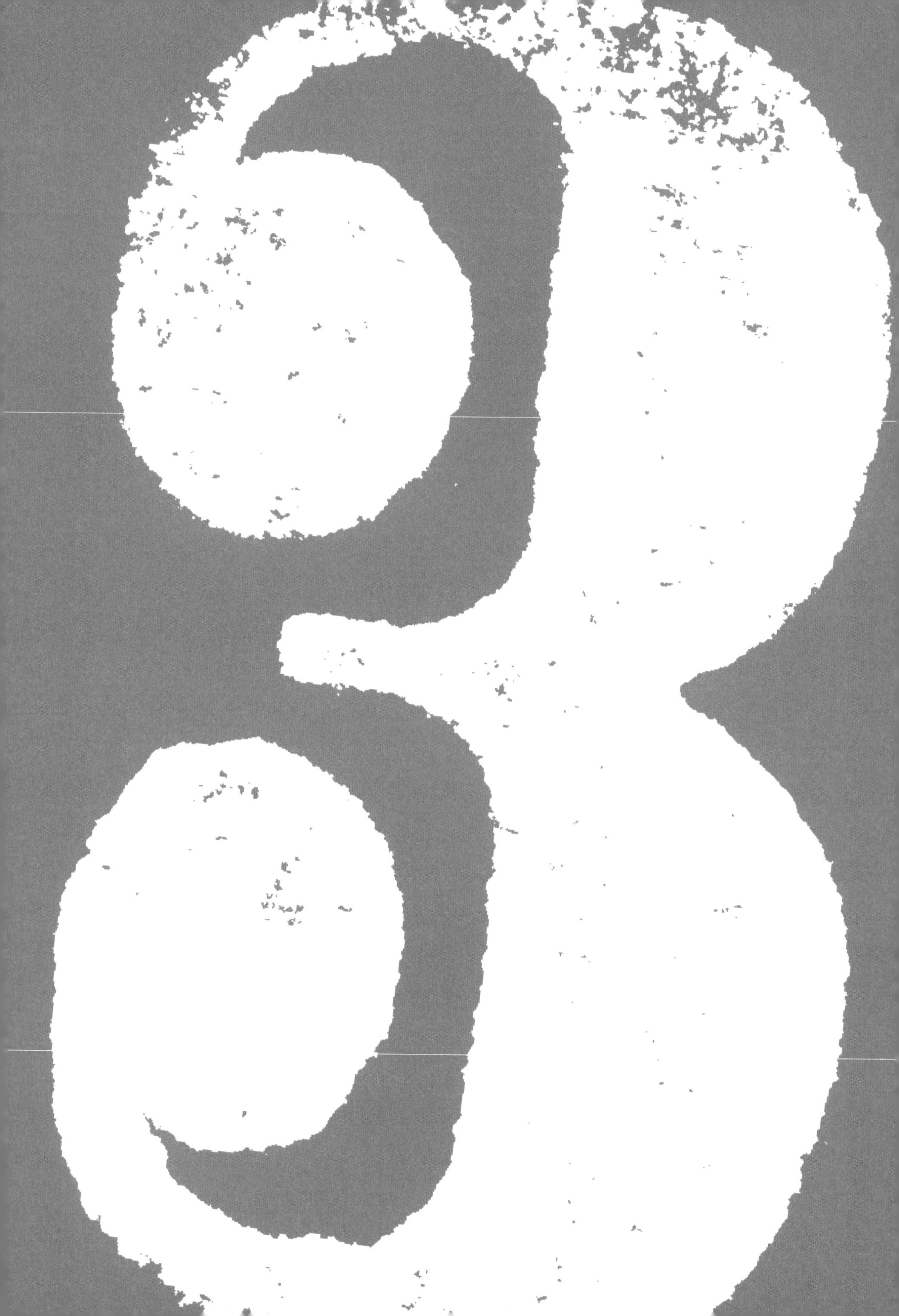

FROM THE MIDDLE AGES TO FRAKTURS

LIBON

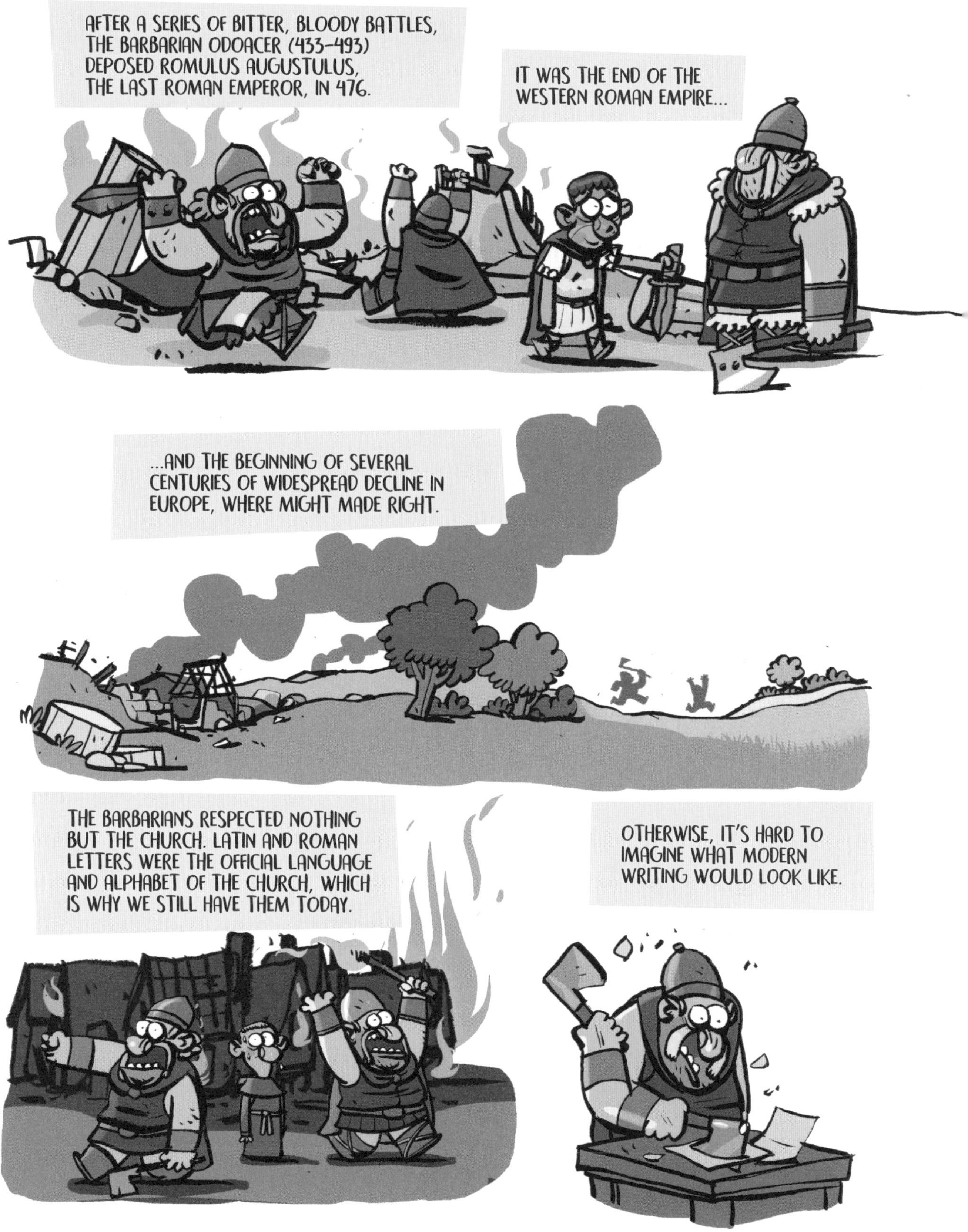
AFTER A SERIES OF BITTER, BLOODY BATTLES, THE BARBARIAN ODOACER (433–493) DEPOSED ROMULUS AUGUSTULUS, THE LAST ROMAN EMPEROR, IN 476.
IT WAS THE END OF THE WESTERN ROMAN EMPIRE...
...AND THE BEGINNING OF SEVERAL CENTURIES OF WIDESPREAD DECLINE IN EUROPE, WHERE MIGHT MADE RIGHT.
THE BARBARIANS RESPECTED NOTHING BUT THE CHURCH. LATIN AND ROMAN LETTERS WERE THE OFFICIAL LANGUAGE AND ALPHABET OF THE CHURCH, WHICH IS WHY WE STILL HAVE THEM TODAY.
OTHERWISE, IT'S HARD TO IMAGINE WHAT MODERN WRITING WOULD LOOK LIKE.

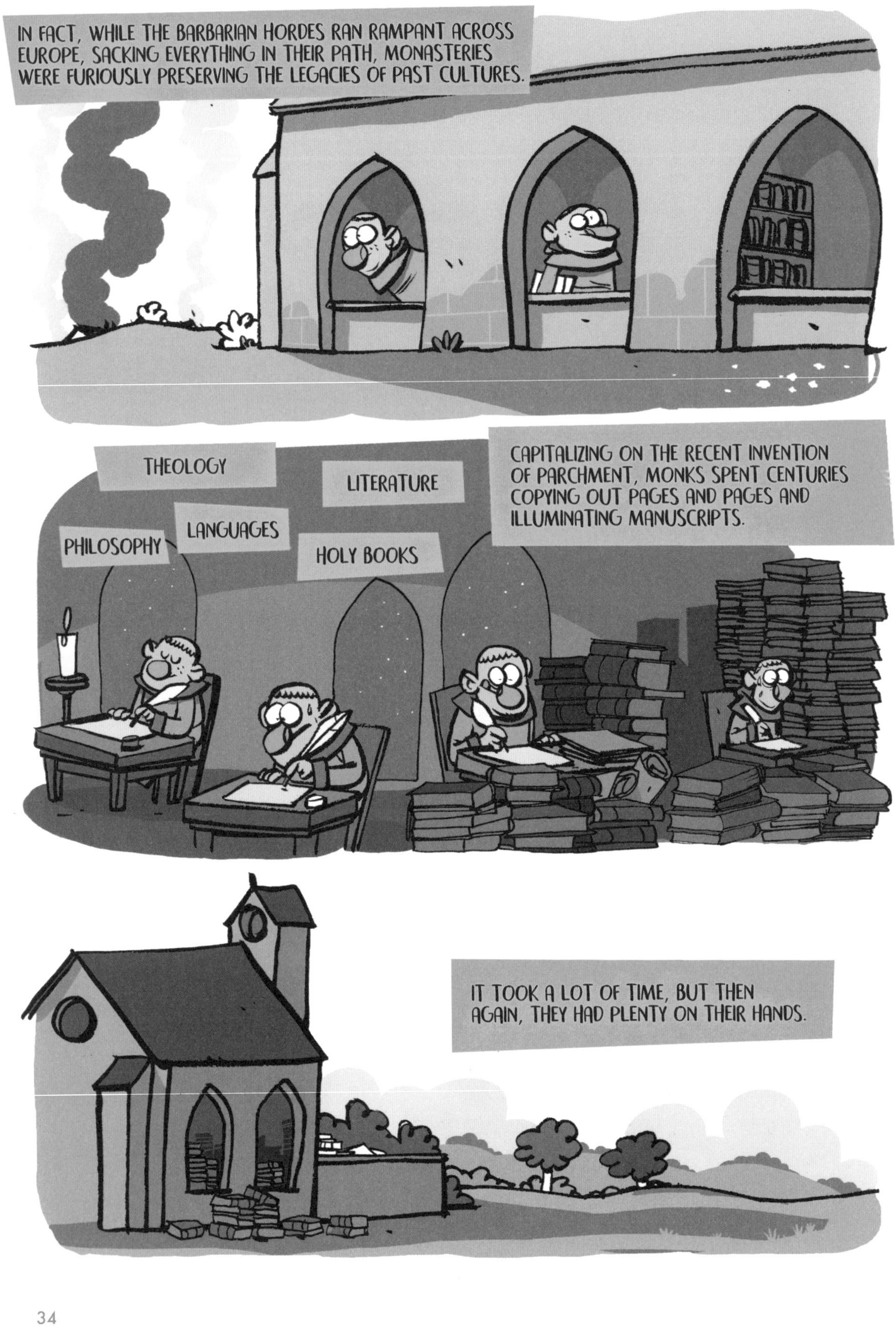
IN FACT, WHILE THE BARBARIAN HORDES RAN RAMPANT ACROSS EUROPE, SACKING EVERYTHING IN THEIR PATH, MONASTERIES WERE FURIOUSLY PRESERVING THE LEGACIES OF PAST CULTURES.
THEOLOGY
PHILOSOPHY
LANGUAGES
LITERATURE
HOLY BOOKS
CAPITALIZING ON THE RECENT INVENTION OF PARCHMENT, MONKS SPENT CENTURIES COPYING OUT PAGES AND PAGES AND ILLUMINATING MANUSCRIPTS.
IT TOOK A LOT OF TIME, BUT THEN AGAIN, THEY HAD PLENTY ON THEIR HANDS.

OUTSIDE, CHAOS REIGNED. EVERY REGION–PRETTY MUCH EVERY SOCIAL GROUP, IN FACT–DEVELOPED ITS OWN WAY OF WRITING, THROUGH IGNORANCE AND THE LACK OF ANY STANDARD RULES.
HERE, READ THIS, PAL!
HERE!
COMMUNICATION WAS LIMITED, AND AS A RESULT, STANDARDIZATION IMPOSSIBLE.
?
?
WHAT'S THIS?
SOMETHING I WROTE.
WHAT? YOU CALL THIS WRITING?!
WELL, YEAH! DUH!
OR SO, AT LEAST, CHARLEMAGNE (742–814), THE YOUNG KING OF THE FRANKS, BELIEVED UPON TAKING POWER IN 771.
NO, BUT SERIOUSLY! WHAT DO YOU THINK?
ME? I CAN'T READ. SO, UH...
HE COULDN'T WRITE EITHER, BUT KNEW FULL WELL THAT ONLY BY IMPOSING A SINGLE WRITING SYSTEM AND STRICT RULES COULD HE "DISPEL IGNORANCE AND MAKE ORDER AND CLARITY PREVAIL", TO USE HIS OWN WORDS.
OKAY, WE'RE GONNA START FROM SCRATCH.

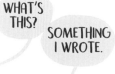

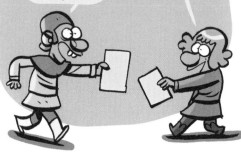

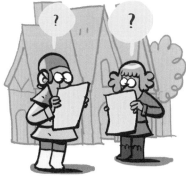

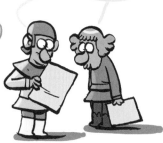

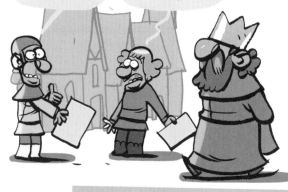

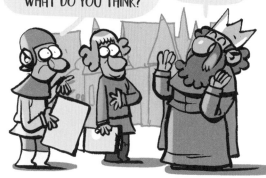

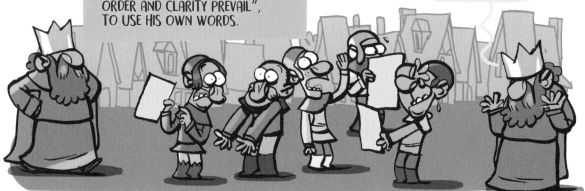

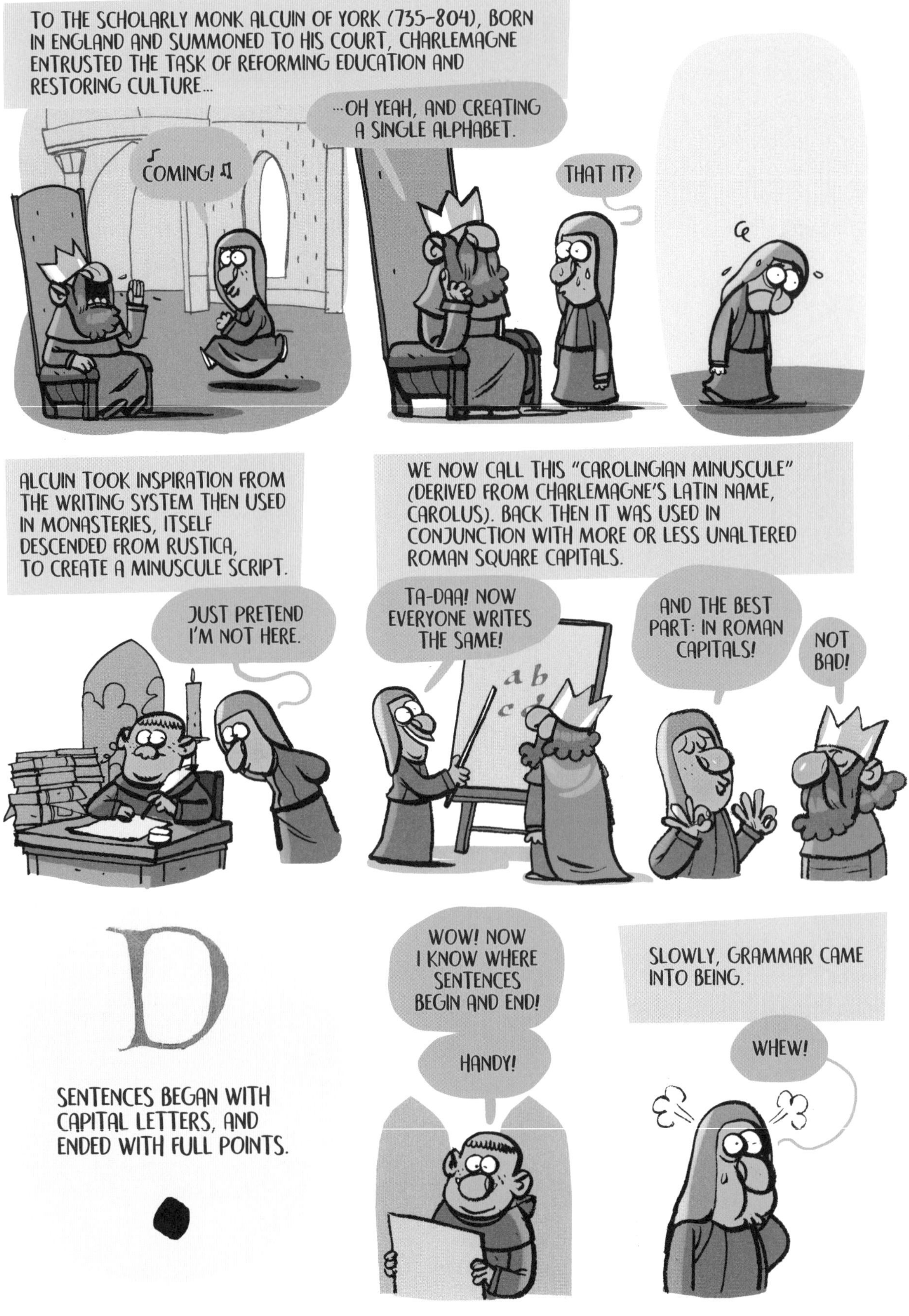
TO THE SCHOLARLY MONK ALCUIN OF YORK (735-804), BORN IN ENGLAND AND SUMMONED TO HIS COURT, CHARLEMAGNE ENTRUSTED THE TASK OF REFORMING EDUCATION AND RESTORING CULTURE...
COMING!
...OH YEAH, AND CREATING A SINGLE ALPHABET.
THAT IT?
ALCUIN TOOK INSPIRATION FROM THE WRITING SYSTEM THEN USED IN MONASTERIES, ITSELF DESCENDED FROM RUSTICA, TO CREATE A MINUSCULE SCRIPT.
JUST PRETEND I'M NOT HERE.
WE NOW CALL THIS "CAROLINGIAN MINUSCULE" (DERIVED FROM CHARLEMAGNE'S LATIN NAME, CAROLUS). BACK THEN IT WAS USED IN CONJUNCTION WITH MORE OR LESS UNALTERED ROMAN SQUARE CAPITALS.
TA-DAA! NOW EVERYONE WRITES THE SAME!
a b
c
AND THE BEST PART: IN ROMAN CAPITALS!
NOT BAD!
D
SENTENCES BEGAN WITH CAPITAL LETTERS, AND ENDED WITH FULL POINTS.
WOW! NOW I KNOW WHERE SENTENCES BEGIN AND END!
HANDY!
SLOWLY, GRAMMAR CAME INTO BEING.
WHEW!

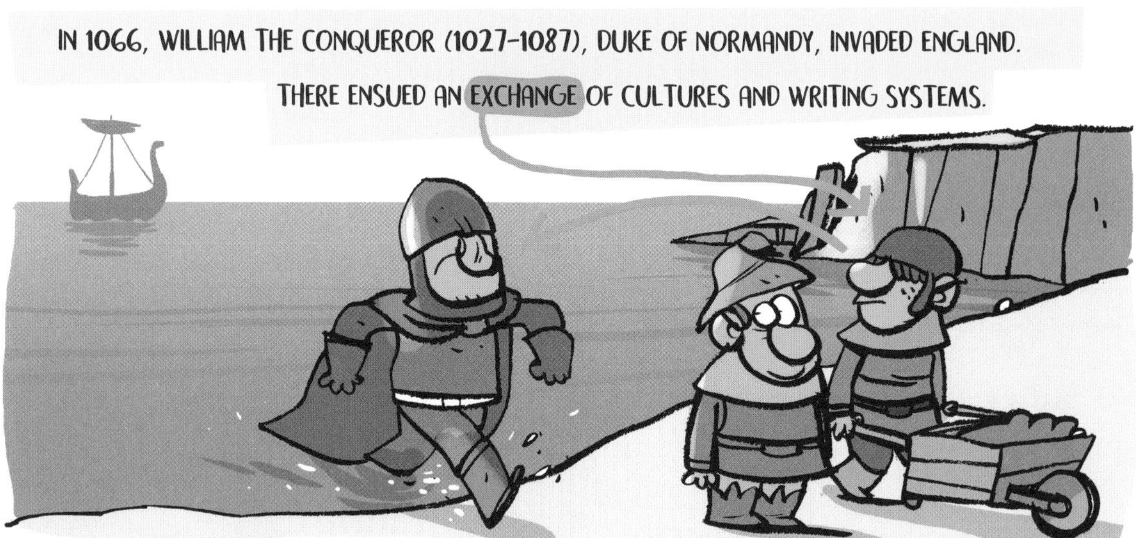
IN 1066, WILLIAM THE CONQUEROR (1027–1087), DUKE OF NORMANDY, INVADED ENGLAND.
THERE ENSUED AN EXCHANGE OF CULTURES AND WRITING SYSTEMS.

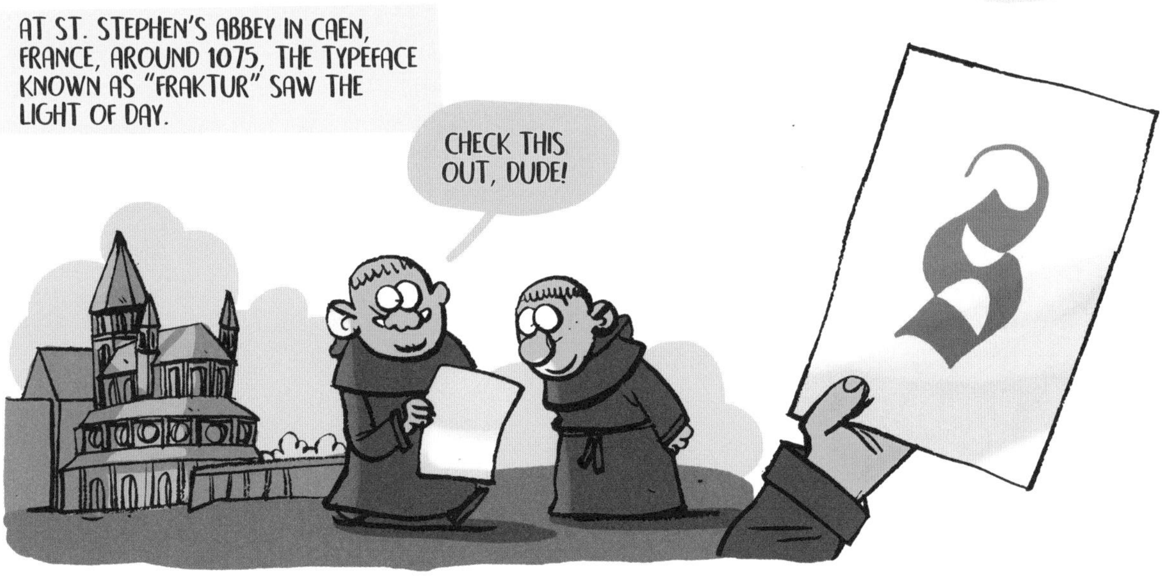
AT ST. STEPHEN'S ABBEY IN CAEN, FRANCE, AROUND 1075, THE TYPEFACE KNOWN AS "FRAKTUR" SAW THE LIGHT OF DAY.
CHECK THIS OUT, DUDE!
S

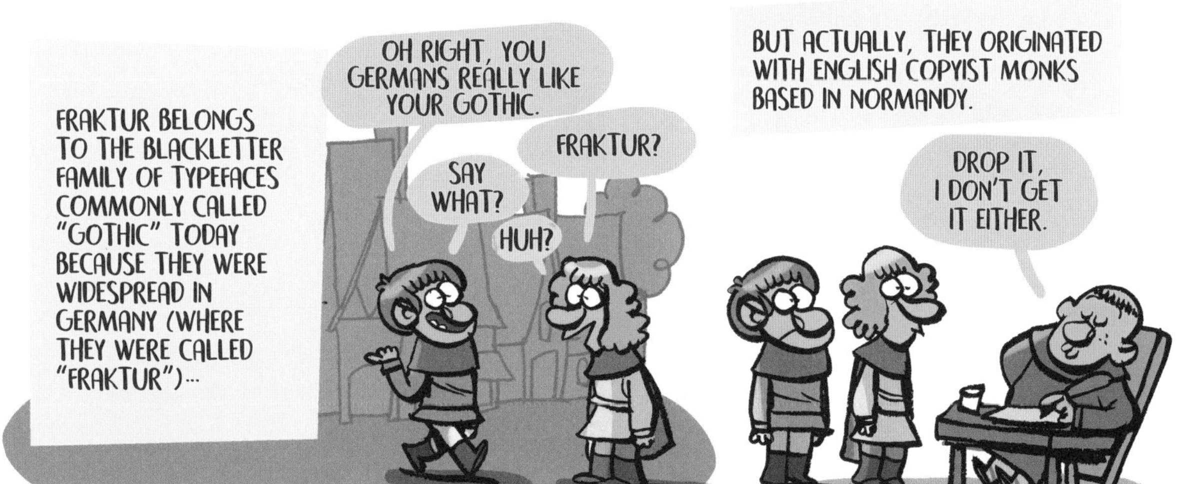
FRAKTUR BELONGS TO THE BLACKLETTER FAMILY OF TYPEFACES COMMONLY CALLED "GOTHIC" TODAY BECAUSE THEY WERE WIDESPREAD IN GERMANY (WHERE THEY WERE CALLED "FRAKTUR")...
OH RIGHT, YOU GERMANS REALLY LIKE YOUR GOTHIC.
FRAKTUR?
SAY WHAT?
HUH?
BUT ACTUALLY, THEY ORIGINATED WITH ENGLISH COPYIST MONKS BASED IN NORMANDY.
DROP IT, I DON'T GET IT EITHER.

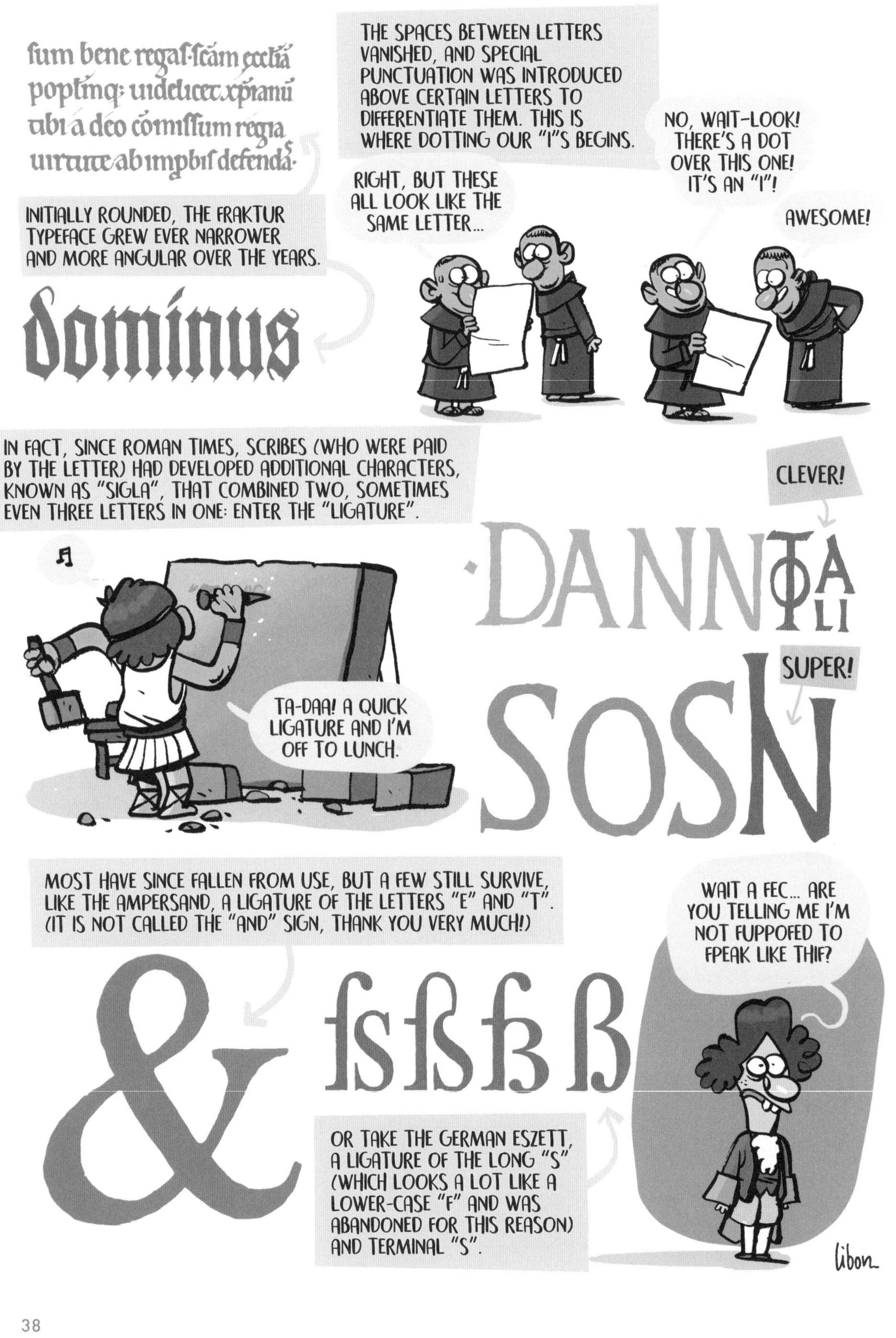

ſum bene regaſ·ſcām ecclīā
poplmq: uidelicet·xpianū
tibi a deo cōmiſſum regia
uirtute ab impbiſ defendā·
INITIALLY ROUNDED, THE FRAKTUR TYPEFACE GREW EVER NARROWER AND MORE ANGULAR OVER THE YEARS.
dominus
THE SPACES BETWEEN LETTERS VANISHED, AND SPECIAL PUNCTUATION WAS INTRODUCED ABOVE CERTAIN LETTERS TO DIFFERENTIATE THEM. THIS IS WHERE DOTTING OUR "I"S BEGINS.
RIGHT, BUT THESE ALL LOOK LIKE THE SAME LETTER...
NO, WAIT–LOOK! THERE'S A DOT OVER THIS ONE! IT'S AN "I"!
AWESOME!
IN FACT, SINCE ROMAN TIMES, SCRIBES (WHO WERE PAID BY THE LETTER) HAD DEVELOPED ADDITIONAL CHARACTERS, KNOWN AS "SIGLA", THAT COMBINED TWO, SOMETIMES EVEN THREE LETTERS IN ONE: ENTER THE "LIGATURE".
TA-DAA! A QUICK LIGATURE AND I'M OFF TO LUNCH.
CLEVER!
DANNTALI
SUPER!
SOSN
MOST HAVE SINCE FALLEN FROM USE, BUT A FEW STILL SURVIVE, LIKE THE AMPERSAND, A LIGATURE OF THE LETTERS "E" AND "T". (IT IS NOT CALLED THE "AND" SIGN, THANK YOU VERY MUCH!)
&
ſs ſß ß ß
OR TAKE THE GERMAN ESZETT, A LIGATURE OF THE LONG "S" (WHICH LOOKS A LOT LIKE A LOWER-CASE "F" AND WAS ABANDONED FOR THIS REASON) AND TERMINAL "S".
WAIT A FEC... ARE YOU TELLING ME I'M NOT FUPPOFED TO FPEAK LIKE THIF?
libon

Pñs spalm
Rubricat
Adimuétione arti
ablqz calamivilla
biam dei industrie
Cíué magutinú. E
Anno dñi Mille

THE GUTENBERG BIBLE

SEYHAN ARGUN

AS EARLY AS THE BEGINNING OF THE 15TH CENTURY, MONASTIC COPYISTS BEGAN ENGRAVING WHOLE PAGES ON WOODEN BLOCKS, WHICH THEY THEN PRINTED ON RAG PAPER USING A MANUAL SCREW PRESS.

IT WAS BOTH IMPRACTICAL AND LABORIOUS.

JUST ONE MISTAKE, AND THE ENTIRE PAGE HAD TO BE REDONE.

NOT UNTIL THE MIDDLE OF THE 15TH CENTURY DID A GERMAN IN MAINZ INVENT PRINTING WITH REUSABLE MOVABLE TYPE.

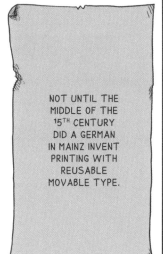

JOHANNES GENSFLEISCH, WHO ADOPTED THE NAME OF HIS ANCESTRAL HOME — GUTENBERG — PERFECTED HIS INVENTION IN AROUND 1450.

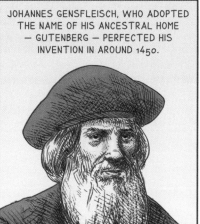

HE THEN SET OUT IN SEARCH OF FUNDING, AND SPECIALIST CRAFTSMEN.

HE APPROACHED JOHANN FUST, A BURGHER WITH LITTLE MONEY BUT A GREAT DEAL OF PROPERTY.

HELLO, FUST!

FUST BORROWED 800 GUILDERS* AND INVESTED THEM IN GUTENBERG'S PRINT WORKS, USING HIS PRINTING-PRESS AS COLLATERAL.

* ABOUT £80,000 OR $100,000 TODAY.

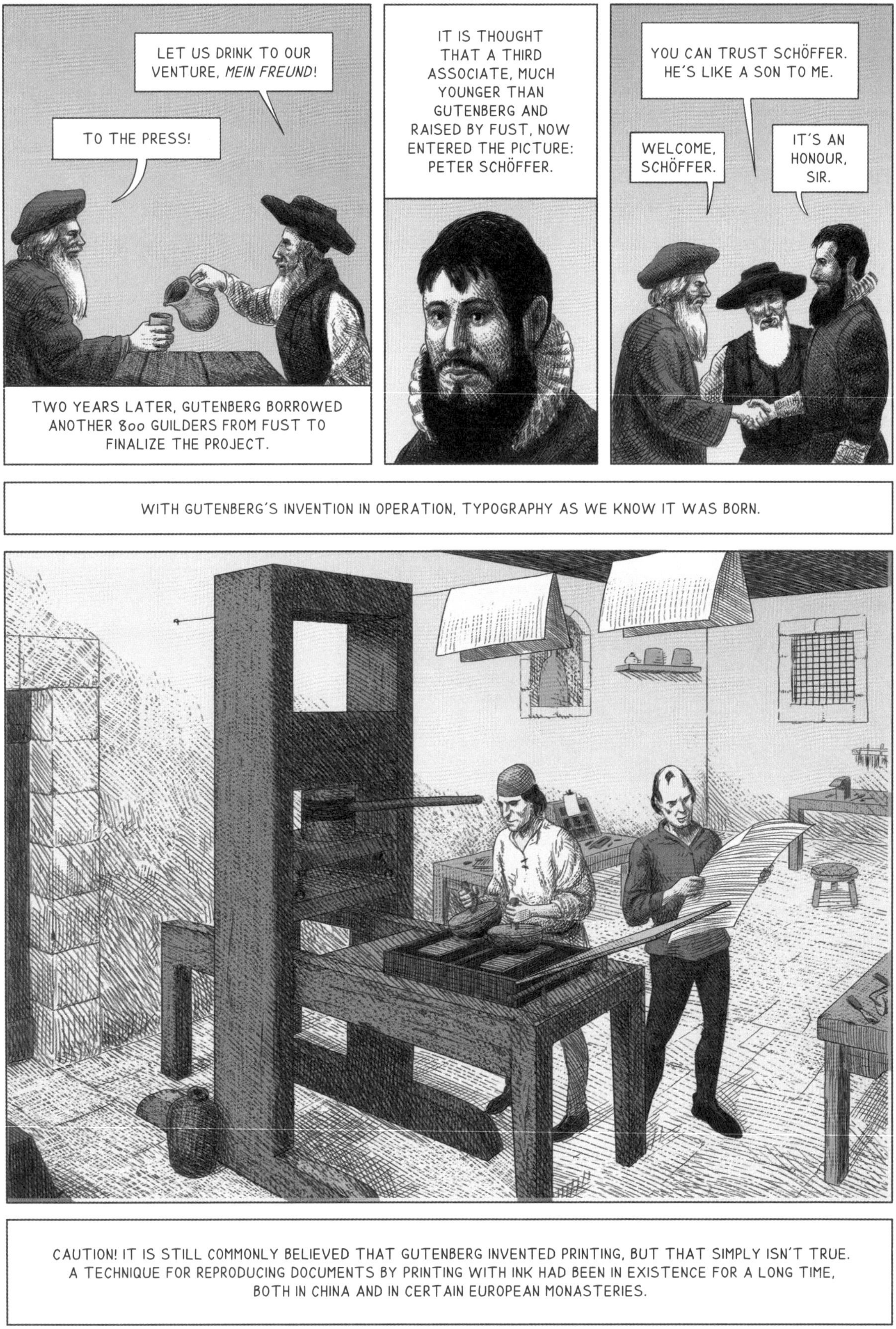
LET US DRINK TO OUR VENTURE, *MEIN FREUND*!
TO THE PRESS!
TWO YEARS LATER, GUTENBERG BORROWED ANOTHER 800 GUILDERS FROM FUST TO FINALIZE THE PROJECT.
IT IS THOUGHT THAT A THIRD ASSOCIATE, MUCH YOUNGER THAN GUTENBERG AND RAISED BY FUST, NOW ENTERED THE PICTURE: PETER SCHÖFFER.
YOU CAN TRUST SCHÖFFER. HE'S LIKE A SON TO ME.
WELCOME, SCHÖFFER.
IT'S AN HONOUR, SIR.
WITH GUTENBERG'S INVENTION IN OPERATION, TYPOGRAPHY AS WE KNOW IT WAS BORN.
CAUTION! IT IS STILL COMMONLY BELIEVED THAT GUTENBERG INVENTED PRINTING, BUT THAT SIMPLY ISN'T TRUE. A TECHNIQUE FOR REPRODUCING DOCUMENTS BY PRINTING WITH INK HAD BEEN IN EXISTENCE FOR A LONG TIME, BOTH IN CHINA AND IN CERTAIN EUROPEAN MONASTERIES.

AT FIRST I TRIED WOODEN BLOCKS, BUT THEY SOON WORE OUT AND BECAME UNUSABLE.

METAL BLOCKS ARE MORE DURABLE. AND WHEN THEY WEAR OUT OR GET DAMAGED, YOU CAN JUST MELT THEM DOWN AND MAKE NEW ONES.

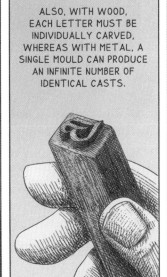

ALSO, WITH WOOD, EACH LETTER MUST BE INDIVIDUALLY CARVED, WHEREAS WITH METAL, A SINGLE MOULD CAN PRODUCE AN INFINITE NUMBER OF IDENTICAL CASTS.

WE START BY CUTTING THE CHARACTER, IN REVERSE, INTO ONE END OF A SHORT AND VERY HARD STEEL BAR.

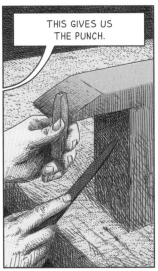

THIS GIVES US THE PUNCH.

WE STAMP THE PUNCH INTO A BAR OF SOFTER METAL, SUCH AS COPPER...

...WHICH RESULTS IN A MATRIX, WHICH IS LOCKED INTO A HAND MOULD.

MOLTEN TYPE METAL (A LEAD ALLOY) IS POURED IN...

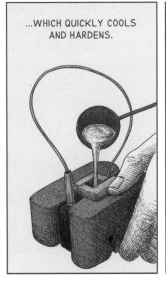

...WHICH QUICKLY COOLS AND HARDENS.

OPEN THE MOULD, AND YOUR LETTER BLOCK IS READY TO USE.

FROM NOW ON, THE MATRIX CAN BE REUSED TO PRODUCE MORE OF THE SAME, QUICKLY AND EASILY.

THEN YOU STORE THE LETTERS IN A "TYPE CASE"—A WOODEN CABINET DIVIDED INTO SMALL COMPARTMENTS, EACH MEANT FOR A SINGLE CHARACTER OR PUNCTUATION MARK.*

* CAPITAL (OR "UPPER-CASE") LETTERS WERE ALWAYS PLACED ON THE HIGHER SHELVES, AND LOWER-CASE LETTERS ON THE LOWER ONES, HENCE THE TERMS STILL IN USE TODAY.

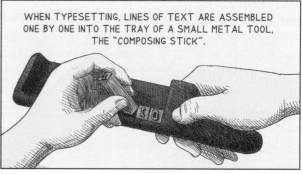

WHEN TYPESETTING, LINES OF TEXT ARE ASSEMBLED ONE BY ONE INTO THE TRAY OF A SMALL METAL TOOL, THE "COMPOSING STICK".

SUCCESSIVE LINES OF TEXT ARE THEN LAID OUT ON AN "IMPOSING-STONE", TRADITIONALLY OF SMOOTH MARBLE.

THE IMPOSING-STONE IS PLACED INTO A "BED" OR "COFFIN", AND COATED WITH VISCOUS INK.

A SHEET OF PAPER IS LAID OVER THE TOP.

WANT TO GIVE IT A TRY?

SURE, THANKS!

THE VERY FIRST BOOK GUTENBERG PRINTED ON HIS NEW INVENTION WAS A BIBLE.

IT WAS PRINTED USING A TYPEFACE OF THE "FRAKTUR" (OR GOTHIC, A.K.A. "BLACKLETTER") FAMILY, IN TWO COLUMNS OF 42 LINES PER PAGE, AS BECAME COMMON AT THE TIME.

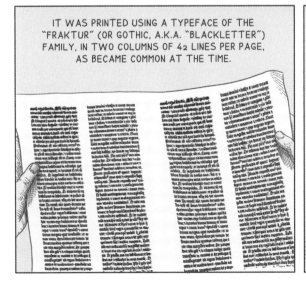

TODAY, THERE ARE 49 KNOWN SURVIVING COPIES (ONLY 21 OF WHICH ARE COMPLETE), IN THE WORLD'S MOST PRESTIGIOUS LIBRARIES.

OF THESE, 13 ARE IN GERMANY, 11 IN THE U.S., 8 IN THE U.K., AND 4 IN FRANCE.

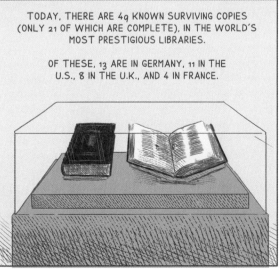

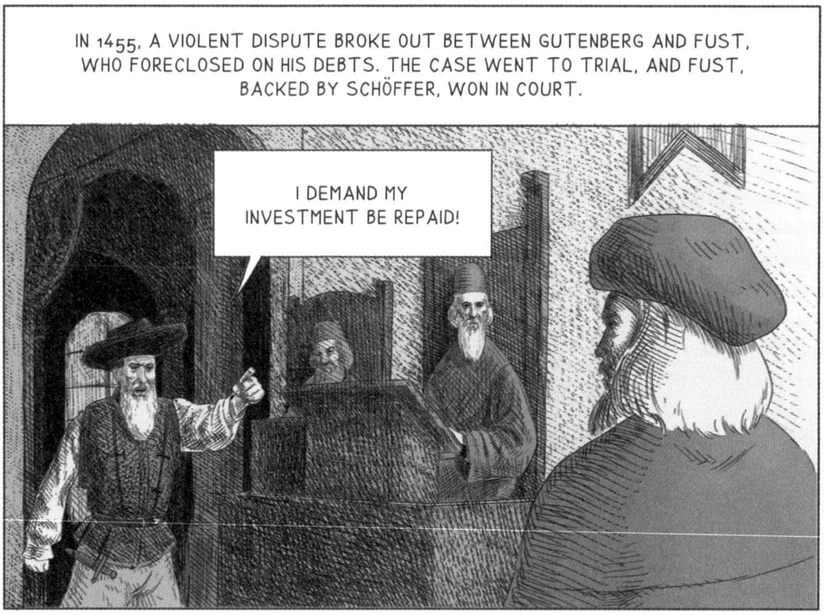
IN 1455, A VIOLENT DISPUTE BROKE OUT BETWEEN GUTENBERG AND FUST, WHO FORECLOSED ON HIS DEBTS. THE CASE WENT TO TRIAL, AND FUST, BACKED BY SCHÖFFER, WON IN COURT.
I DEMAND MY INVESTMENT BE REPAID!

FUST KEPT THE PRINTING-PRESS, THE TYPE, AND THE BIBLES THAT HAD ALREADY BEEN PRINTED.

GUTENBERG MAY THEN HAVE PURCHASED A SECOND PRESS AND PRINTED A SECOND BIBLE IN 1459...

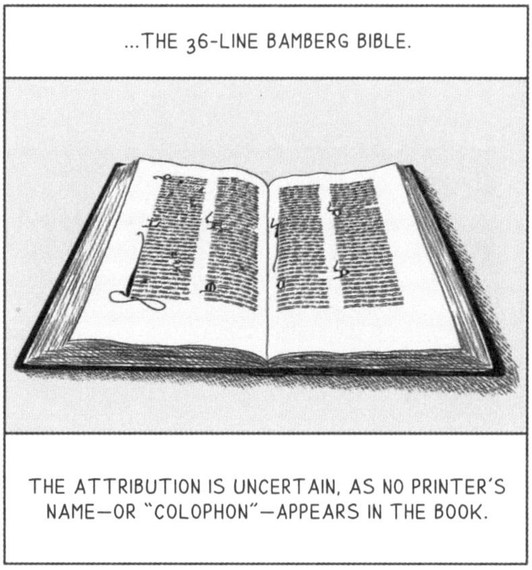
...THE 36-LINE BAMBERG BIBLE.
THE ATTRIBUTION IS UNCERTAIN, AS NO PRINTER'S NAME—OR "COLOPHON"—APPEARS IN THE BOOK.

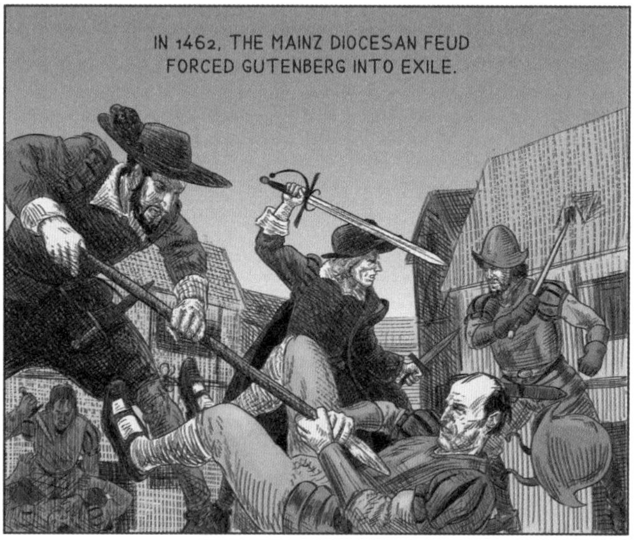
IN 1462, THE MAINZ DIOCESAN FEUD FORCED GUTENBERG INTO EXILE.

HE RETURNED A FEW YEARS LATER, UNDER THE PROTECTION OF ARCHBISHOP VON NASSAU, WHO HONOURED HIM WITH A STIPEND.

GUTENBERG DIED ON 3 FEBRUARY 1468. HE WAS BURIED IN A CHURCH THAT WAS LATER DESTROYED IN 1793. HIS GRAVE IS NOW LOST, AND HIS MEMORY MIGHT HAVE SUFFERED THE SAME FATE HAD HIS NAME NOT BEEN CITED, AS EARLY AS 1499, IN A WORK PUBLISHED IN MAINZ, AS "THE INVENTOR OF THE ART OF PRINTING".

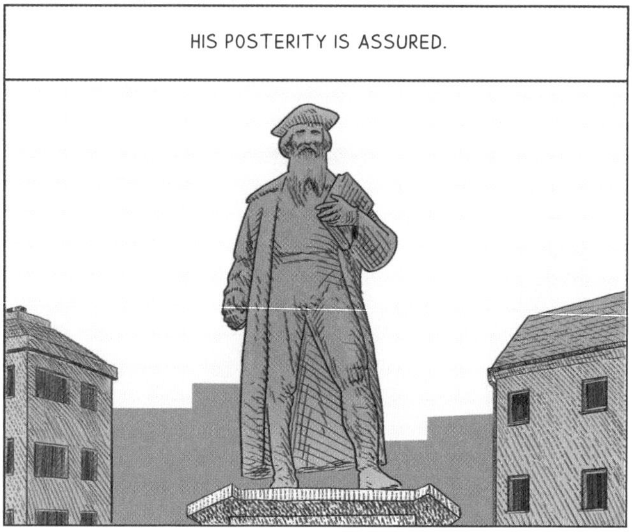
HIS POSTERITY IS ASSURED.

reulationis in agnitione ei

illuminatos oculos cordis

cut sciatis que sit spes voca

nis eius ⁊ que diuitie glori

reditatis eius in sanctis: et

supeminēs magnitudo vi

tis ei⁹ in nos q̃ credim⁹ sed

patione potētie virtutis q

patus ē in cristo: suscitās il

mortuis • et cōstituēs ad dx

am suā in celestibz supra o

ncipatū et potestatē ⁊ virt

et dnatione • ⁊ omē nomen

FROM HUMANIST
TO DIDONE

DELPHINE PANIQUE

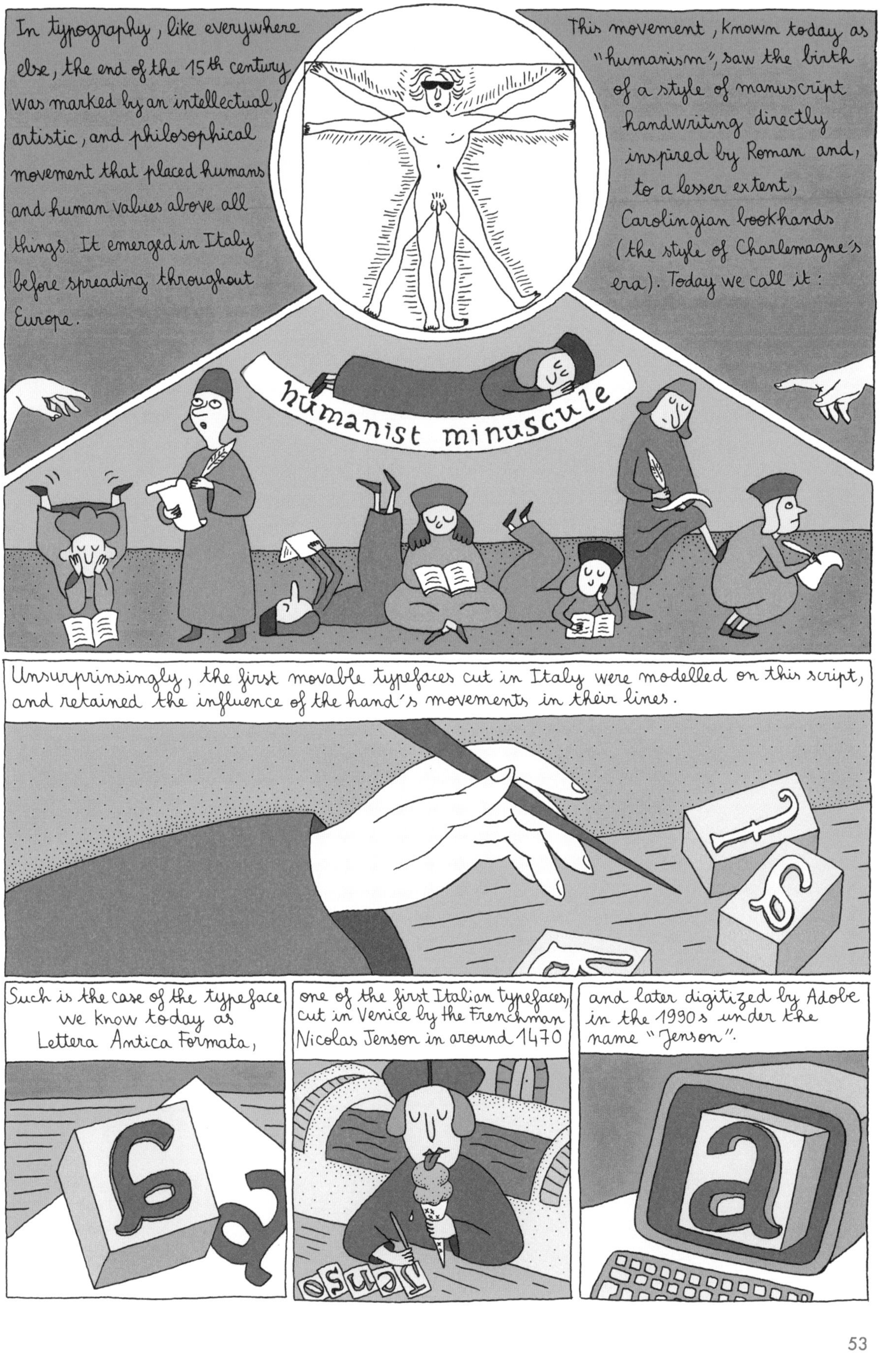
In typography, like everywhere else, the end of the 15th century was marked by an intellectual, artistic, and philosophical movement that placed humans and human values above all things. It emerged in Italy before spreading throughout Europe.
This movement, known today as "humanism", saw the birth of a style of manuscript handwriting directly inspired by Roman and, to a lesser extent, Carolingian bookhands (the style of Charlemagne's era). Today we call it:
humanist minuscule
Unsurprinsingly, the first movable typefaces cut in Italy were modelled on this script, and retained the influence of the hand's movements in their lines.
Such is the case of the typeface we know today as Lettera Antica Formata,
one of the first Italian typefaces, cut in Venice by the Frenchman Nicolas Jenson in around 1470
and later digitized by Adobe in the 1990s under the name "Jenson".

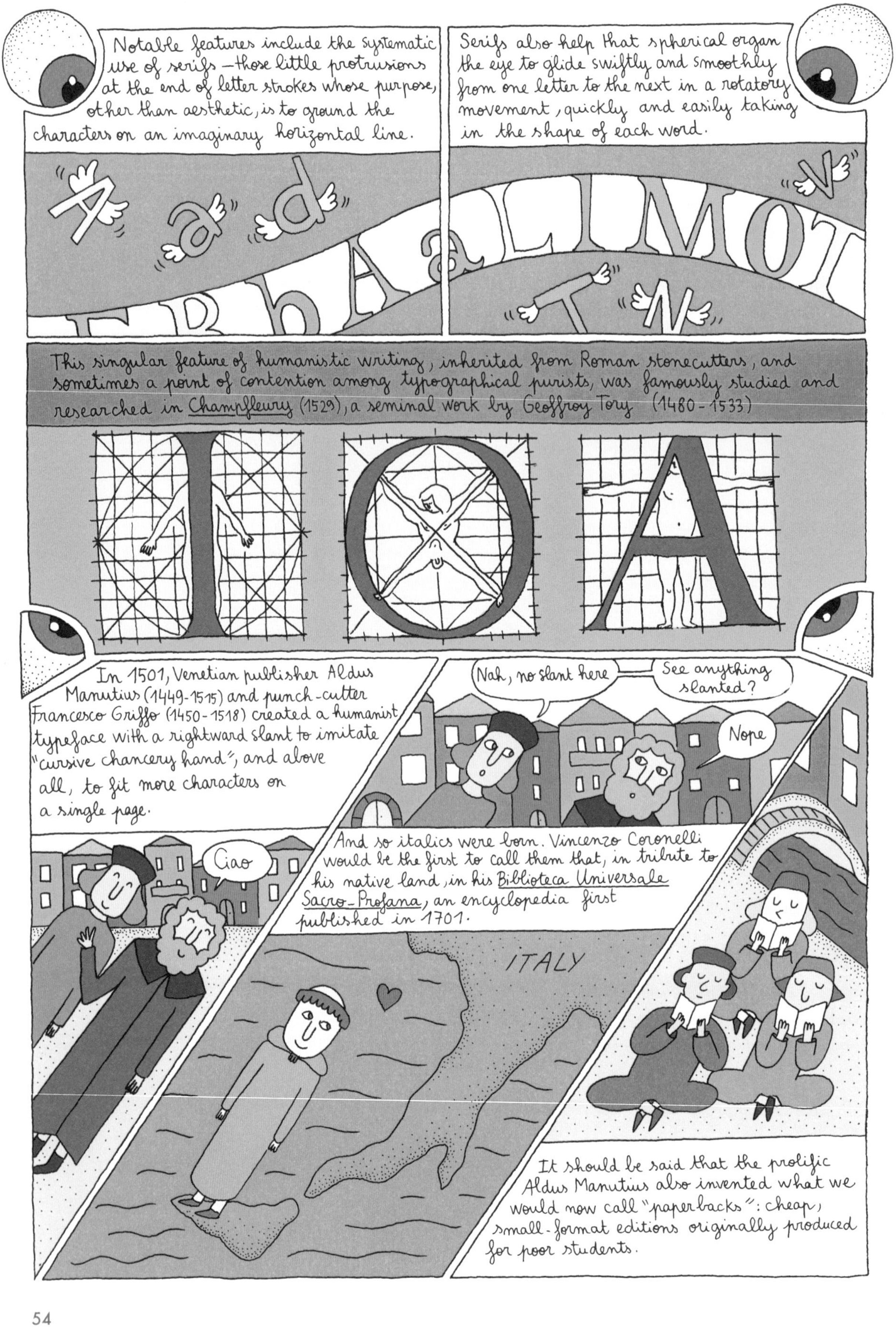
Notable features include the systematic use of serifs — those little protrusions at the end of letter strokes whose purpose, other than aesthetic, is to ground the characters on an imaginary horizontal line.
Serifs also help that spherical organ the eye to glide swiftly and smoothly from one letter to the next in a rotatory movement, quickly and easily taking in the shape of each word.
This singular feature of humanistic writing, inherited from Roman stonecutters, and sometimes a point of contention among typographical purists, was famously studied and researched in Champfleury (1529), a seminal work by Geoffroy Tory (1480-1533)
In 1501, Venetian publisher Aldus Manutius (1449-1515) and punch-cutter Francesco Griffo (1450-1518) created a humanist typeface with a rightward slant to imitate "cursive chancery hand", and above all, to fit more characters on a single page.
Nah, no slant here
See anything slanted?
Nope
Ciao
And so italics were born. Vincenzo Coronelli would be the first to call them that, in tribute to his native land, in his Biblioteca Universale Sacro-Profana, an encyclopedia first published in 1701.
ITALY
It should be said that the prolific Aldus Manutius also invented what we would now call "paperbacks": cheap, small-format editions originally produced for poor students.

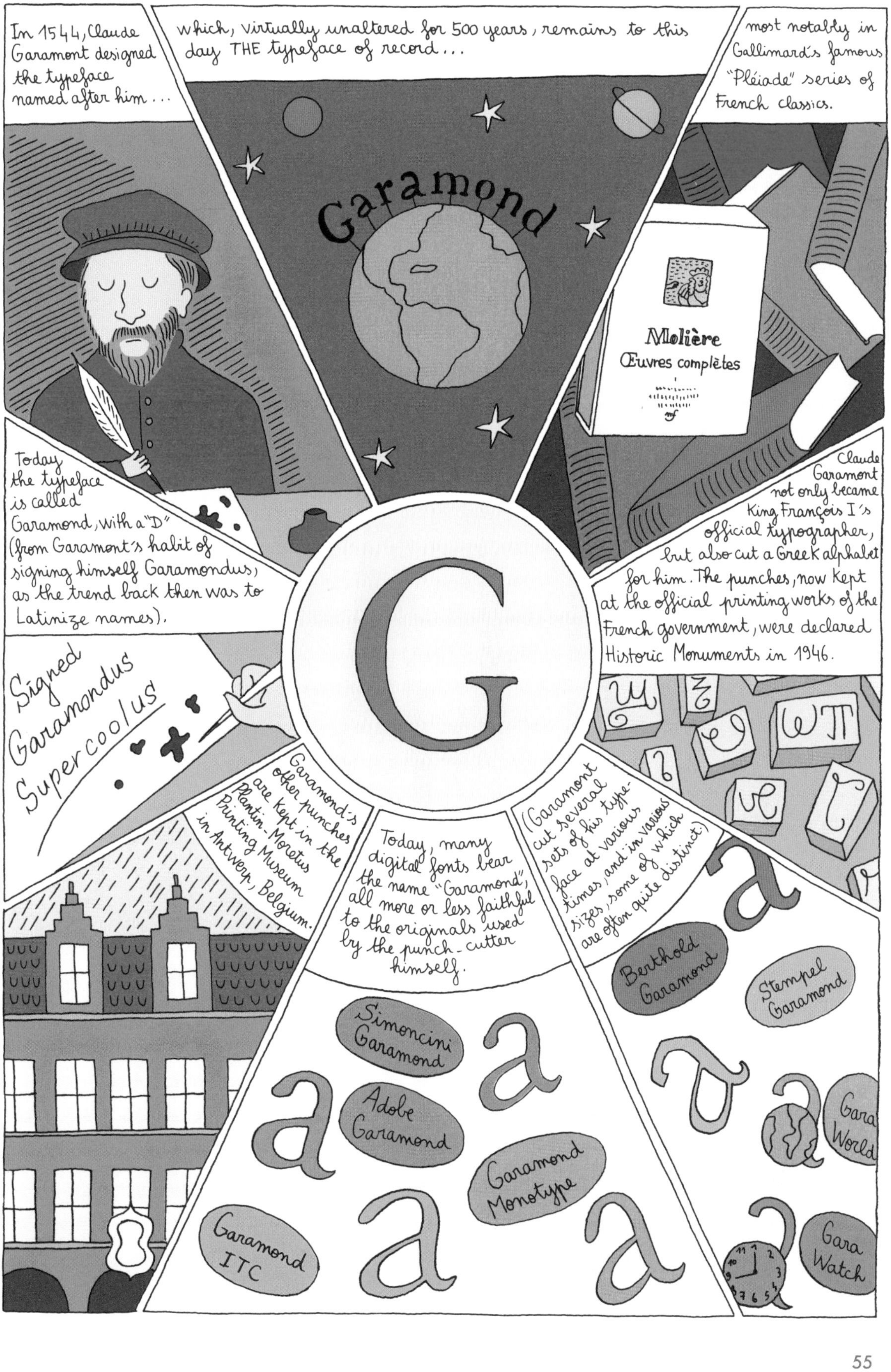

In 1544, Claude Garamont designed the typeface named after him ...
which, virtually unaltered for 500 years, remains to this day THE typeface of record ...
most notably in Gallimard's famous "Pléiade" series of French classics.
Garamond
Molière
Œuvres complètes
Today the typeface is called Garamond, with a "D" (from Garamont's habit of signing himself Garamondus, as the trend back then was to Latinize names).
G
Claude Garamont not only became King François I's official typographer, but also cut a Greek alphabet for him. The punches, now kept at the official printing works of the French government, were declared Historic Monuments in 1946.
Signed Garamondus Supercoolus
Garamond's other punches are kept in the Plantin-Moretus Printing Museum in Antwerp, Belgium.
Today, many digital fonts bear the name "Garamond", all more or less faithful to the originals used by the punch-cutter himself.
(Garamont cut several sets of his typeface at various times, and in various sizes, some of which are often quite distinct.)
Berthold Garamond
Stempel Garamond
Simoncini Garamond
Adobe Garamond
Garamond Monotype
Garamond ITC
Gara World
Gara Watch

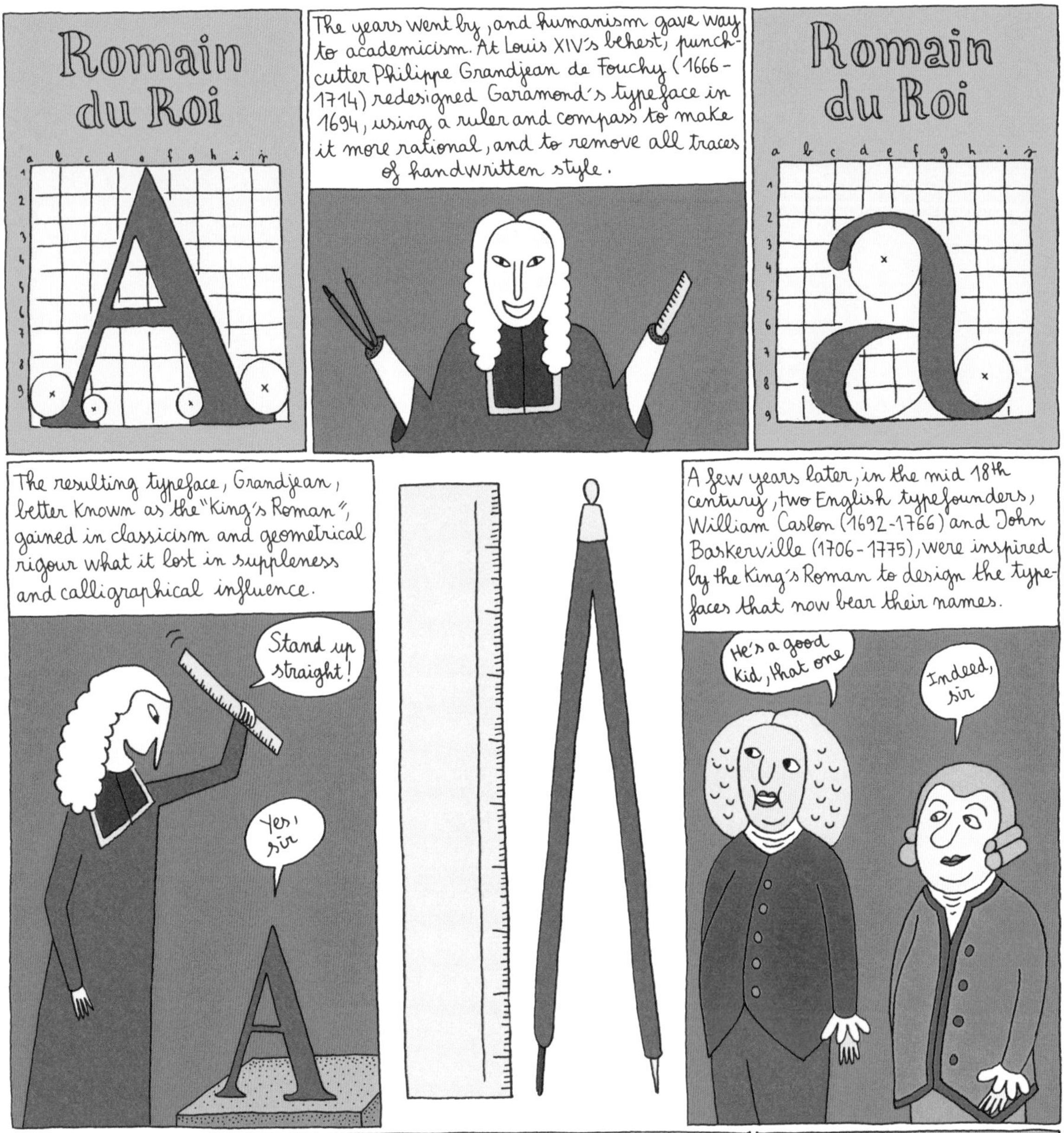
Romain du Roi
The years went by, and humanism gave way to academicism. At Louis XIV's behest, punch-cutter Philippe Grandjean de Fouchy (1666-1714) redesigned Garamond's typeface in 1694, using a ruler and compass to make it more rational, and to remove all traces of handwritten style.
Romain du Roi
The resulting typeface, Grandjean, better known as the "King's Roman", gained in classicism and geometrical rigour what it lost in suppleness and calligraphical influence.
Stand up straight!
Yes, sir
A few years later, in the mid 18th century, two English typefounders, William Caslon (1692-1766) and John Baskerville (1706-1775), were inspired by the King's Roman to design the typefaces that now bear their names.
He's a good kid, that one
Indeed, sir
Caslon
By century's end, Baskerville had also developed the highly durable paper known as "wove" or "vellum", which, combined with later technological advances, enabled the design of new typefaces with very thick pull-strokes, hairline cross-strokes, and spindly serifs.
Who'll last longer?
I WILL!
Baskerville

The best-known of these typefaces were designed by the Frenchman Firmin Didot (1764-1838)...
DIDOT
the German Justus Erich Walbaum (1768-1837)...
WALBA
and above all, the Italian Giambattista Bodoni (1740-1813), nicknamed the "King of Typographers", who was knighted by no less a figure than Napoleon himself.
BODONI
The first typefaces Bodoni created were very close to John Baskerville's, but he soon altered his designs, venturing ever deeper into more radical waters.
Andiamo!
The contrast he developed between a letter's thick, dark downward strokes and its thin, light, horizontal ones grew ever more pronounced, along with his serifs, which shrank to mere lines.
His signature typeface was born, austere and majestic, vertical and immovable.
Towards the end of the 18th century and at the start of the 19th, the French Revolution, Empire and Restoration applied Bodoni or Didot on their decrees and assignats...
conferring upon them an incontestable aura of public rigour and severity. Not to mention the aftertaste of bureaucracy and effortless authority.
TREMBLE TYRANTS LIGHTNING SHALL SOON STRIKE
TREMB
TYRANT

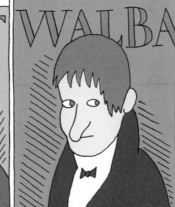

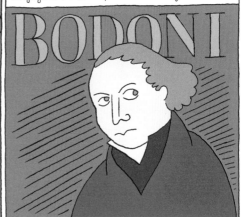

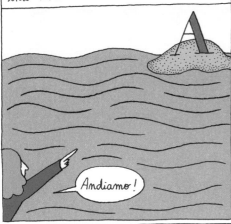

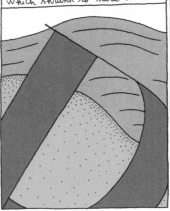

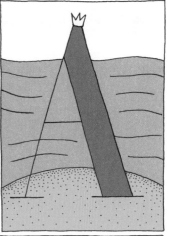

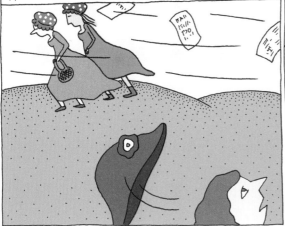

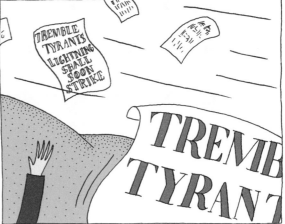

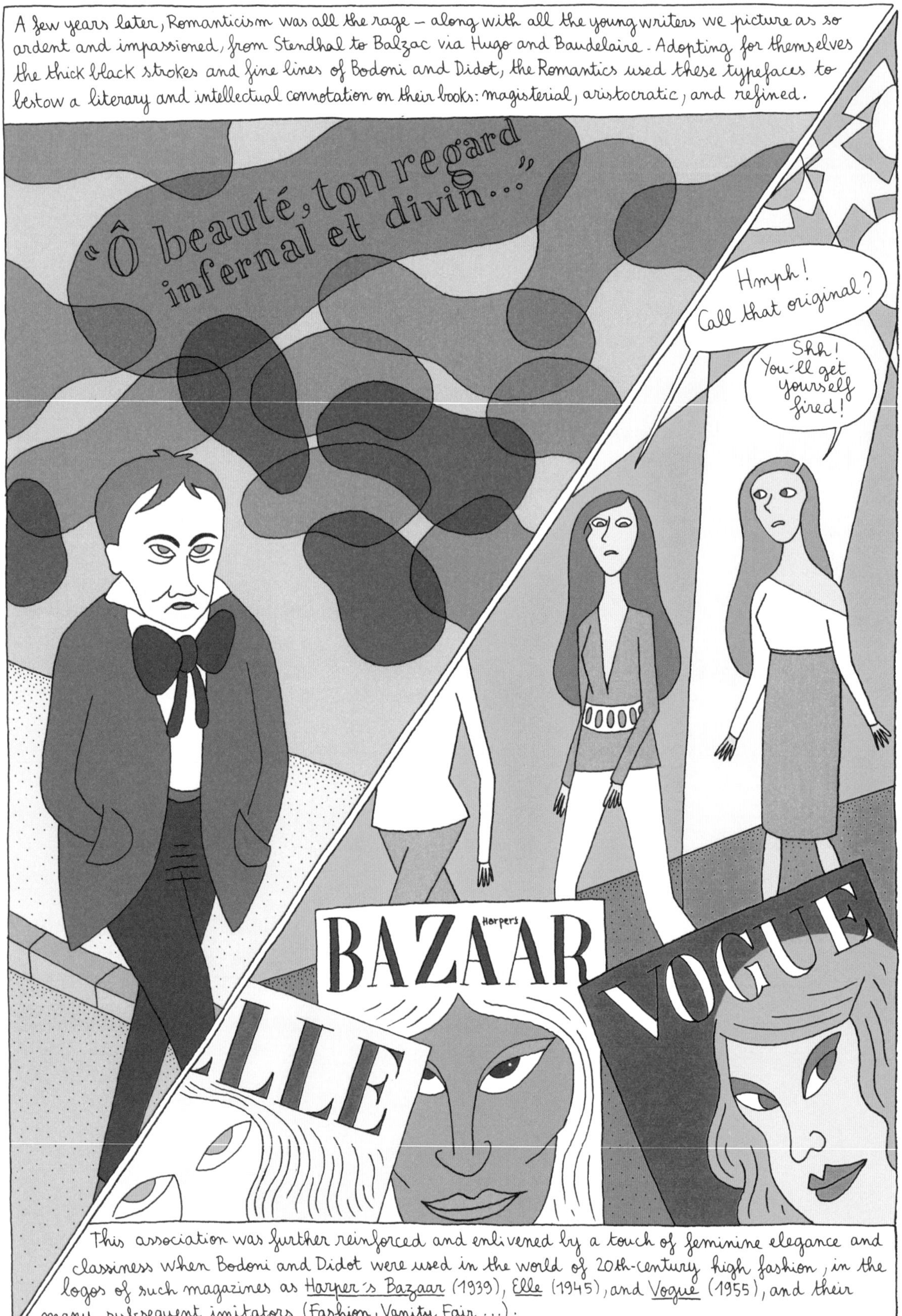
A few years later, Romanticism was all the rage – along with all the young writers we picture as so ardent and impassioned, from Stendhal to Balzac via Hugo and Baudelaire. Adopting for themselves the thick black strokes and fine lines of Bodoni and Didot, the Romantics used these typefaces to bestow a literary and intellectual connotation on their books: magisterial, aristocratic, and refined.
"Ô beauté, ton regard infernal et divin..."
Hmph! Call that original?
Shh! You'll get yourself fired!
Harper's BAZAAR
LLE
VOGUE
This association was further reinforced and enlivened by a touch of feminine elegance and classiness when Bodoni and Didot were used in the world of 20th-century high fashion, in the logos of such magazines as Harper's Bazaar (1939), Elle (1945), and Vogue (1955), and their many subsequent imitators (Fashion, Vanity Fair ...).

ETVSTATE
lissimæ Vicecomit
liæ qui ambitiosius
Romanorū Cæsar
ne, Longobardísq
deducto stemmate
re contédunt, fabu
nè initiis inuoluer
tur. Nos autem re
illustrioráque, vti ab omnibus recepta, seque
tentique erimus insigni memoria Heriprand
uanii nepotis, qui eximia cum laude rei mili
uilísque prudentiæ, Mediolani principem lo
nuerunt. Incidit Galuanius in id tempus quo
lanum à Federico AEnobarbo deletū est, vir
rerum gestarum gloria, & quod in fatis fuit,
calamitate memorabilis. Captus enim, & ad
phum in Germaniam ductus fuisse traditur: s
multo pòst carceris catenas fregit, ingentíque
virtute non semel cæsis Barbaris, vltus iniurias
restituit. Fuit hic (vt Annales ferunt) Othonis
cius qui ab insigni pietate magni liæ (

NEWSPAPERS AND MACHINES

OLIVIER DELOYE

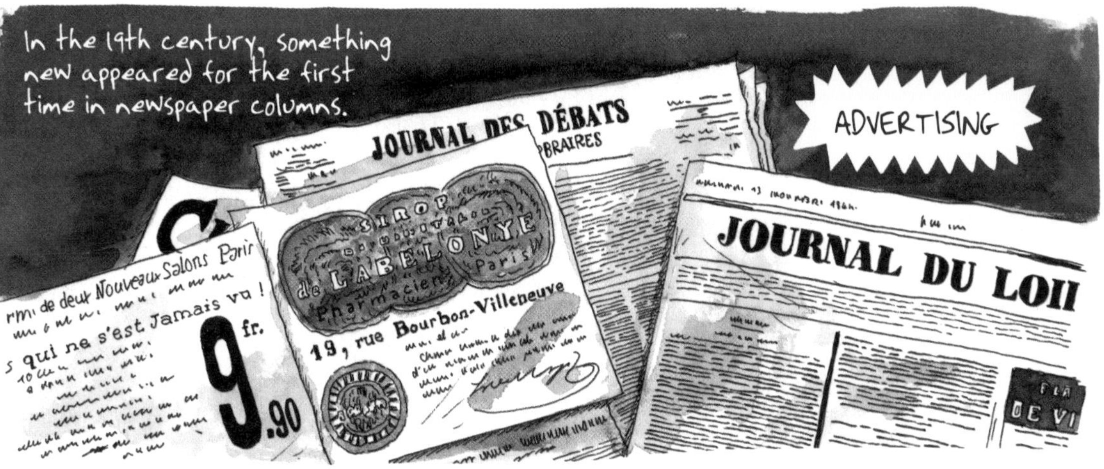
In the 19th century, something new appeared for the first time in newspaper columns.
ADVERTISING
JOURNAL DES DÉBATS
SIROP DE LABELONYE Pharmacien Paris
19, rue Bourbon-Villeneuve
de deux Nouveaux Salons Paris
qui ne s'est jamais vu !
9.90 fr.
JOURNAL DU LOII

But ad space was very expensive. Advertisers wanted to make it worthwhile by fitting in as many words as they could.

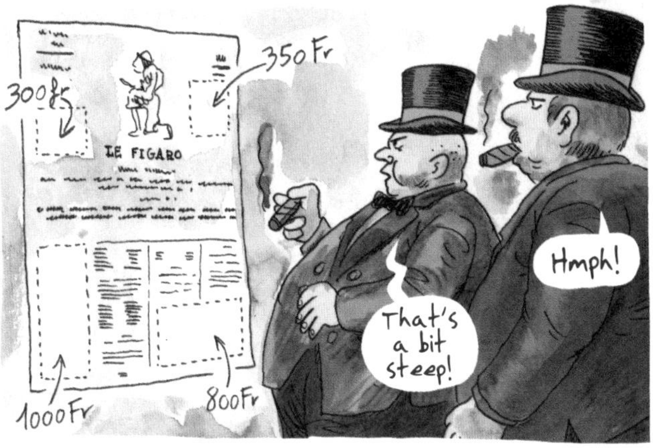
350 Fr
300 Fr
LE FIGARO
1000 Fr
800 Fr
Hmph!
That's a bit steep!

The fact is, letter serifs in those days took up a lot of space "for no reason", and the lack of any alternatives drove type foundries to innovate.

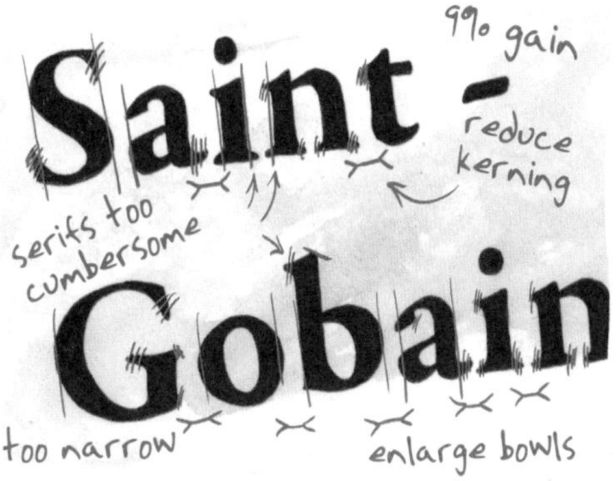
Saint-Gobain
9% gain
reduce kerning
serifs too cumbersome
too narrow
enlarge bowls

And so the first typefaces specifically intended for publicity came into being: sans serif, and very weighty (so they'd be first to catch the eye).

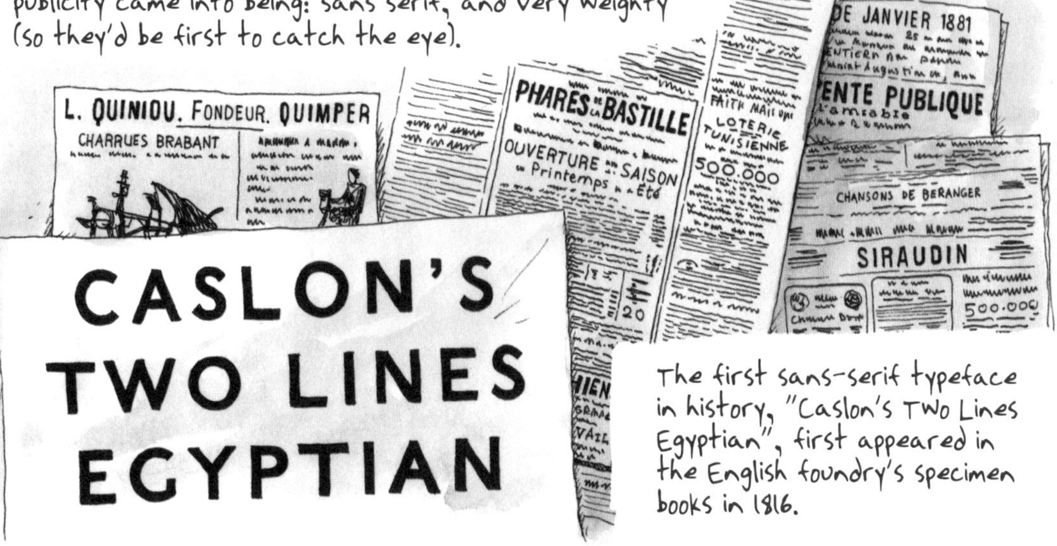
L. QUINIOU. FONDEUR. QUIMPER
CHARRUES BRABANT
PHARES DE LA BASTILLE
OUVERTURE DE LA SAISON Printemps & Été
LOTERIE TUNISIENNE
500.000
DE JANVIER 1881
VENTE PUBLIQUE
CHANSONS DE BERANGER
SIRAUDIN
500.000
CASLON'S TWO LINES EGYPTIAN

The first sans-serif typeface in history, "Caslon's Two Lines Egyptian", first appeared in the English foundry's specimen books in 1816.

The proliferation of newspapers and other periodicals saw a rise in the use of display typefaces, meant for use in headings, designed to draw in a reader's eyes to each section.

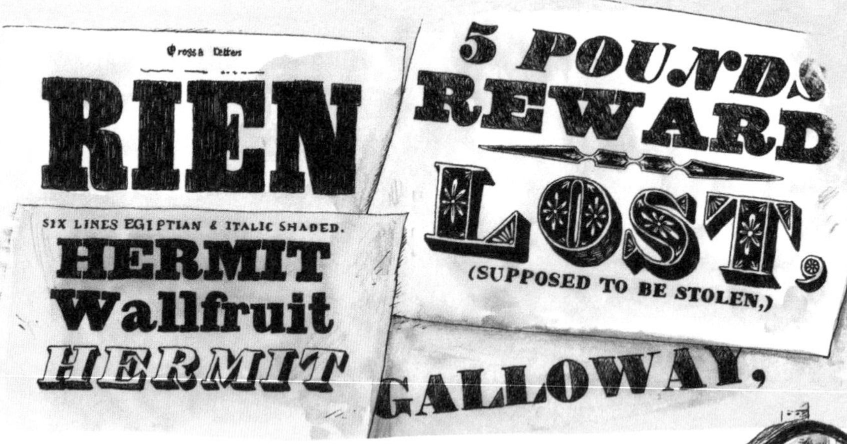
RIEN
SIX LINES EGIPTIAN & ITALIC SHADED.
HERMIT
Wallfruit
HERMIT
5 POUNDS
REWARD
LOST,
(SUPPOSED TO BE STOLEN,)
GALLOWAY,

This was a first. Previously, headings were merely "text" typefaces* writ large.

*See Glossary.

Characteristics of display typeface characters:

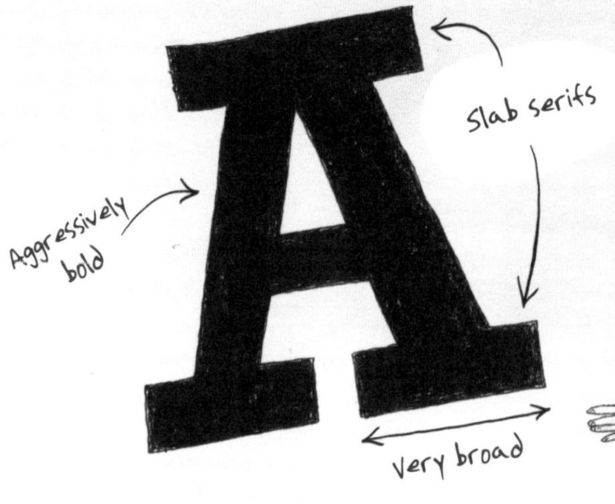
A
Slab serifs
Aggressively bold
Very broad

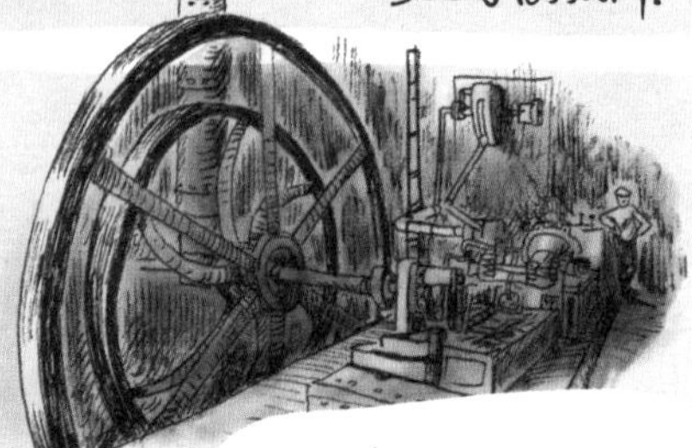

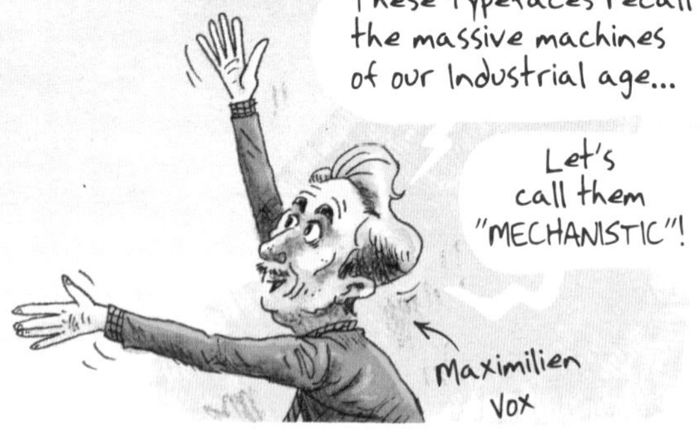
These typefaces recall the massive machines of our Industrial age...
Let's call them "MECHANISTIC"!
Maximilien Vox

The finest example of these typefaces remains Clarendon, designed by Robert Besley of London's Fann Street Foundry in 1845–a monster hit, back in the day.

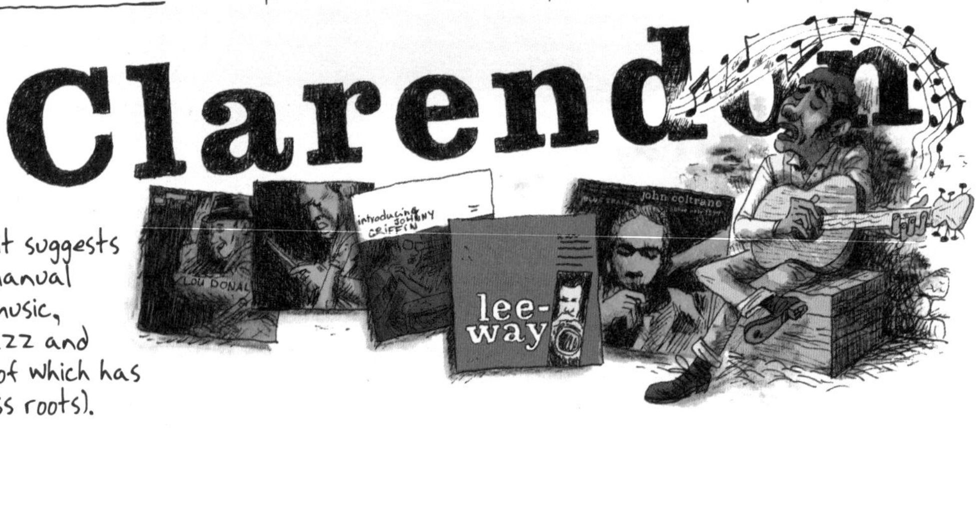
Clarendon
introducing JOHNNY GRIFFIN
john coltrane
lee-way

These days it suggests a world of manual labour and music, especially jazz and blues (each of which has working-class roots).

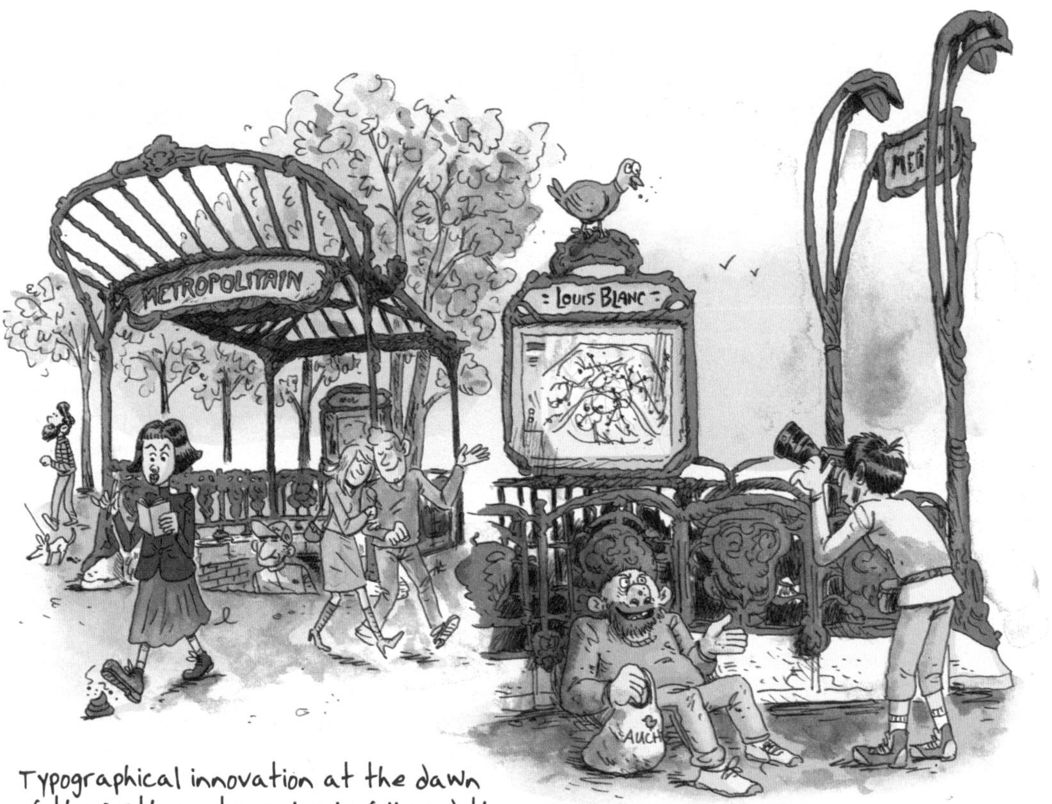
METROPOLITAIN
LOUIS BLANC

Typographical innovation at the dawn of the 20th century closely followed the trends in fashion and architecture: typographers from 1900 to 1920 were directly inspired by the organic, plantlike curves of Art Nouveau and the Japanese-like ornaments of the day.

Two such typefaces are especially noteworthy:

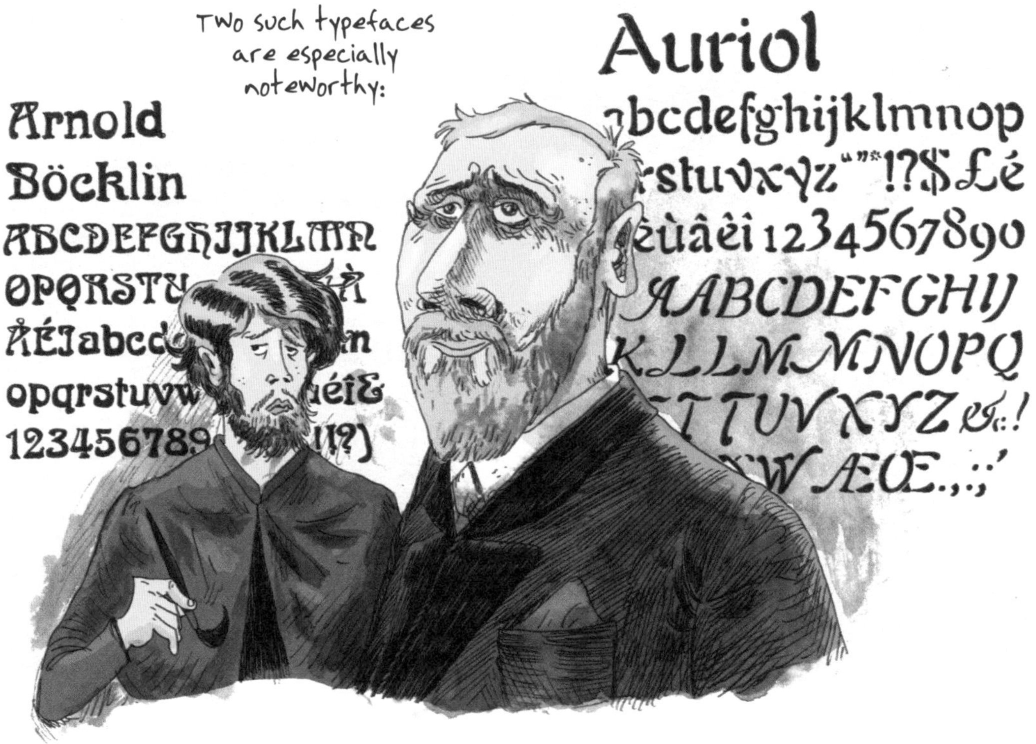
Arnold Böcklin
Auriol
abcdefghijklmnop
1234567890
AABCDEFGHIJ
KLLMMNOPQ
TTUVXYZ

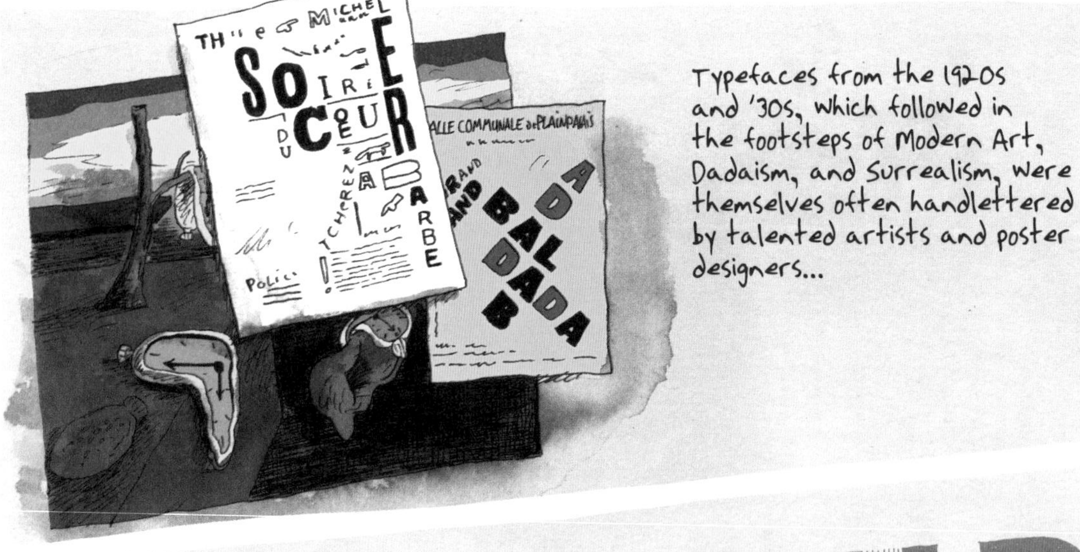
Typefaces from the 1920s and '30s, which followed in the footsteps of Modern Art, Dadaism, and Surrealism, were themselves often handlettered by talented artists and poster designers...

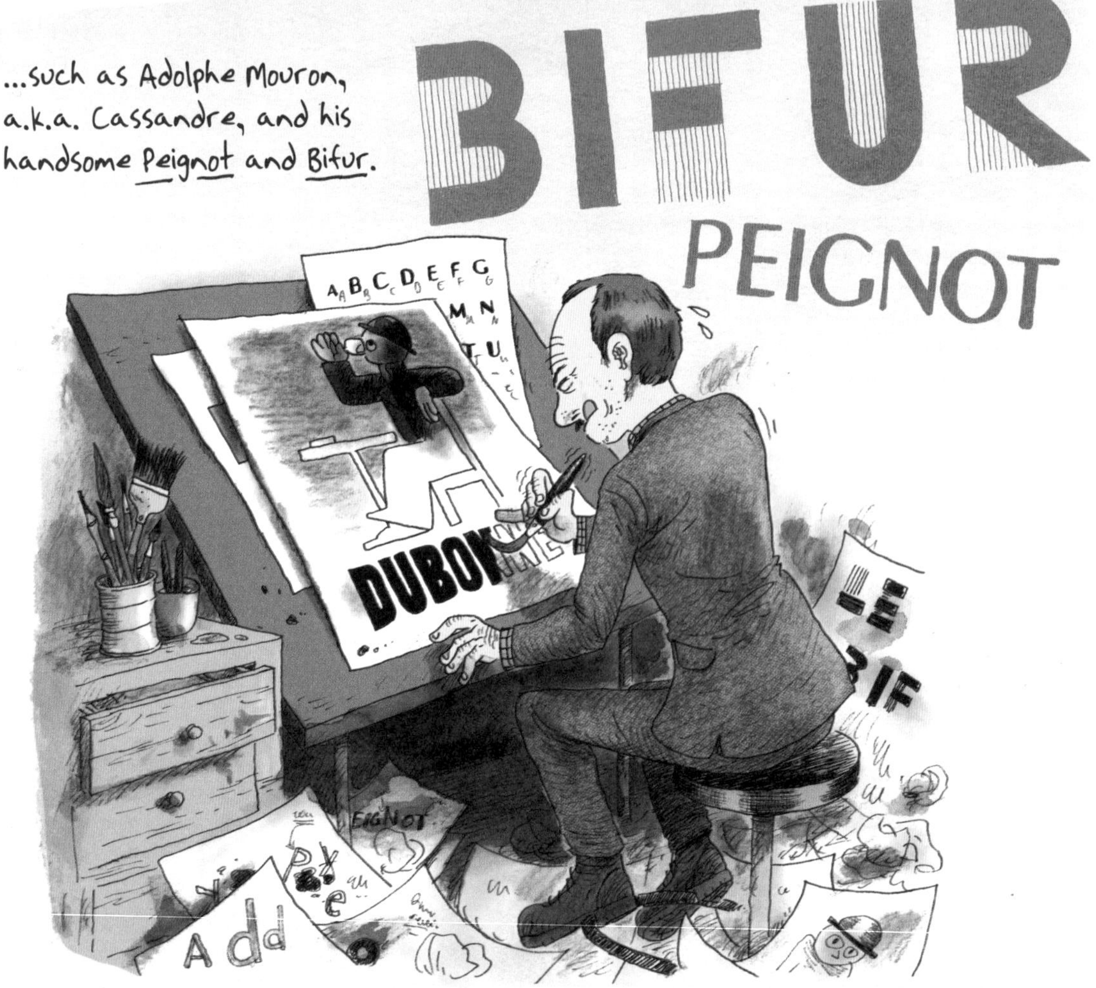
...such as Adolphe Mouron, a.k.a. Cassandre, and his handsome Peignot and Bifur.
BIFUR
PEIGNOT

The resulting fonts were often very decorative (perfect for short titles, but hard work to read in the small print of long texts).

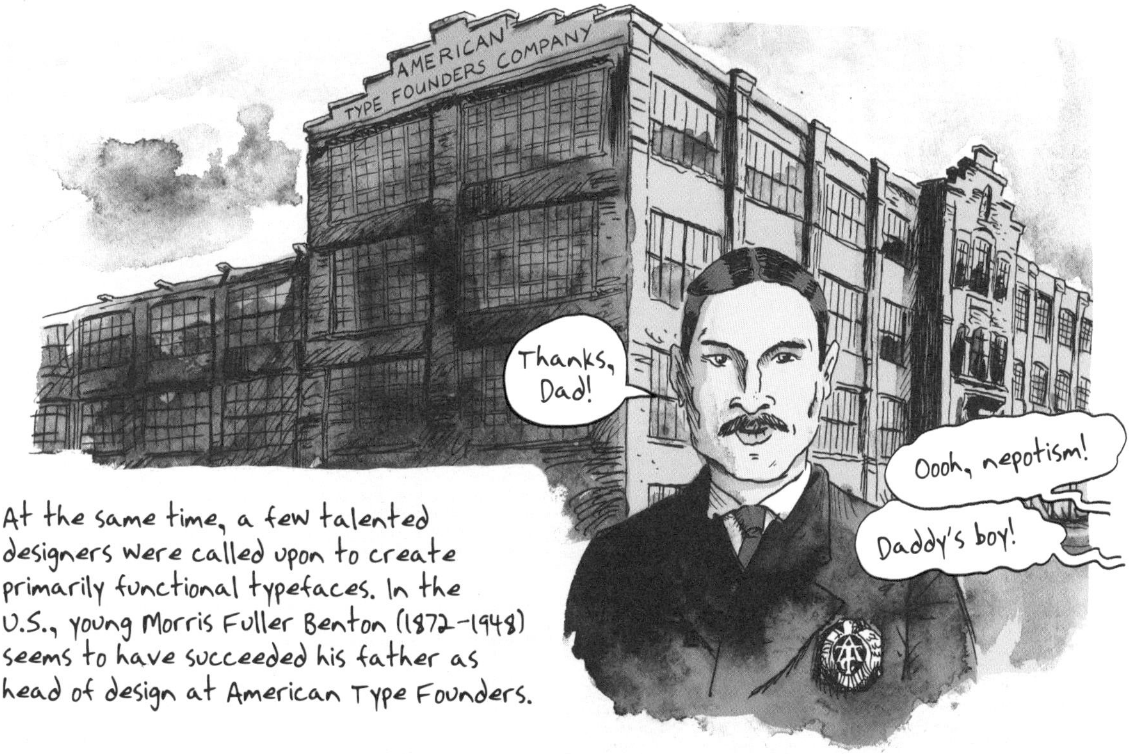
AMERICAN TYPE FOUNDERS COMPANY
Thanks, Dad!
Oooh, nepotism!
Daddy's boy!
At the same time, a few talented designers were called upon to create primarily functional typefaces. In the U.S., young Morris Fuller Benton (1872–1948) seems to have succeeded his father as head of design at American Type Founders.

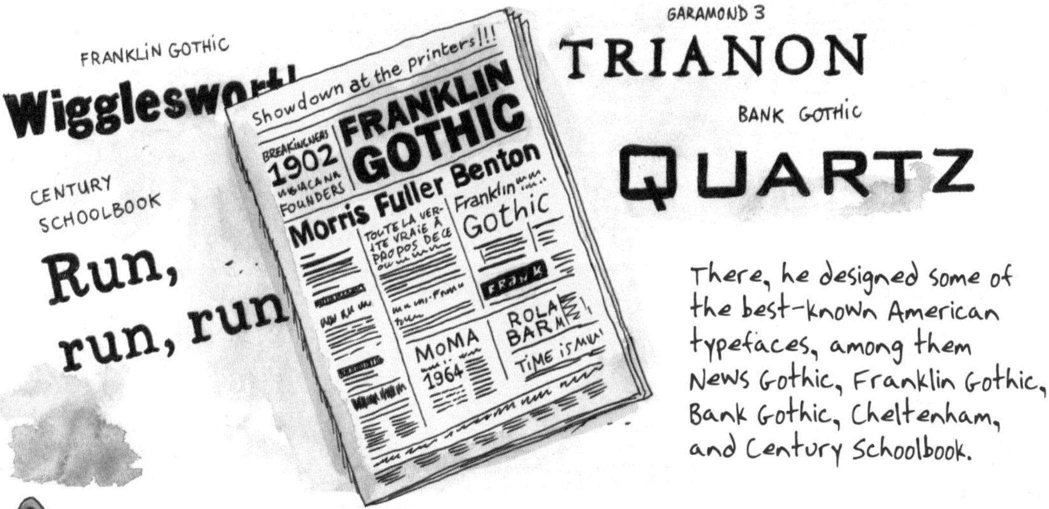
FRANKLIN GOTHIC
Wigglesworth!
CENTURY SCHOOLBOOK
Run, run, run
Showdown at the printers!!!
FRANKLIN GOTHIC
1902
Morris Fuller Benton
Franklin Gothic
MoMA 1964
GARAMOND 3
TRIANON
BANK GOTHIC
QUARTZ
There, he designed some of the best-known American typefaces, among them News Gothic, Franklin Gothic, Bank Gothic, Cheltenham, and Century Schoolbook.

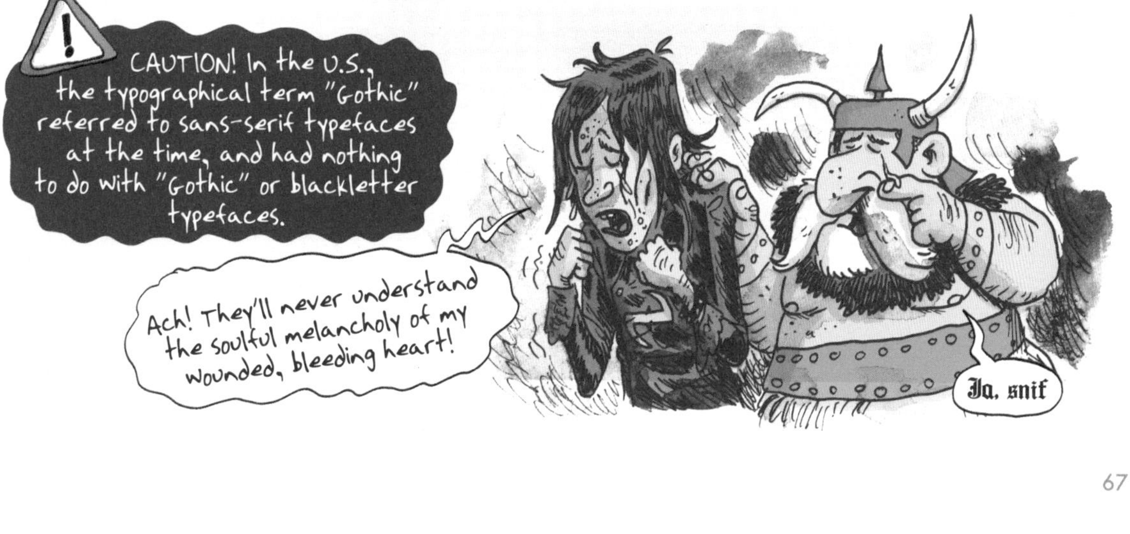
CAUTION! In the U.S., the typographical term "Gothic" referred to sans-serif typefaces at the time, and had nothing to do with "Gothic" or blackletter typefaces.
Ach! They'll never understand the soulful melancholy of my wounded, bleeding heart!
Ja, snif

Meanwhile, in England, the British daily *The Times* (of London) asked Stanley Morison to adapt and revise his house typeface, Times Roman, for better legibility in small print, so more lines could fit into a single column.

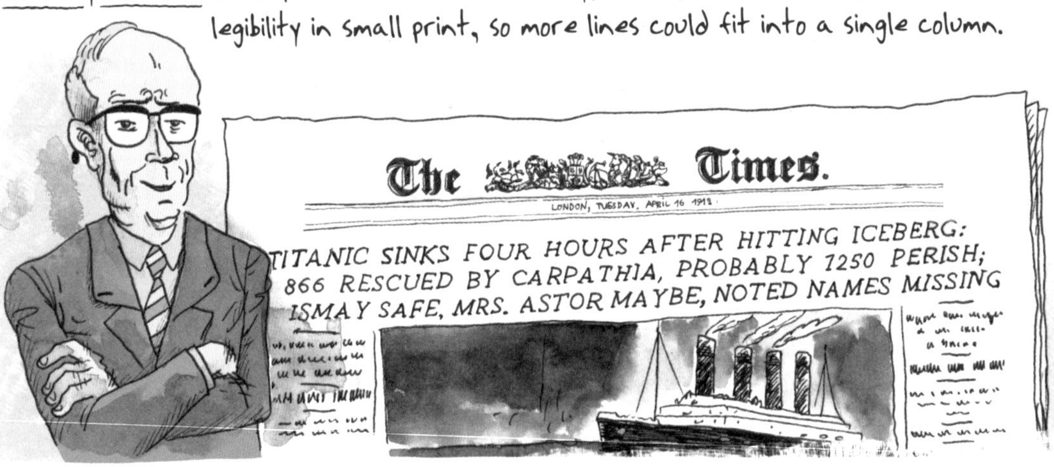

The Times.
LONDON, TUESDAY, APRIL 16 1912
TITANIC SINKS FOUR HOURS AFTER HITTING ICEBERG: 866 RESCUED BY CARPATHIA, PROBABLY 1250 PERISH; ISMAY SAFE, MRS. ASTOR MAYBE, NOTED NAMES MISSING

Morison reworked the shapes of the letters in partnership with young advertising and graphic designer Victor Lardent, perfecting them in a few weeks.

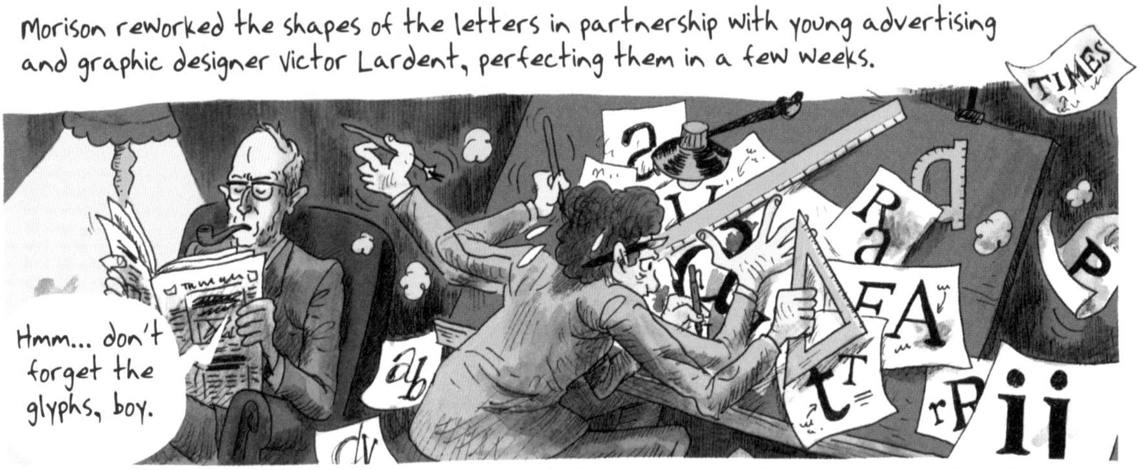

TIMES
Hmm... don't forget the glyphs, boy.

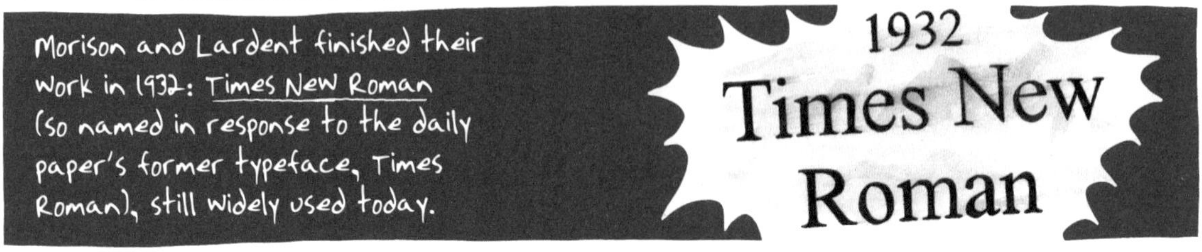

Morison and Lardent finished their work in 1932: Times New Roman (so named in response to the daily paper's former typeface, Times Roman), still widely used today.
1932
Times New Roman

For a long time, this was the default typeface of many word-processing programs.

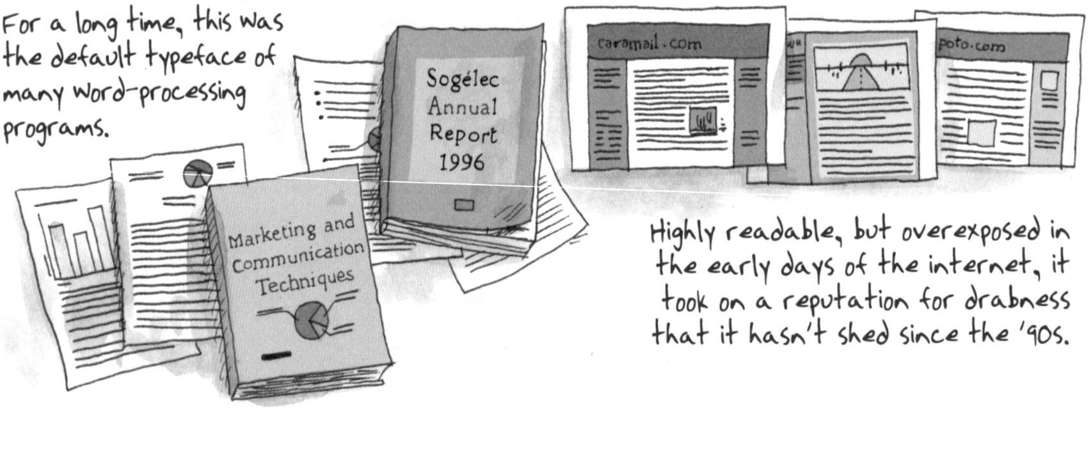

Sogélec Annual Report 1996
caramail.com
poto.com
Marketing and Communication Techniques

Highly readable, but overexposed in the early days of the internet, it took on a reputation for drabness that it hasn't shed since the '90s.

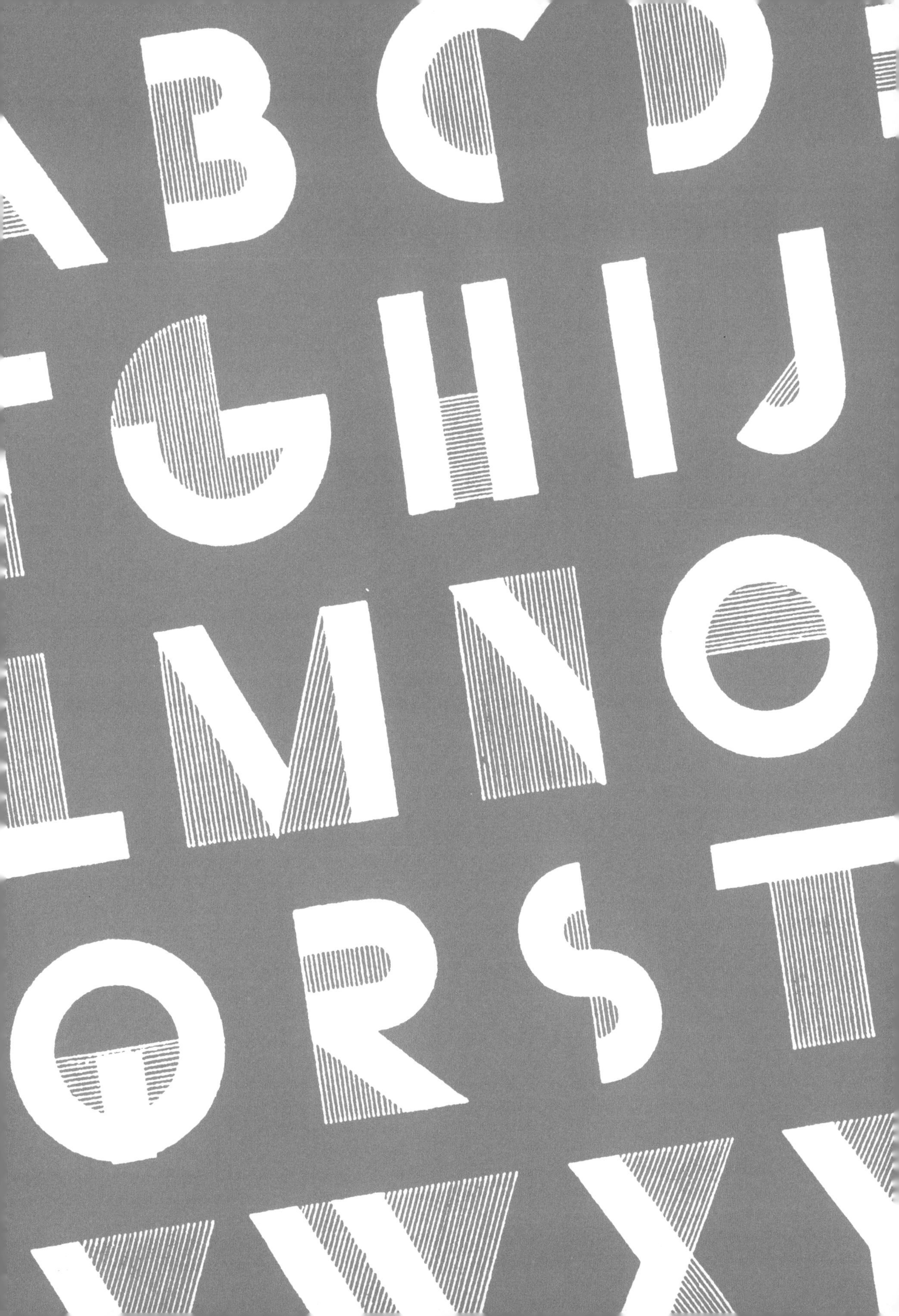
ABCD
GHIJ
LMNO
QRST
VWXY

FROM GILL SANS
TO BAUHAUS

HERVÉ BOURHIS

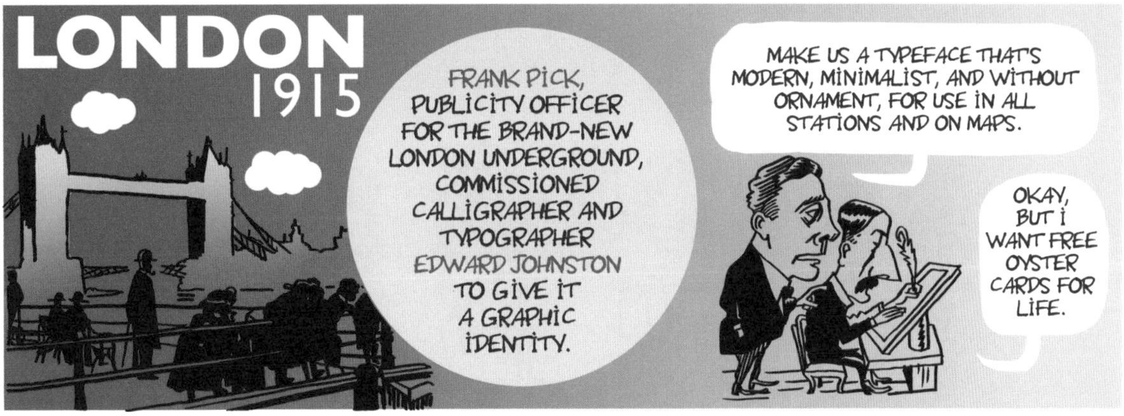
LONDON 1915
FRANK PICK, PUBLICITY OFFICER FOR THE BRAND-NEW LONDON UNDERGROUND, COMMISSIONED CALLIGRAPHER AND TYPOGRAPHER EDWARD JOHNSTON TO GIVE IT A GRAPHIC IDENTITY.
MAKE US A TYPEFACE THAT'S MODERN, MINIMALIST, AND WITHOUT ORNAMENT, FOR USE IN ALL STATIONS AND ON MAPS.
OKAY, BUT I WANT FREE OYSTER CARDS FOR LIFE.

ERIC GILL

JOHNSTON, WHO WAS ALSO A TEACHER, WAS AIDED IN HIS TASK BY ONE OF HIS STUDENTS, ERIC GILL, AND DELIVERED HIS TYPEFACE, A HUMANIST LINEAL WITH NEITHER SERIFS NOR FLARING, AND VERY LITTLE HANDWRITTEN INFLUENCE.

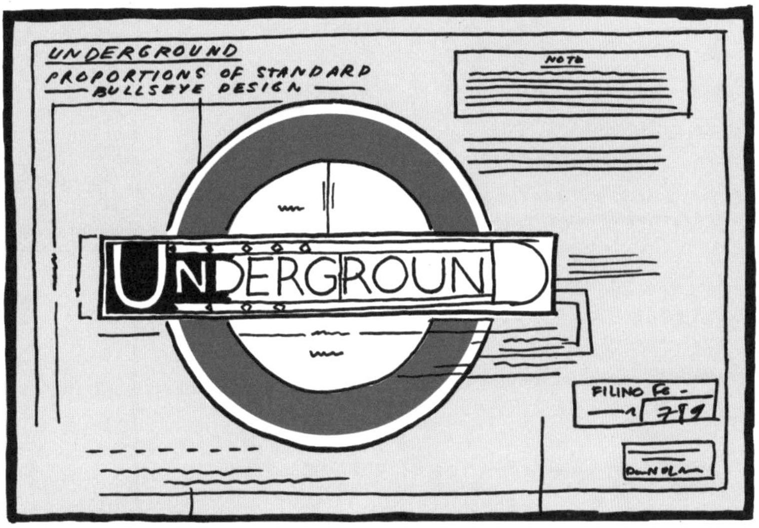
UNDERGROUND
PROPORTIONS OF STANDARD BULLSEYE DESIGN
UNDERGROUND

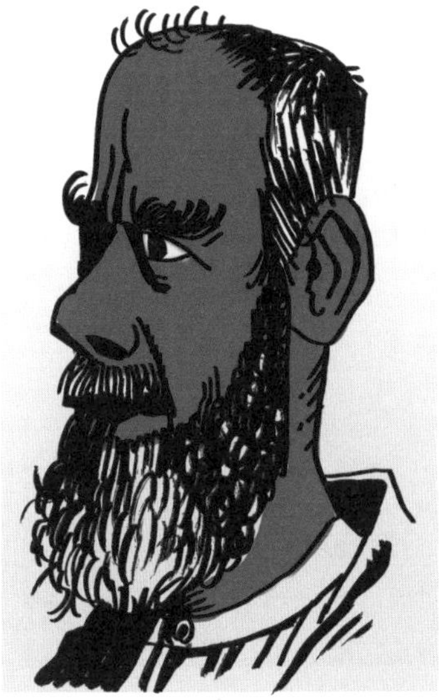

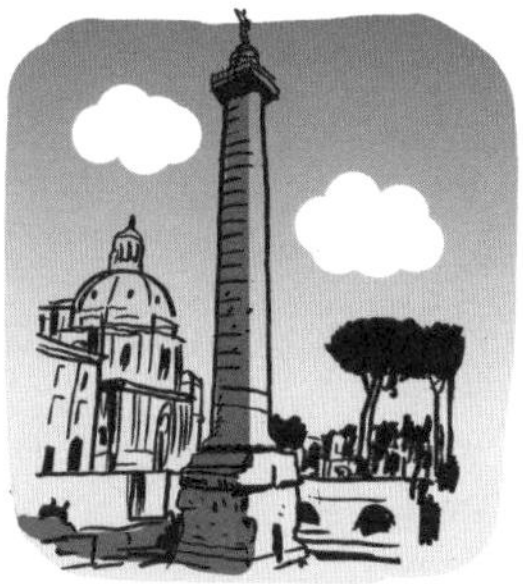

TRAJAN

THE PROPORTIONS OF ITS CAPITAL LETTERS WERE BASED ON THOSE OF TRAJAN'S COLUMN; THE PROPORTIONS OF ITS LOWER CASE BASED ON THOSE OF CAROLINGIAN MINUSCULE. THE RESULTING TYPEFACE WAS AT ONCE CONTEMPORARY AND ELEGANT, NEITHER MASCULINE NOR FEMININE, MULTIPURPOSE, AND AT THE SAME TIME, VERY, VERY CLASSY.

A BIT LATER, ERIC GILL WOULD REWORK THIS TYPEFACE AT STANLEY MORISON'S SUGGESTION (SEE PREVIOUS CHAPTER). THE RESULT WAS GILL SANS, IN 1927.

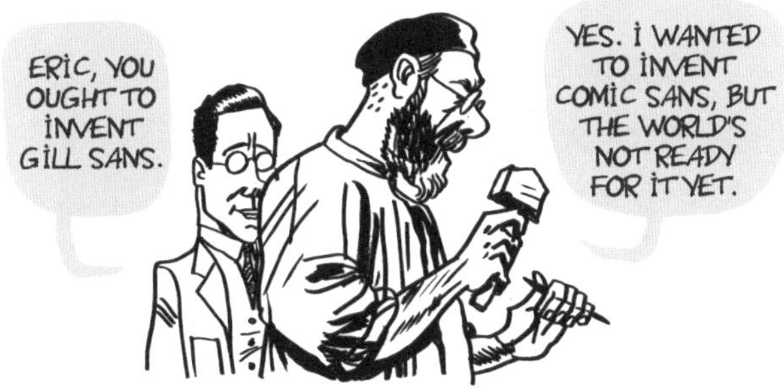
ERIC, YOU OUGHT TO INVENT GILL SANS.
YES. I WANTED TO INVENT COMIC SANS, BUT THE WORLD'S NOT READY FOR IT YET.

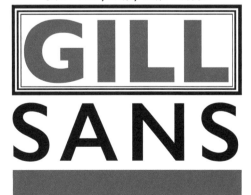

GILL SANS

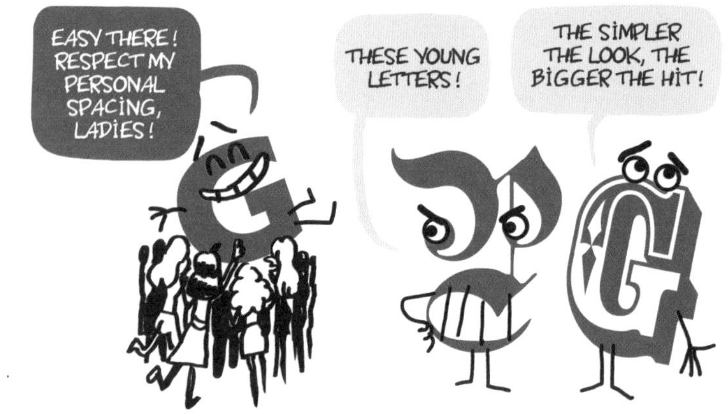
EASY THERE! RESPECT MY PERSONAL SPACING, LADIES!
THESE YOUNG LETTERS!
THE SIMPLER THE LOOK, THE BIGGER THE HIT!

SUCCESS STORY

WARMER THAN FUTURA* (BECAUSE LESS GEOMETRICAL, AND MORE HUMANIST-INSPIRED), MORE MODERN THAN GARAMOND (BECAUSE WITHOUT SERIFS), GILL SANS MET WITH GREAT SUCCESS AS SOON AS IT WAS MARKETED.

* WE'LL GET BACK TO THAT.

SO BRITISH

THE UBIQUITY OF GILL SANS IN THE LONDON UNDERGROUND (OKAY, SO IT'S NOT EXACTLY THE SAME TYPEFACE AS JOHNSTON'S, BUT THEY'RE VERY CLOSE) AND ITS USE, NOTABLY BY TYPOGRAPHER AND DESIGNER JAN TSCHICHOLD ON PENGUIN BOOK COVERS, SOON MADE IT THE SYMBOL OF ENGLAND, A VERY STRONG CONNOTATION IT STILL CARRIES TODAY.

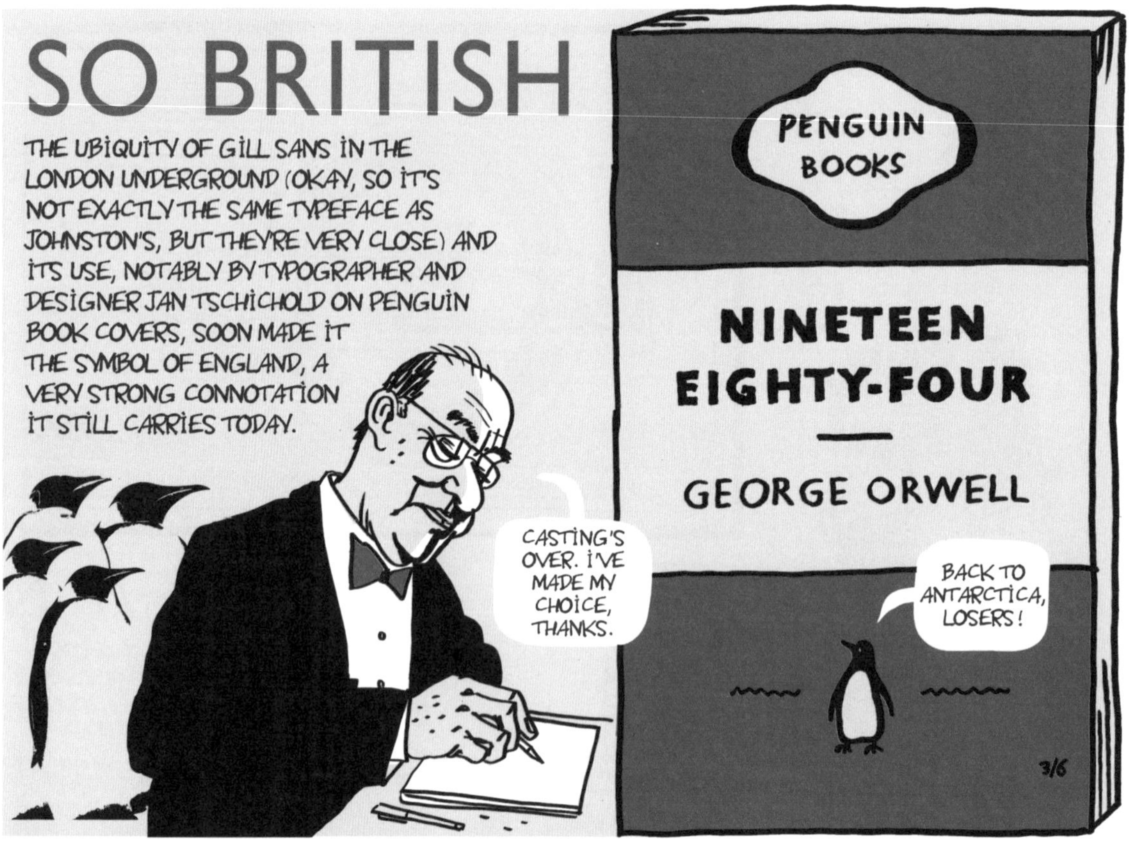
PENGUIN BOOKS
NINETEEN EIGHTY-FOUR
GEORGE ORWELL
CASTING'S OVER. I'VE MADE MY CHOICE, THANKS.
BACK TO ANTARCTICA, LOSERS!
3/6

B B C

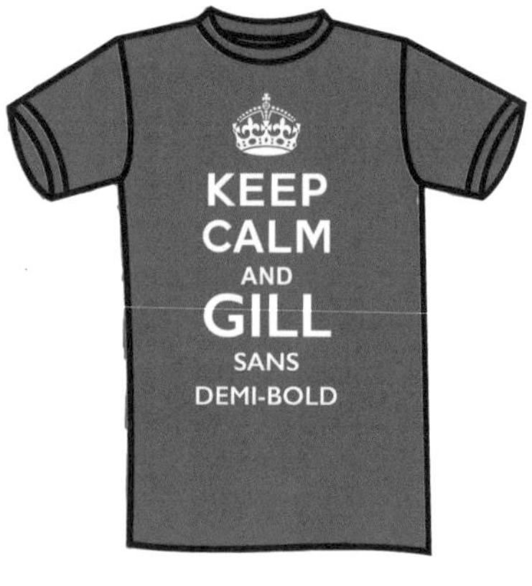
KEEP CALM AND GILL SANS DEMI-BOLD

IT CAN EVEN BE FOUND IN THE BBC'S LOGO. IT ALSO RECALLS AN ALMOST ARISTOCRATIC ELEGANCE, A HIGH LEVEL OF QUALITY AND SERIOUSNESS, WHILE AT THE SAME TIME REMAINING CONVIVIAL AND EFFICIENT, FUNCTIONAL, CONTEMPORARY.

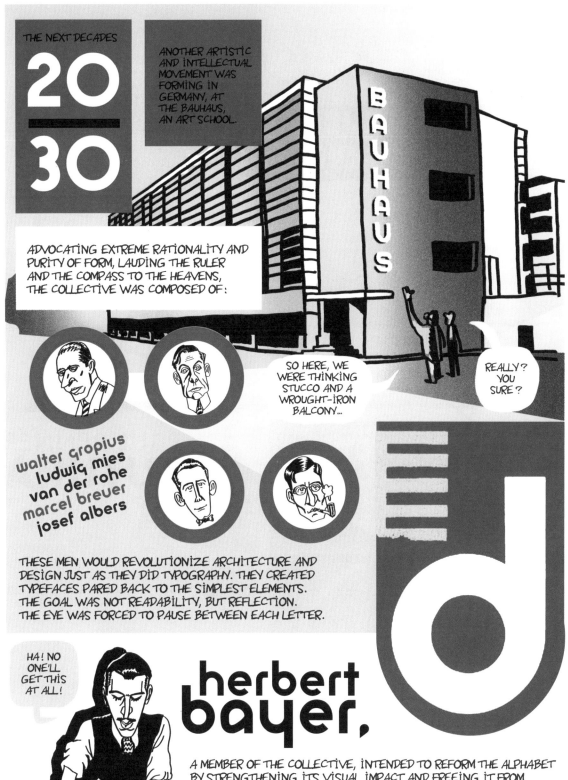

THE NEXT DECADES

20
30

ANOTHER ARTISTIC AND INTELLECTUAL MOVEMENT WAS FORMING IN GERMANY, AT THE BAUHAUS, AN ART SCHOOL.

BAUHAUS

ADVOCATING EXTREME RATIONALITY AND PURITY OF FORM, LAUDING THE RULER AND THE COMPASS TO THE HEAVENS, THE COLLECTIVE WAS COMPOSED OF:

SO HERE, WE WERE THINKING STUCCO AND A WROUGHT-IRON BALCONY...

REALLY? YOU SURE?

walter gropius
ludwig mies van der rohe
marcel breuer
josef albers

THESE MEN WOULD REVOLUTIONIZE ARCHITECTURE AND DESIGN JUST AS THEY DID TYPOGRAPHY. THEY CREATED TYPEFACES PARED BACK TO THE SIMPLEST ELEMENTS. THE GOAL WAS NOT READABILITY, BUT REFLECTION. THE EYE WAS FORCED TO PAUSE BETWEEN EACH LETTER.

HA! NO ONE'LL GET THIS AT ALL!

herbert bayer,

A MEMBER OF THE COLLECTIVE, INTENDED TO REFORM THE ALPHABET BY STRENGTHENING ITS VISUAL IMPACT AND FREEING IT FROM CONSTRAINTS OF CULTURAL CONNOTATION. IN PRINCIPLE, THIS WAS TO MAKE READING HARDER: READERS WOULD HAVE TO RE-READ EACH SENTENCE TO ASSIMILATE THE MEANING, THUS GIVING RISE TO MORE SUSTAINED REFLECTION.

RADICALISM

ABCDEFGHIJKLMNO PQRSTUVWXYZ 123

MANY OF THESE TYPEFACES, DESIGNED BY HERBERT BAYER OR JOSEF ALBERS, VANISHED MORE OR LESS BECAUSE OF THEIR RADICAL FORM. HOWEVER, PAUL RENNER'S FUTURA, ALSO BORN OF THIS MOVEMENT, HAS BECOME A WORLDWIDE CLASSIC.

NOT BAD... CAREFUL, THOUGH: A FEW LETTERS ARE ACTUALLY LEGIBLE!

AFTER TEACHING IN FRANKFURT AND DESIGNING IN MUNICH, PAUL RENNER (1878–1956) BECAME SIMULTANEOUSLY THE PRINCIPAL AND DIRECTOR OF TWO DIFFERENT PRINTING SCHOOLS IN THE SAME TOWN. HE WAS NEVER OFFICIALLY AFFILIATED WITH THE BAUHAUS, BUT HE ESPOUSED ITS PRINCIPLES, AND IN 1924 BEGAN DESIGNING A RADICALLY GEOMETRICAL ALPHABET.

PAUL RENNER
FUTURA

BAUER ALPHABETS INC.

FUTURA

AT FIRST, IT WAS WHOLLY COMPOSED USING THE BAUHAUS'S THREE KEY SYMBOLS: THE TRIANGLE, THE CIRCLE, AND THE SQUARE. PURIFYING THE FORMS SUPERSEDED READABILITY, AND HIS TYPEFACE WAS ALMOST ILLEGIBLE—AND SO CONSIDERED AN UNQUALIFIED SUCCESS.

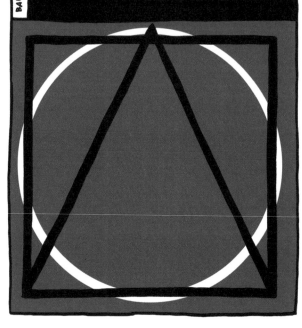

WHY, YOUR TYPEFACE IS UTTERLY UNREADABLE!

AW, SHUCKS! ENOUGH WITH THE FLATTERY!

FUTURA

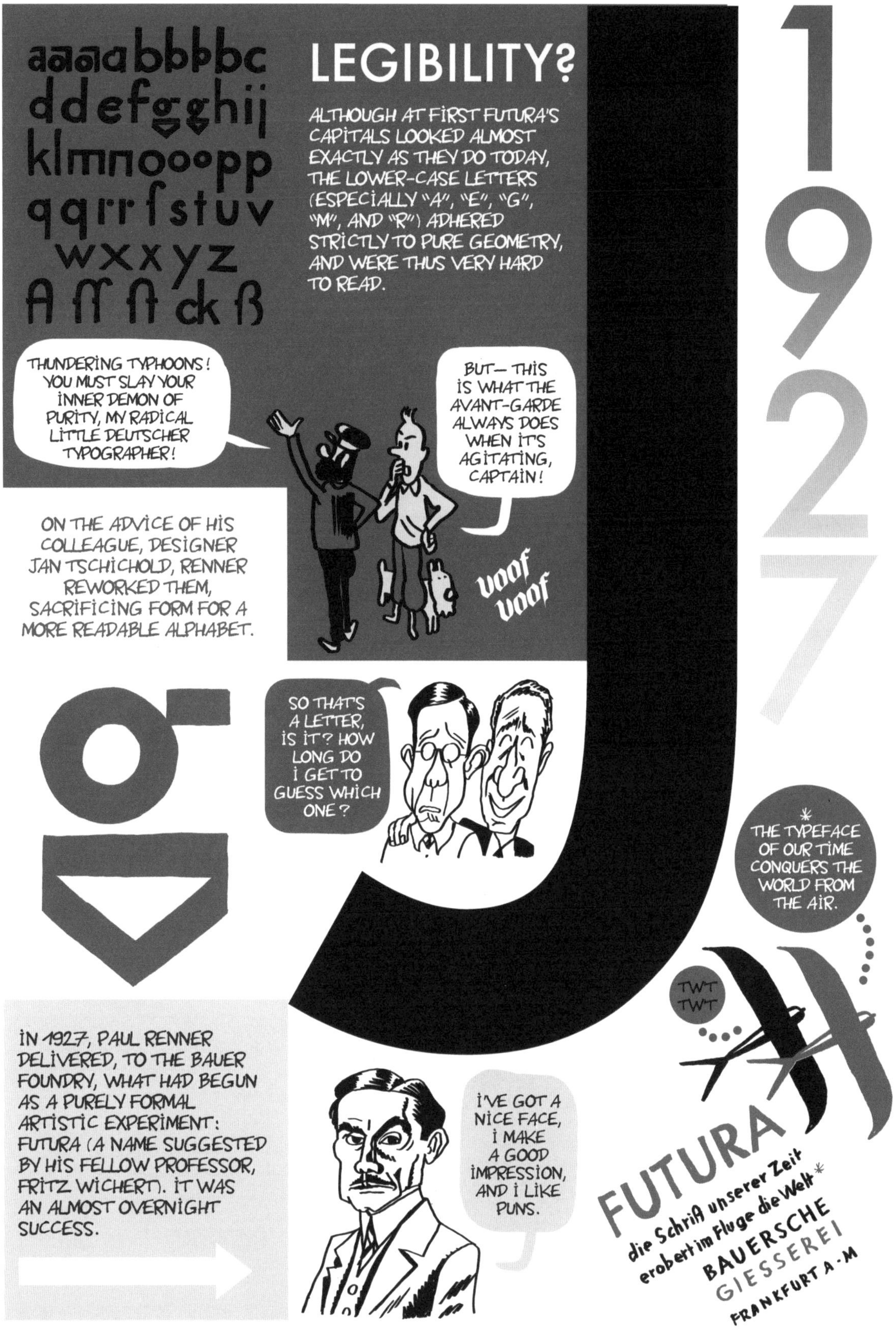
aaaabbbbc
ddefgghij
klmnooopp
qqrrſstuv
wxxyz
A ſſ ſt ck ß
LEGIBILITY?
ALTHOUGH AT FIRST FUTURA'S CAPITALS LOOKED ALMOST EXACTLY AS THEY DO TODAY, THE LOWER-CASE LETTERS (ESPECIALLY "A", "E", "G", "M", AND "R") ADHERED STRICTLY TO PURE GEOMETRY, AND WERE THUS VERY HARD TO READ.
1927
THUNDERING TYPHOONS! YOU MUST SLAY YOUR INNER DEMON OF PURITY, MY RADICAL LITTLE DEUTSCHER TYPOGRAPHER!
BUT— THIS IS WHAT THE AVANT-GARDE ALWAYS DOES WHEN IT'S AGITATING, CAPTAIN!
ON THE ADVICE OF HIS COLLEAGUE, DESIGNER JAN TSCHICHOLD, RENNER REWORKED THEM, SACRIFICING FORM FOR A MORE READABLE ALPHABET.
voof voof
SO THAT'S A LETTER, IS IT? HOW LONG DO I GET TO GUESS WHICH ONE?
* THE TYPEFACE OF OUR TIME CONQUERS THE WORLD FROM THE AIR.
TW'T TW'T
IN 1927, PAUL RENNER DELIVERED, TO THE BAUER FOUNDRY, WHAT HAD BEGUN AS A PURELY FORMAL ARTISTIC EXPERIMENT: FUTURA (A NAME SUGGESTED BY HIS FELLOW PROFESSOR, FRITZ WICHERT). IT WAS AN ALMOST OVERNIGHT SUCCESS.
I'VE GOT A NICE FACE, I MAKE A GOOD IMPRESSION, AND I LIKE PUNS.
FUTURA
die Schrift unserer Zeit erobert im Fluge die Welt*
BAUERSCHE GIESSEREI
FRANKFURT A·M

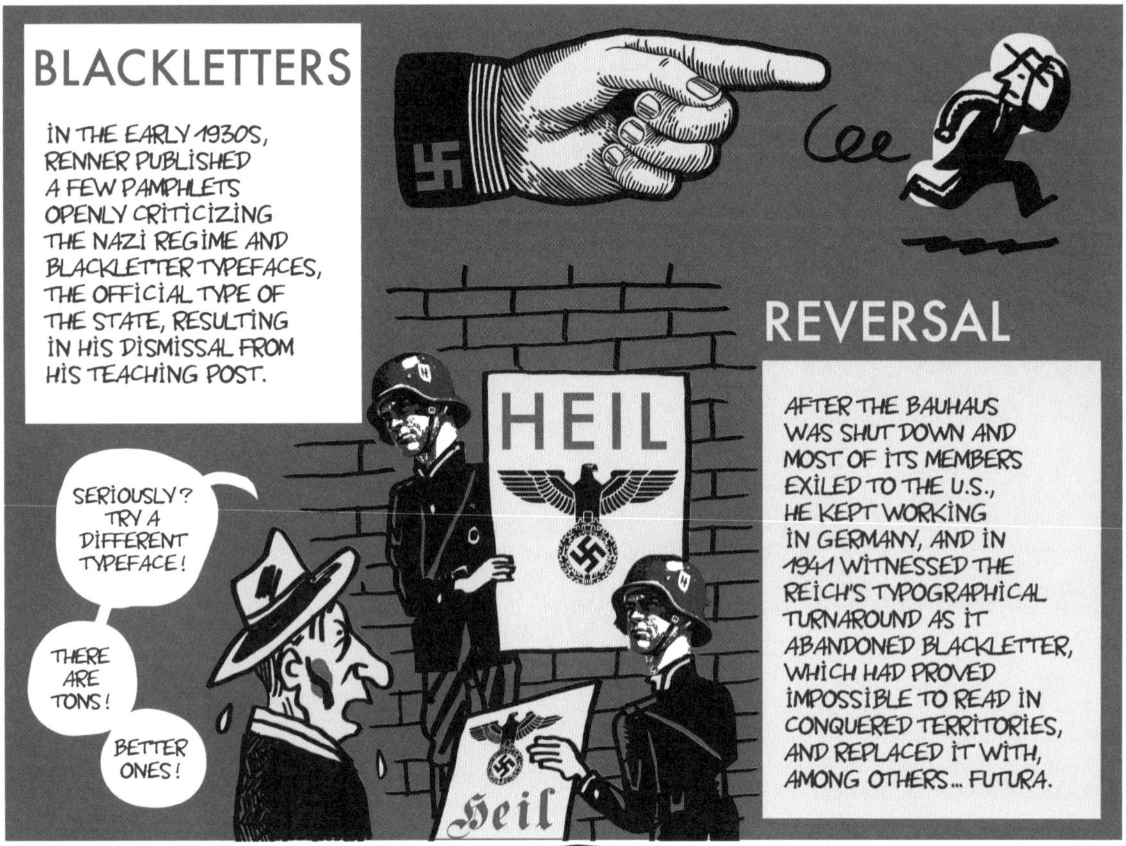
BLACKLETTERS
IN THE EARLY 1930S, RENNER PUBLISHED A FEW PAMPHLETS OPENLY CRITICIZING THE NAZI REGIME AND BLACKLETTER TYPEFACES, THE OFFICIAL TYPE OF THE STATE, RESULTING IN HIS DISMISSAL FROM HIS TEACHING POST.
SERIOUSLY? TRY A DIFFERENT TYPEFACE!
THERE ARE TONS!
BETTER ONES!
HEIL
Heil
REVERSAL
AFTER THE BAUHAUS WAS SHUT DOWN AND MOST OF ITS MEMBERS EXILED TO THE U.S., HE KEPT WORKING IN GERMANY, AND IN 1941 WITNESSED THE REICH'S TYPOGRAPHICAL TURNAROUND AS IT ABANDONED BLACKLETTER, WHICH HAD PROVED IMPOSSIBLE TO READ IN CONQUERED TERRITORIES, AND REPLACED IT WITH, AMONG OTHERS... FUTURA.

VOX

WHEN THE WAR WAS OVER, FUTURA WAS LITERALLY BOYCOTTED IN FRANCE FOR ITS GERMAN CONNOTATIONS.

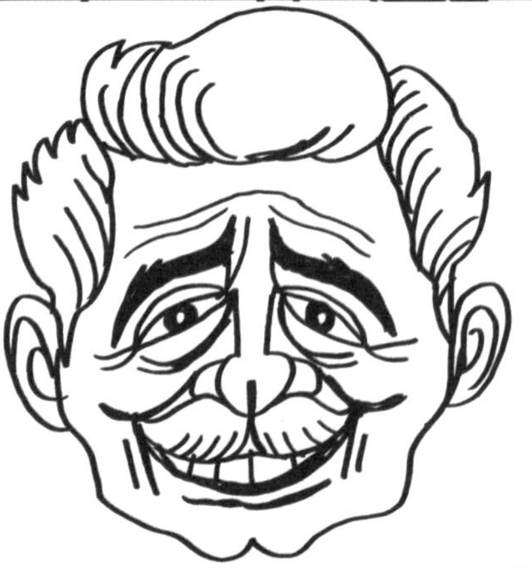

EUROPE

BUT THE OPINIONATED MAXIMILIEN VOX, THEN WORKING FOR THE DEBERNY AND PEIGNOT FOUNDRY, IMPORTED IT ANYWAY, REBRANDING IT "EUROPE". IT MET WITH GROWING SUCCESS BEFORE BEING RENAMED FUTURA AGAIN A FEW YEARS LATER.

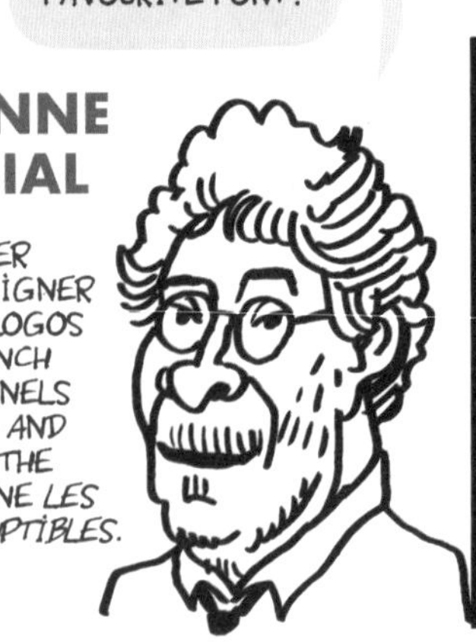
THAT'S MY FAVOURITE FONT!

ÉTIENNE ROBIAL

PUBLISHER AND DESIGNER OF THE LOGOS FOR FRENCH TV CHANNELS CANAL + AND M6, AND THE MAGAZINE *LES INROCKUPTIBLES*.

INFLUENCE

FUTURA CAN BE FOUND IN THE LOGOS OF LOUIS VUITTON, FEDEX, AND CANAL +, AND IN IKEA AND VOLKSWAGEN CATALOGUES. STANLEY KUBRICK, WHO LOVED IT WITH A PASSION, FEATURED IT ON POSTERS AND TITLE SEQUENCES OF HIS FILMS, AS DID WES ANDERSON.

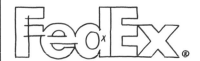

2001:aspaceodyssey

FedEx®

CANAL+

LOUIS VUITTON

The ROYAL TENENBAUMS

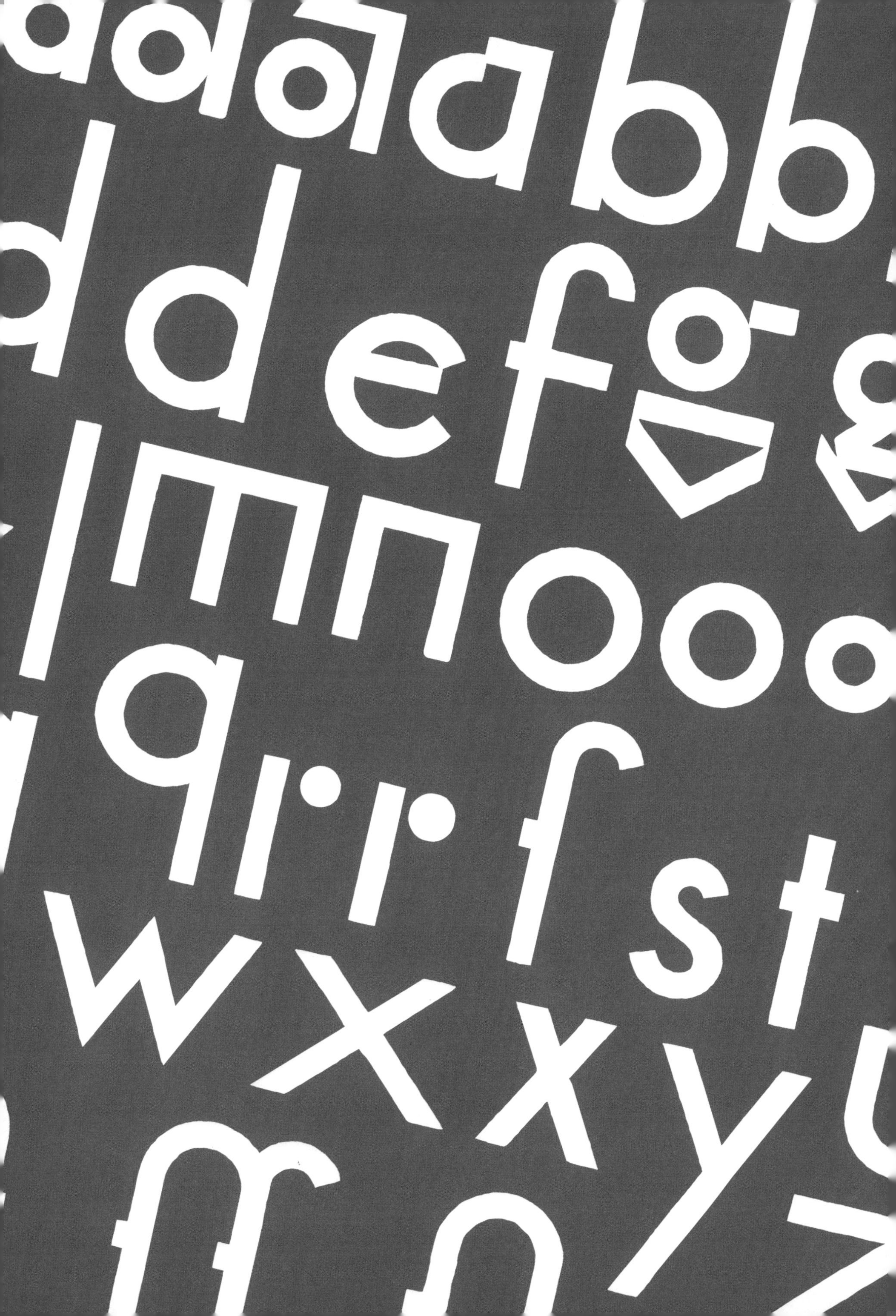

THE "RENCONTRES DE LURE"

ALEXANDRE CLÉRISSE

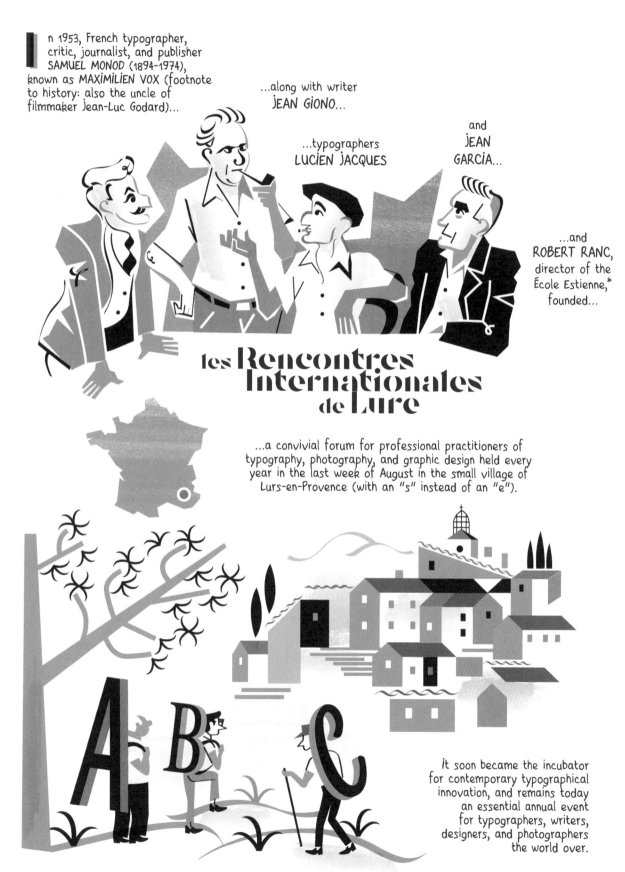

In 1953, French typographer, critic, journalist, and publisher SAMUEL MONOD (1894–1974), known as MAXIMILIEN VOX (footnote to history: also the uncle of filmmaker Jean-Luc Godard)...

...along with writer JEAN GIONO...

...typographers LUCIEN JACQUES

and JEAN GARCIA...

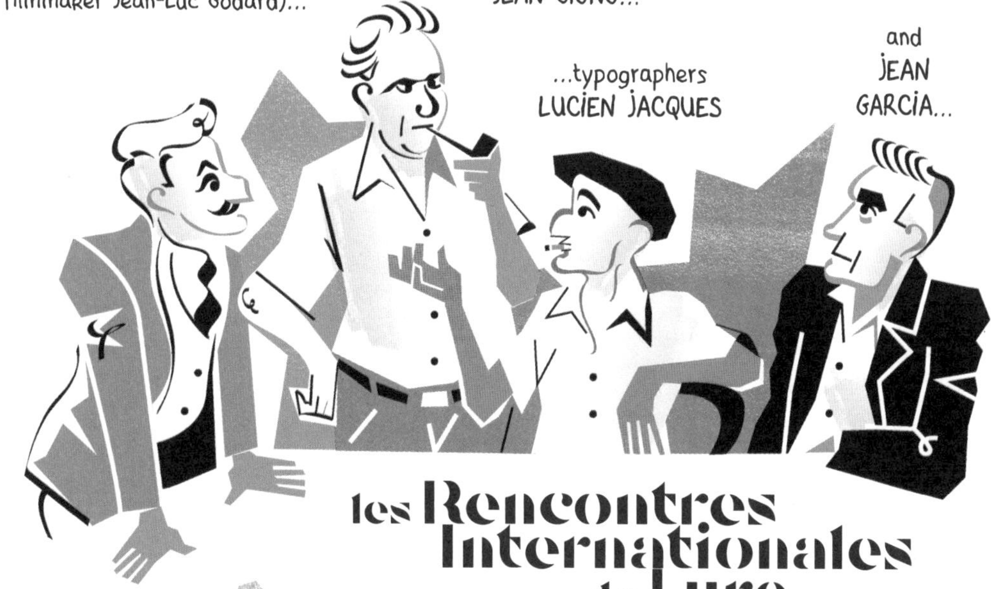

...and ROBERT RANC, director of the École Estienne,* founded...

les Rencontres Internationales de Lure

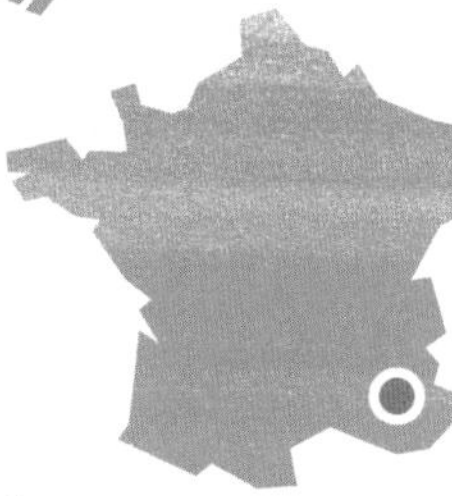

...a convivial forum for professional practitioners of typography, photography, and graphic design held every year in the last week of August in the small village of Lurs-en-Provence (with an "s" instead of an "e").

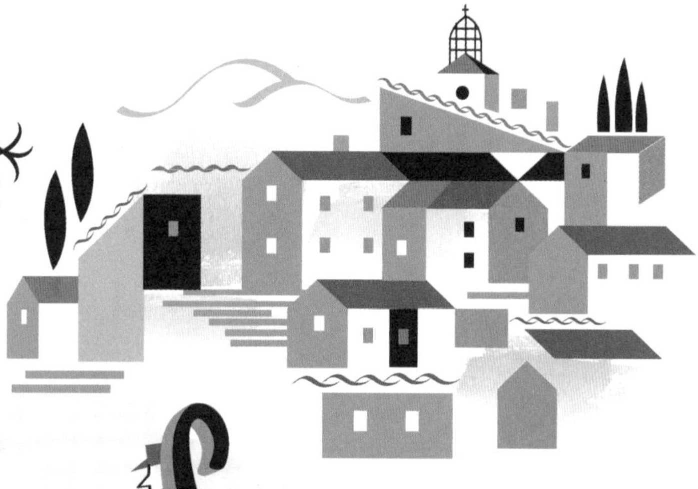

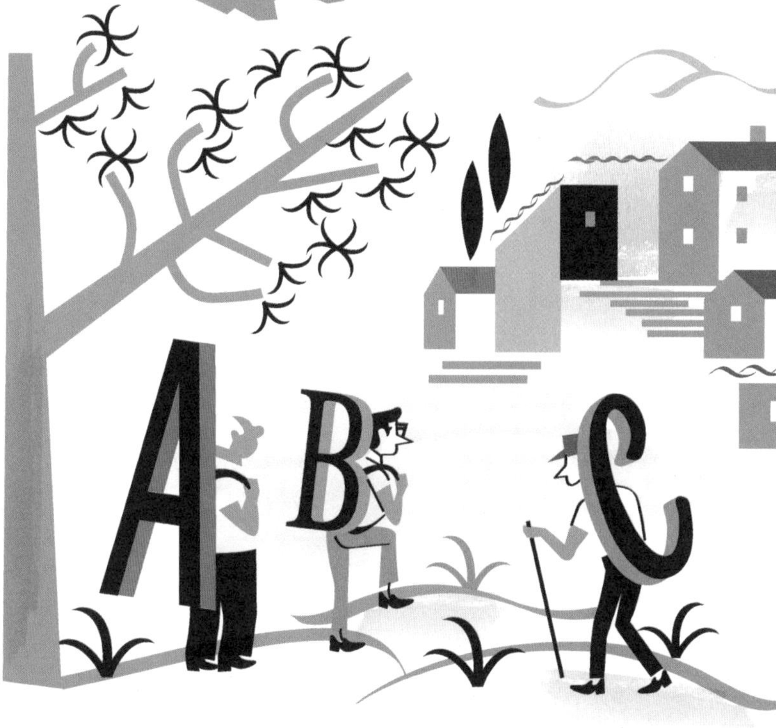
A
B
C

It soon became the incubator for contemporary typographical innovation, and remains today an essential annual event for typographers, writers, designers, and photographers the world over.

* Paris's renowned academy for the printing arts.

Why this little village in Haute-Provence? Because Vox had made his home there, and he wished to lend the place a brighter, more positive image...

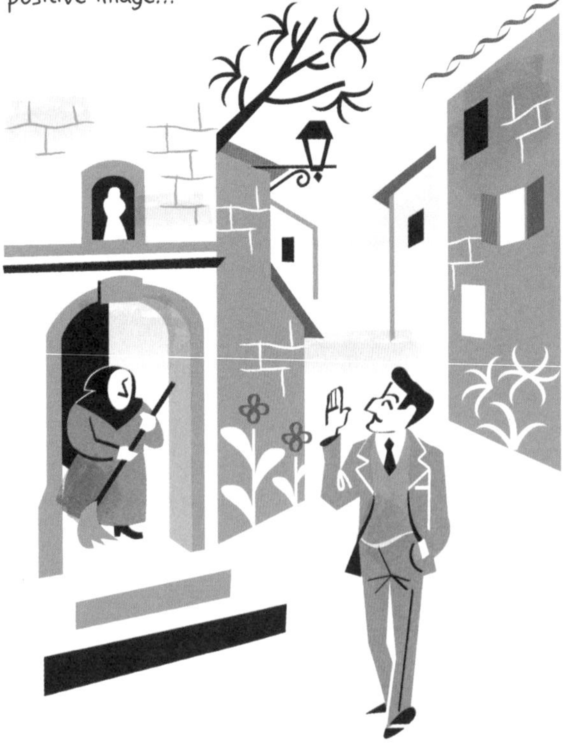

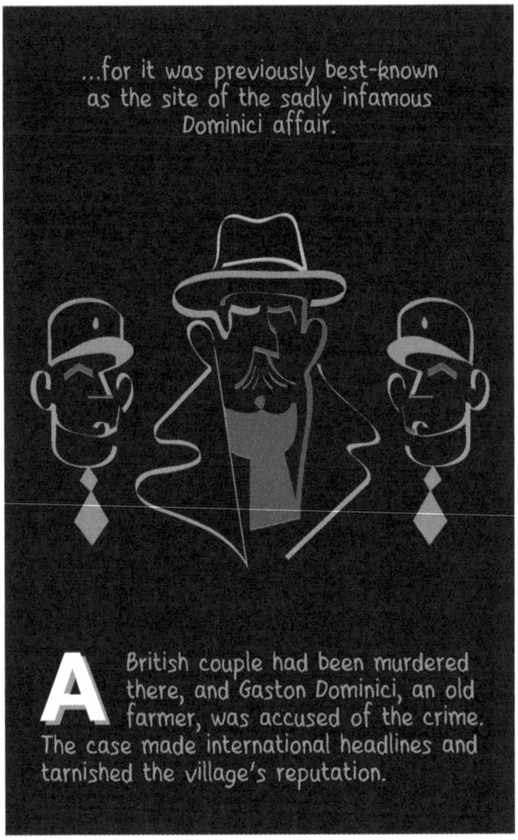
...for it was previously best-known as the site of the sadly infamous Dominici affair.
A British couple had been murdered there, and Gaston Dominici, an old farmer, was accused of the crime. The case made international headlines and tarnished the village's reputation.

Maximilien Vox owned a roomy building in the middle of the village, and donated it to the association that organizes the Rencontres, which renamed it "La Chancellerie".

From then on, conferences and other workshops were held there, hosted by the "Compagnons de Lure". This association swiftly grew from a few dozen to around a hundred members.

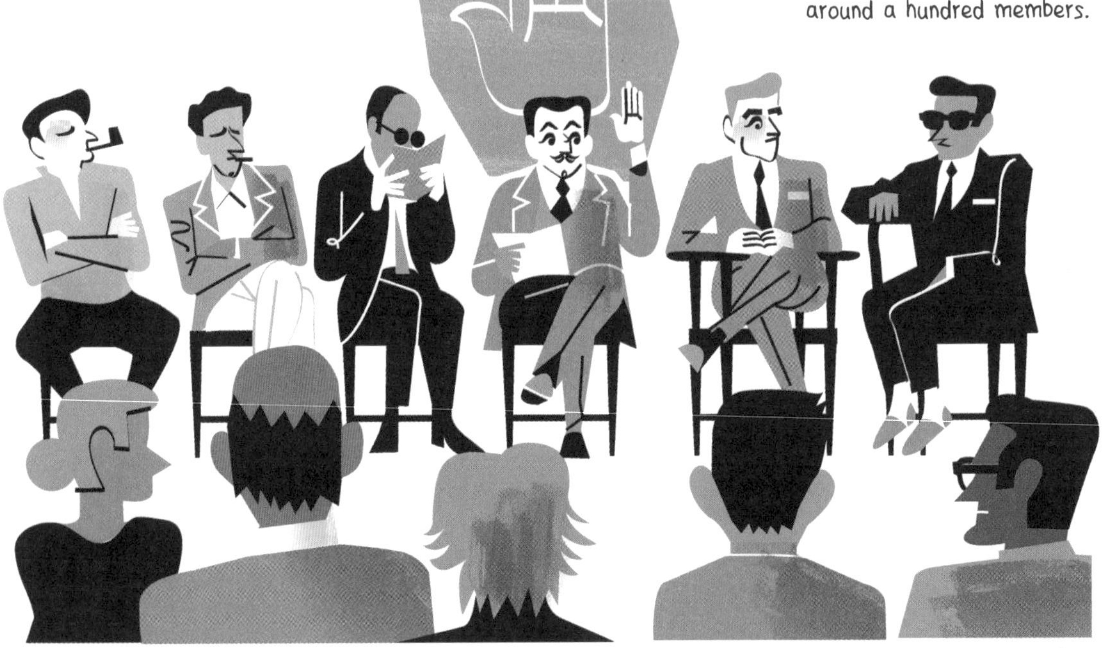

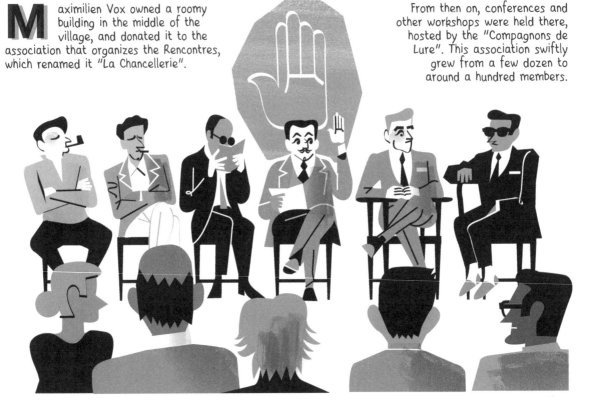

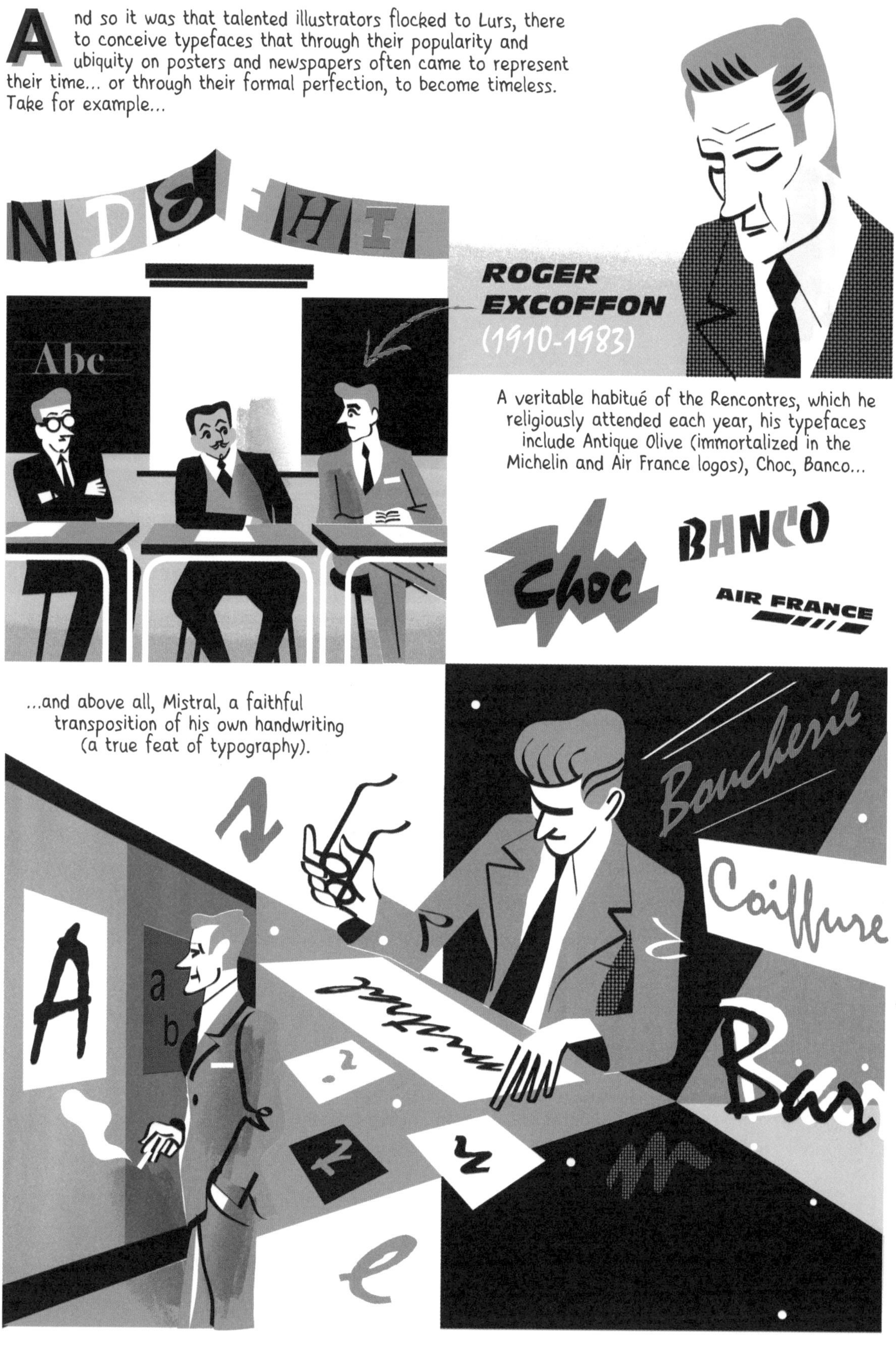
And so it was that talented illustrators flocked to Lurs, there to conceive typefaces that through their popularity and ubiquity on posters and newspapers often came to represent their time... or through their formal perfection, to become timeless. Take for example...
Abc
ROGER EXCOFFON
(1910-1983)
A veritable habitué of the Rencontres, which he religiously attended each year, his typefaces include Antique Olive (immortalized in the Michelin and Air France logos), Choc, Banco...
Choc
BANCO
AIR FRANCE
...and above all, Mistral, a faithful transposition of his own handwriting (a true feat of typography).
A
a
b
Boucherie
Coiffure
Bar

There was also the Swiss

Adrian **Frutiger**

(1928-2015)

His Univers typeface was the precursor to Helvetica...

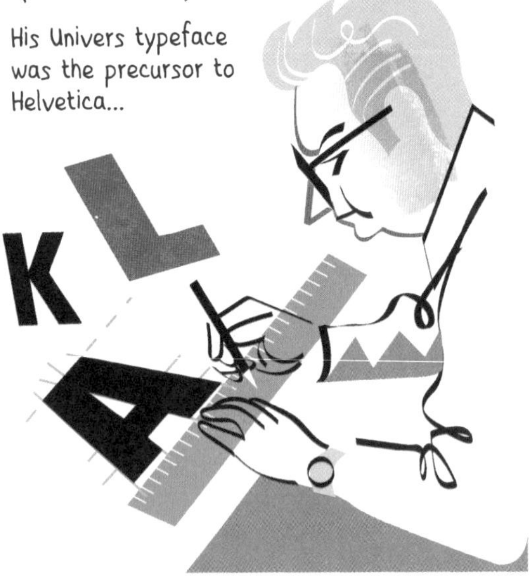

...and the "International Typographic Style" or "Swiss Style", developed according to an almost mathematical system. His Frutiger typeface adorns the signage of many airports all over the world.

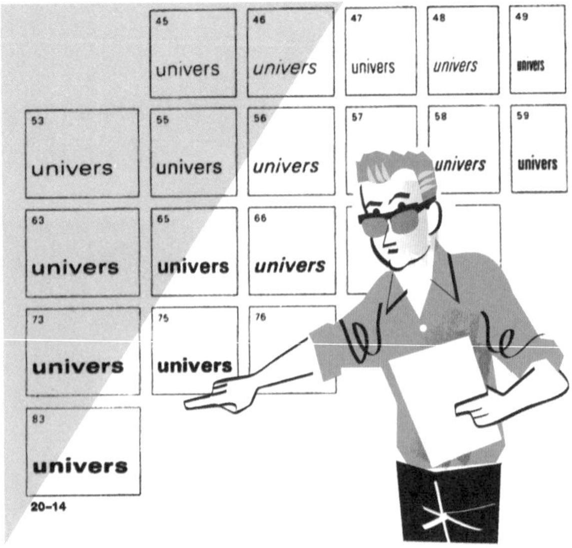
45 univers
46 univers
47 univers
48 univers
49 univers
53 univers
55 univers
56 univers
57
58 univers
59 univers
63 univers
65 univers
66 univers
73 univers
75 univers
76
83 univers
20–14

Last but not least, Italian **Aldo Novarese** (1920-1995), whose Eurostile, the retro-futurist typeface used in the Casio logo, was directly inspired by the shapes of cathode ray tubes in that brand-new invention: television.

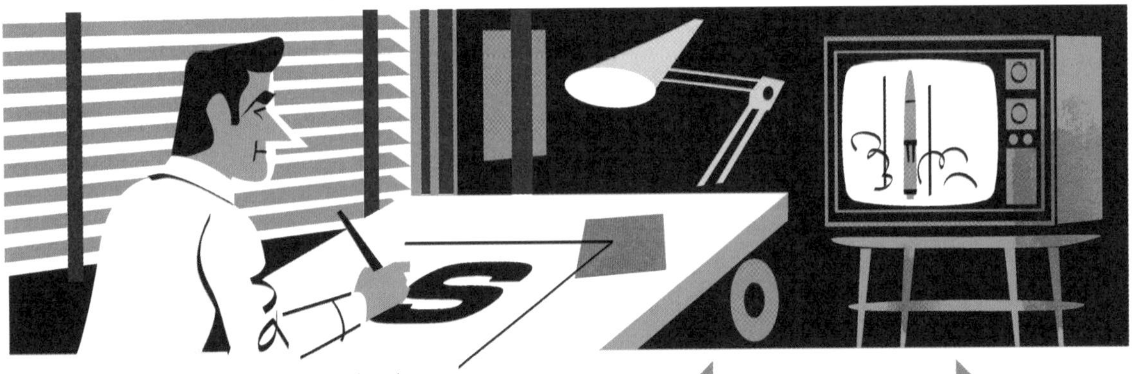

In the '60s and '70s, it remained closely associated with science fiction, and can be found on the spacecraft in, among others, Stanley Kubrick's *2001: A Space Odyssey*...

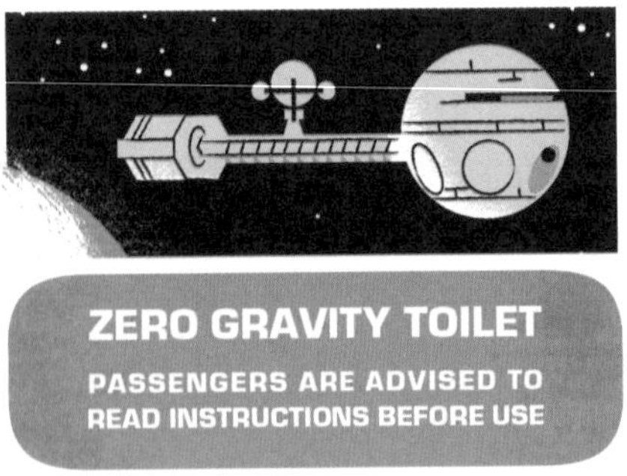
ZERO GRAVITY TOILET
PASSENGERS ARE ADVISED TO READ INSTRUCTIONS BEFORE USE

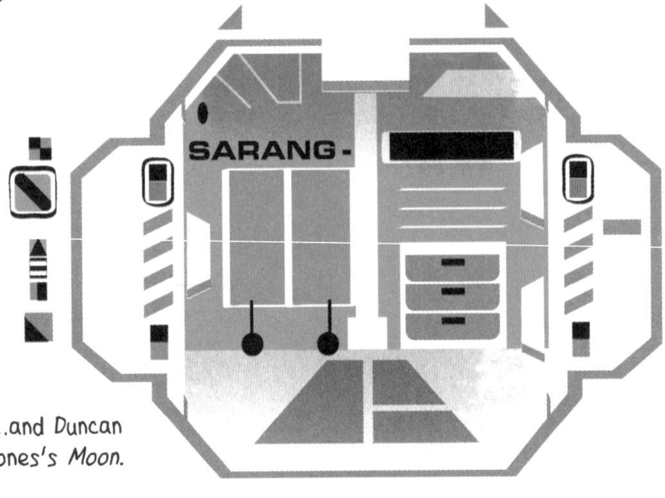
SARANG-

...and Duncan Jones's *Moon*.

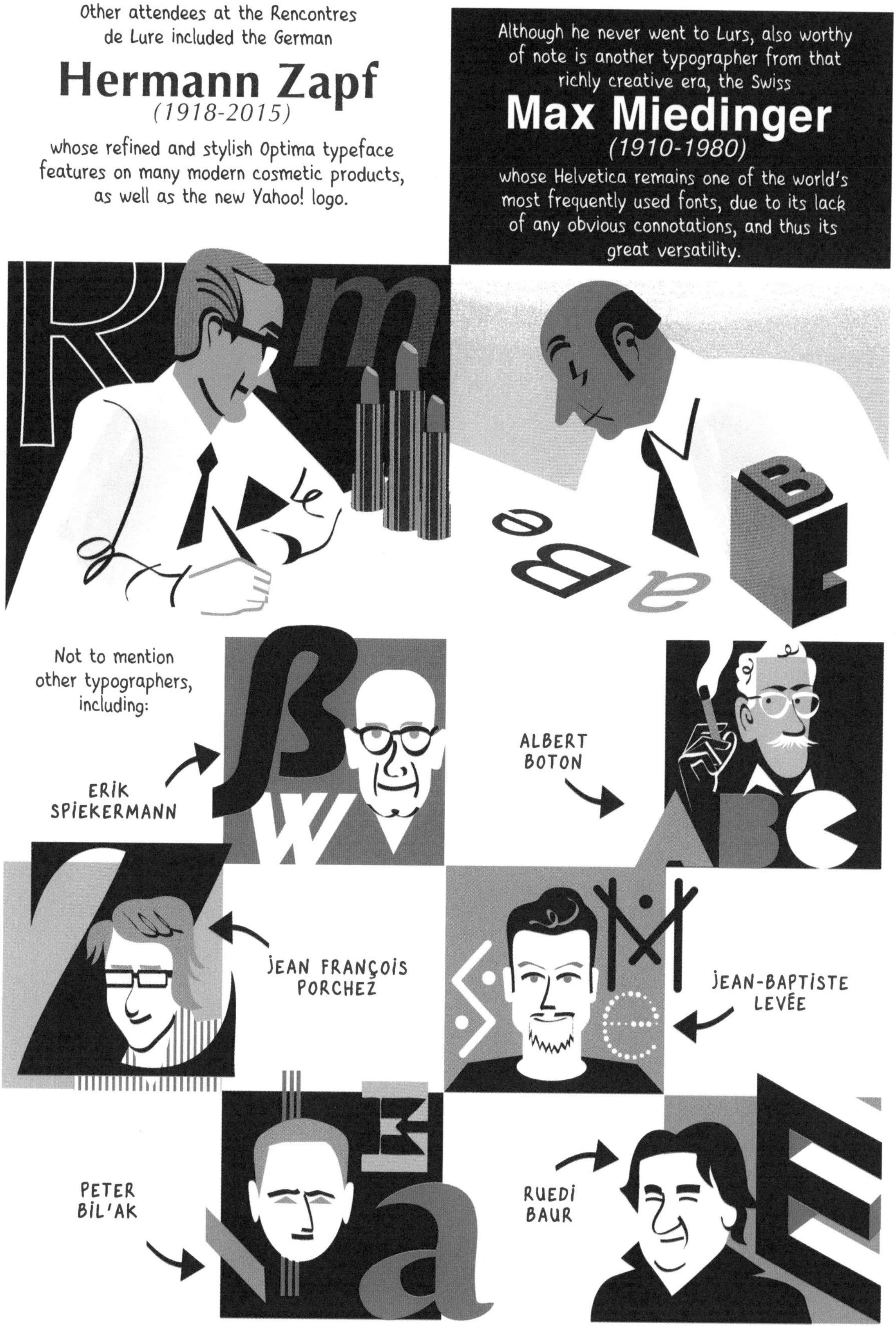
Other attendees at the Rencontres de Lure included the German
Hermann Zapf
(1918-2015)
whose refined and stylish Optima typeface features on many modern cosmetic products, as well as the new Yahoo! logo.
Although he never went to Lurs, also worthy of note is another typographer from that richly creative era, the Swiss
Max Miedinger
(1910-1980)
whose Helvetica remains one of the world's most frequently used fonts, due to its lack of any obvious connotations, and thus its great versatility.
Not to mention other typographers, including:
ERIK SPIEKERMANN
ALBERT BOTON
JEAN FRANÇOIS PORCHEZ
JEAN-BAPTISTE LEVÉE
PETER BIL'AK
RUEDI BAUR

E very year, many artists, designers, and photographers gathered in La Chancellerie.

Of particular note were Robert Massin and Eugène Ionesco

who in 1964 published the idiosyncratic photo-typographical pagespreads of

THE BALD PRIMA DONNA

designer, publisher, and lover of typography (especially Futura)

ÉTIENNE ROBIAL

designers, ad-men, photographers, and video artists

JEAN-PAUL GOUDE and JEAN-CHRISTOPHE AVERTY

writer, illustrator, and typographer

JEAN ALESSANDRINI

creator of a new system for classifying typefaces, Codex 80, highly criticized in its day by the Compagnons de Lure

designer

PHILIPPE APELOIG

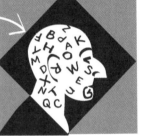

illustrator

RAYMOND SAVIGNAC

whose ads for Perrier, Bic, and Aspro adorned every French wall

creator of fantastical objects

JACQUES CARELMAN

photographer and designer

PETER KNAPP

painter

VICTOR VASARELY,

and many more...

c. 60
10 a 5 A
14 k. 700

EUR

omphante au

RIGUEUR DU

triomphante aux bonne

RIGUEUR DU PLOMB

iomphante aux bonnes d'un

IEUR DU PLOMB OU L'OR

aux bonnes d'un empire

DU PLOMB OU L'

c. 30
24 a 12 A
8 k. 780

MAXIMILIEN VOX'S SYSTEM

ANNE SIMON

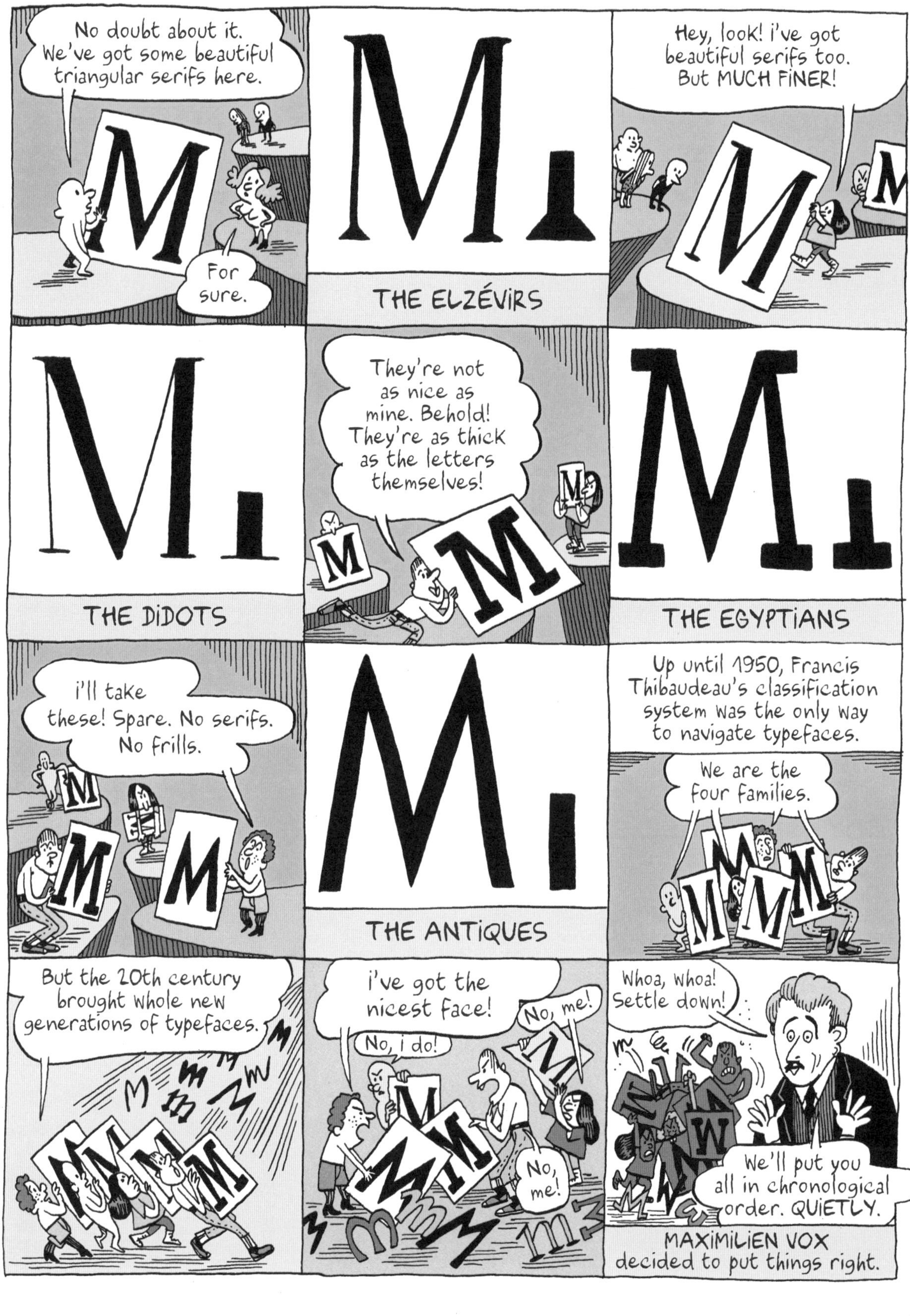

No doubt about it. We've got some beautiful triangular serifs here.
For sure.
THE ELZÉVIRS
Hey, look! I've got beautiful serifs too. But MUCH FINER!
THE DIDOTS
They're not as nice as mine. Behold! They're as thick as the letters themselves!
THE EGYPTIANS
I'll take these! Spare. No serifs. No frills.
THE ANTIQUES
Up until 1950, Francis Thibaudeau's classification system was the only way to navigate typefaces.
We are the four families.
But the 20th century brought whole new generations of typefaces.
I've got the nicest face!
No, me!
No, I do!
No, me!
Whoa, whoa! Settle down!
We'll put you all in chronological order. QUIETLY.
MAXIMILIEN VOX decided to put things right.

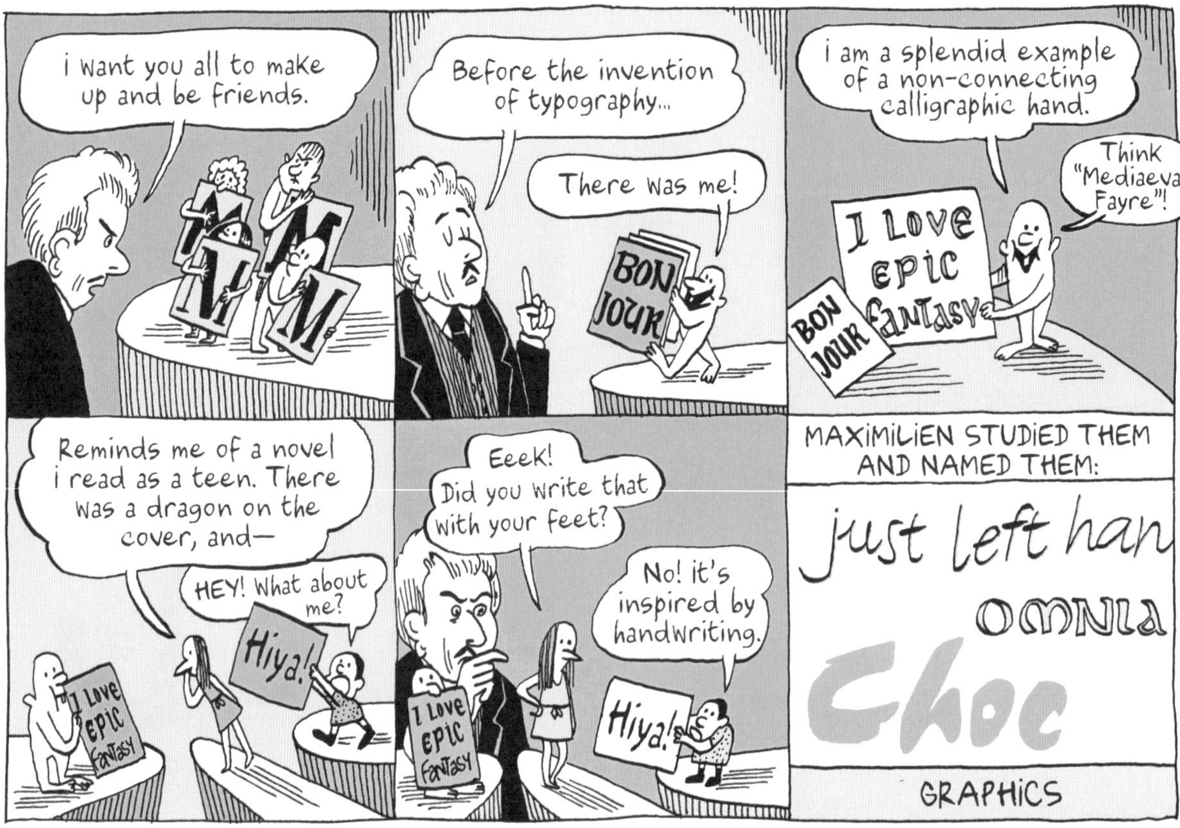
i want you all to make up and be friends.
Before the invention of typography...
There was me!
BON JOUR
i am a splendid example of a non-connecting calligraphic hand.
Think "Mediaeval Fayre"!
I LOVE EPIC FANTASY
BON JOUR
Reminds me of a novel i read as a teen. There was a dragon on the cover, and—
HEY! What about me?
Hiya!
I LOVE EPIC FANTASY
Eeek! Did you write that with your feet?
No! it's inspired by handwriting.
I LOVE EPIC FANTASY
Hiya!
MAXIMILIEN STUDIED THEM AND NAMED THEM:
just left han
OMNIA
Choc
GRAPHICS

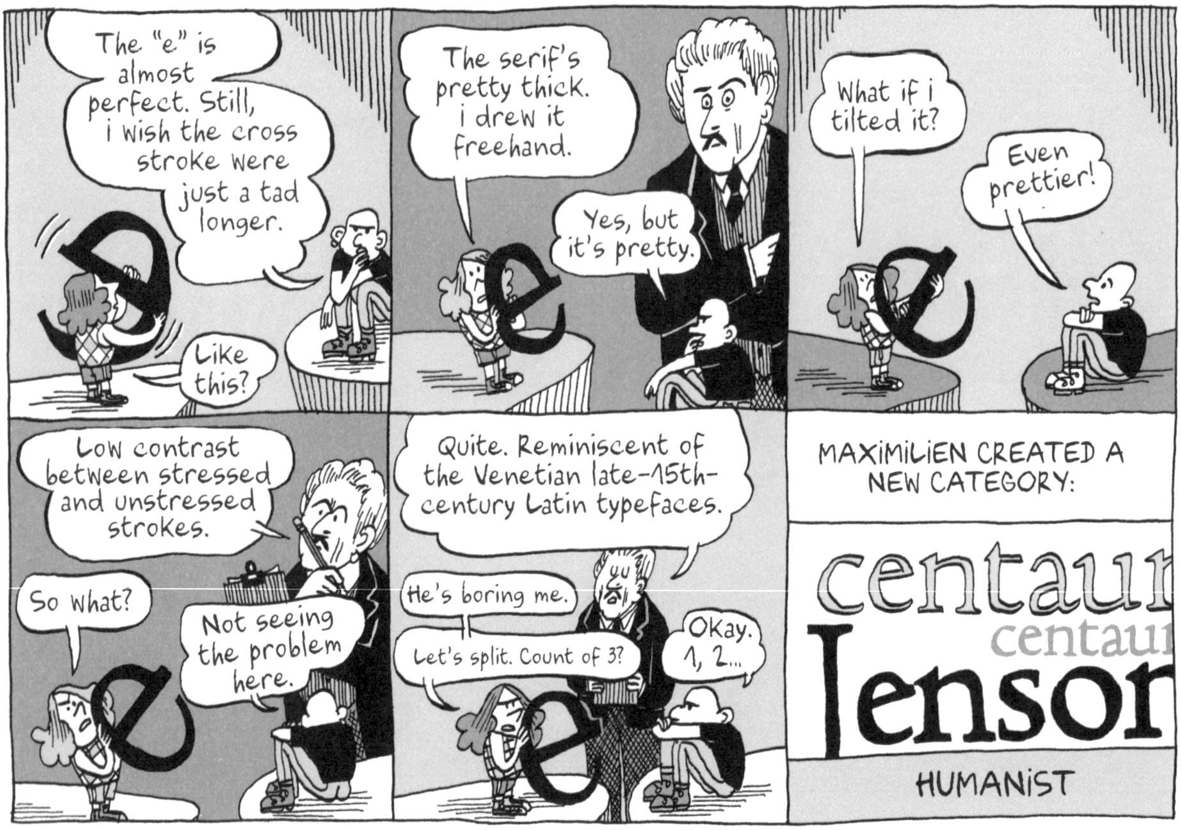
The "e" is almost perfect. Still, i wish the cross stroke were just a tad longer.
Like this?
The serif's pretty thick. i drew it freehand.
Yes, but it's pretty.
What if i tilted it?
Even prettier!
Low contrast between stressed and unstressed strokes.
So what?
Not seeing the problem here.
Quite. Reminiscent of the Venetian late-15th-century Latin typefaces.
He's boring me.
Let's split. Count of 3?
Okay. 1, 2...
MAXIMILIEN CREATED A NEW CATEGORY:
centaur
centaur
Jenson
HUMANIST

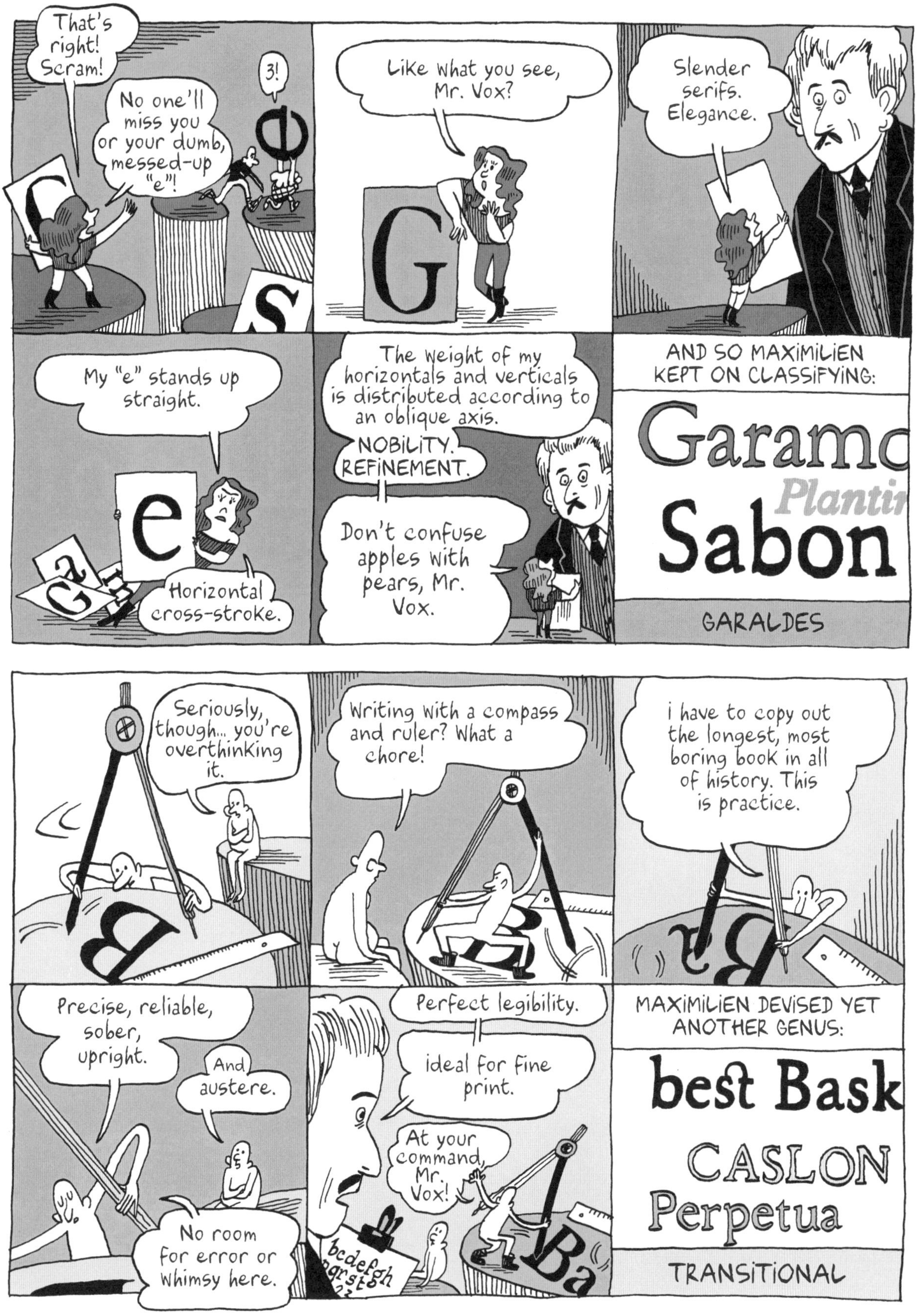
That's right! Scram!
No one'll miss you or your dumb, messed-up "e"!
3!
Like what you see, Mr. Vox?
Slender serifs. Elegance.
My "e" stands up straight.
Horizontal cross-stroke.
The weight of my horizontals and verticals is distributed according to an oblique axis.
NOBILITY. REFINEMENT.
Don't confuse apples with pears, Mr. Vox.
AND SO MAXIMILIEN KEPT ON CLASSIFYING:
Garamo
Plantir
Sabon
GARALDES
Seriously, though... you're overthinking it.
Writing with a compass and ruler? What a chore!
I have to copy out the longest, most boring book in all of history. This is practice.
Precise, reliable, sober, upright.
And austere.
No room for error or whimsy here.
Perfect legibility.
Ideal for fine print.
At your command, Mr. Vox!
MAXIMILIEN DEVISED YET ANOTHER GENUS:
best Bask
CASLON
Perpetua
TRANSITIONAL

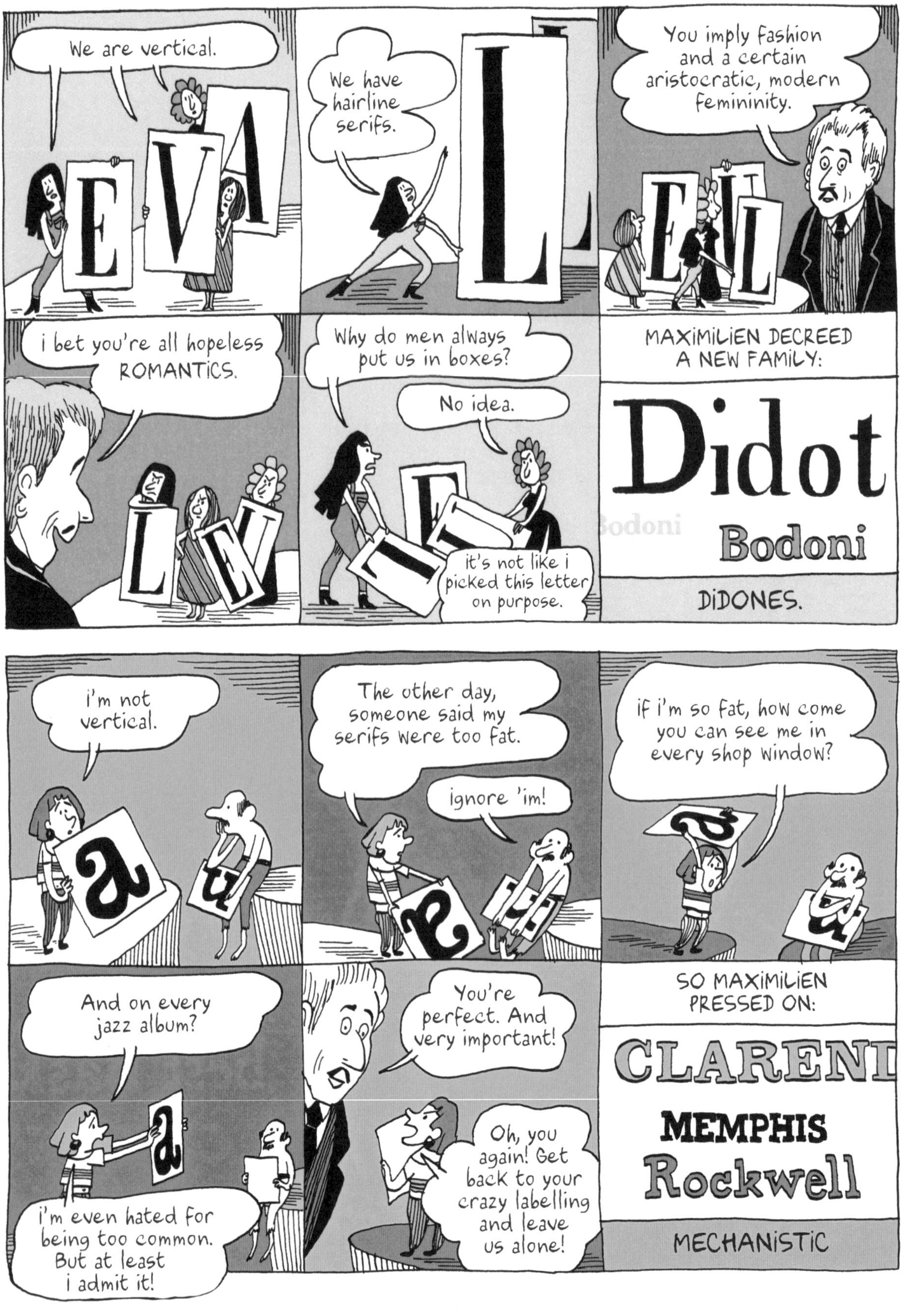
We are vertical.
We have hairline serifs.
You imply fashion and a certain aristocratic, modern femininity.
i bet you're all hopeless ROMANTICS.
Why do men always put us in boxes?
No idea.
it's not like i picked this letter on purpose.
MAXIMILIEN DECREED A NEW FAMILY:
Didot
Bodoni
DIDONES.
i'm not vertical.
The other day, someone said my serifs were too fat.
ignore 'im!
if i'm so fat, how come you can see me in every shop window?
And on every jazz album?
i'm even hated for being too common. But at least i admit it!
You're perfect. And very important!
Oh, you again! Get back to your crazy labelling and leave us alone!
SO MAXIMILIEN PRESSED ON:
MEMPHIS
Rockwell
MECHANISTIC

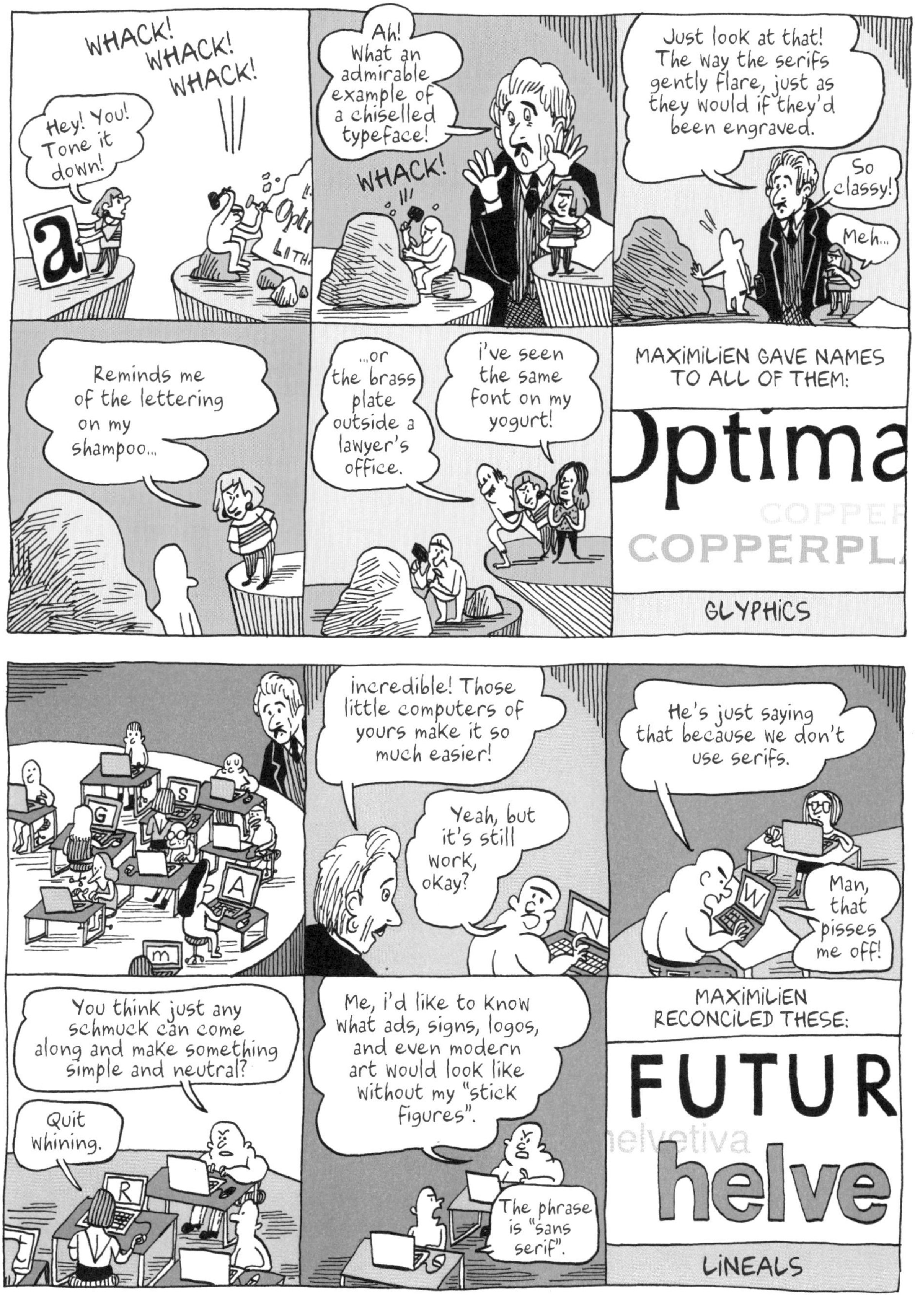

WHACK! WHACK! WHACK!
Hey! You! Tone it down!
Ah! What an admirable example of a chiselled typeface!
WHACK!
Just look at that! The way the serifs gently flare, just as they would if they'd been engraved.
So classy!
Meh...
Reminds me of the lettering on my shampoo...
...or the brass plate outside a lawyer's office.
i've seen the same font on my yogurt!
MAXiMiLiEN GAVE NAMES TO ALL OF THEM:
Optima
COPPER
COPPERPL
GLYPHiCS
incredible! Those little computers of yours make it so much easier!
Yeah, but it's still work, okay?
He's just saying that because we don't use serifs.
Man, that pisses me off!
You think just any schmuck can come along and make something simple and neutral?
Quit whining.
Me, i'd like to know what ads, signs, logos, and even modern art would look like without my "stick figures".
The phrase is "sans serif".
MAXiMiLiEN RECONCiLED THESE:
FUTUR
helve
LiNEALS

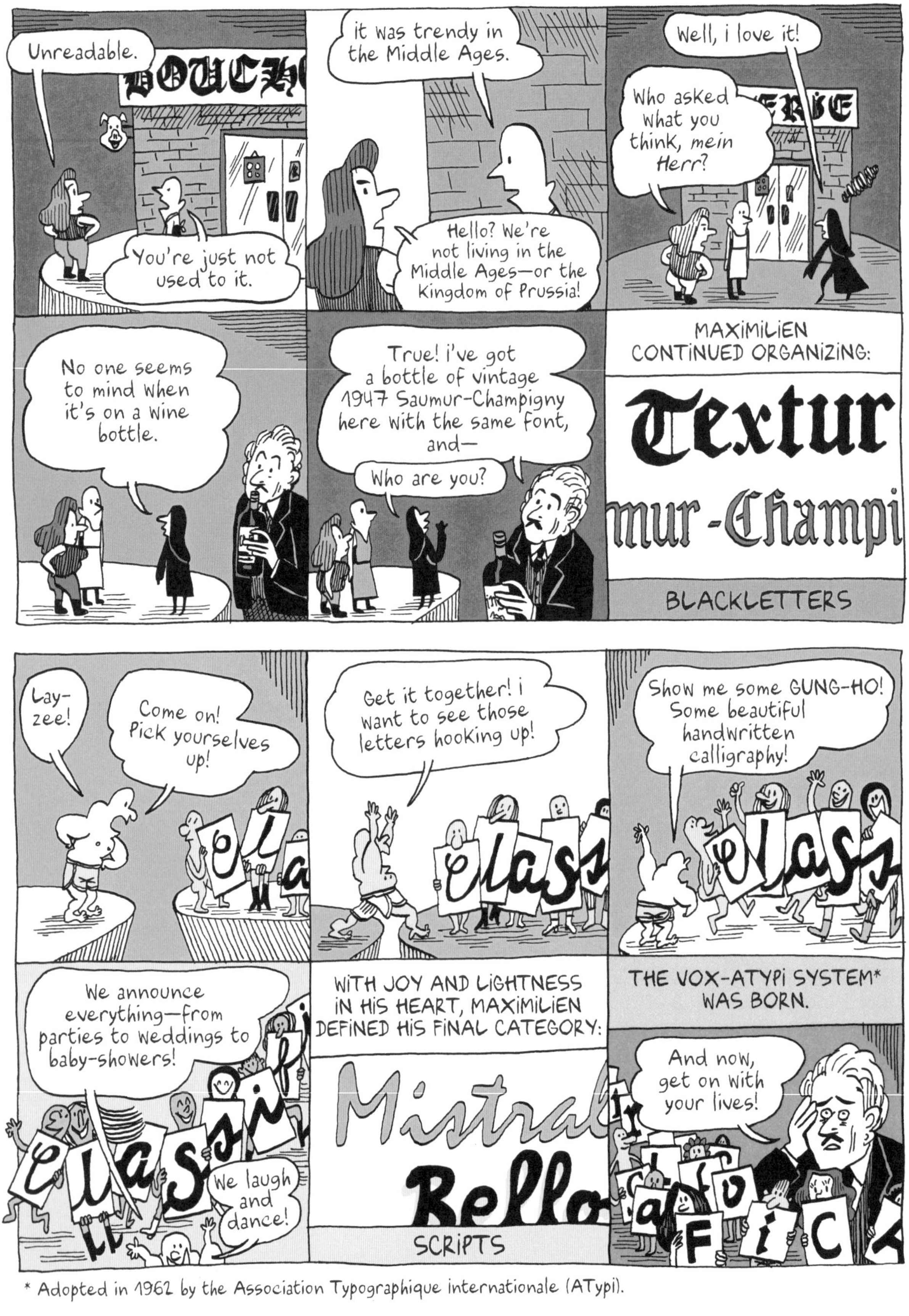
Unreadable.
BOUCH
You're just not used to it.
it was trendy in the Middle Ages.
Hello? We're not living in the Middle Ages—or the Kingdom of Prussia!
Well, i love it!
Who asked what you think, mein Herr?
No one seems to mind when it's on a wine bottle.
True! i've got a bottle of vintage 1947 Saumur-Champigny here with the same font, and—
Who are you?
MAXIMILIEN CONTINUED ORGANIZING:
Textur
mur-Champi
BLACKLETTERS
Lay-zee!
Come on! Pick yourselves up!
Get it together! i want to see those letters hooking up!
Show me some GUNG-HO! Some beautiful handwritten calligraphy!
We announce everything—from parties to weddings to baby-showers!
We laugh and dance!
WITH JOY AND LIGHTNESS IN HIS HEART, MAXIMILIEN DEFINED HIS FINAL CATEGORY:
Mistral
Bello
SCRIPTS
THE VOX-ATYPI SYSTEM* WAS BORN.
And now, get on with your lives!

* Adopted in 1962 by the Association Typographique internationale (ATypi).

XIMILIEN VOX

ES LINÉALES INCISES MANUAIRES

LE ÌL LE Ì

LS NES ERSI La
NES PASCES

IN ICA AUG PO
ICA NES B

sodi abce ci
icn sodi abcm v
nde nord

LETRASET AND PHOTOTYPESETTING

JAKE RAYNAL

Letraset® and PHOTO-TYPESETTING

THE YEARS BETWEEN THE 1960S AND THE MID-1990S SAW THE RISE OF TWO INNOVATIONS THAT WOULD FREE TYPOGRAPHY FROM THE SHACKLES OF LEAD TYPE AND SPECIALIZED STUDIOS.

TRANSFERABLE LETTERS FROM THE LETRASET COMPANY, AND PHOTOTYPESETTING.

PHOTOTYPESETTING ORIGINATED IN FRANCE, VIA THE LUMITYPE MACHINE.

THIS WAS FIRST BROUGHT TO MARKET IN 1944 BY ITS INVENTORS LOUIS MOYROUD AND RENÉ HIGONNET.

IN 1967, THE IMPRESSIVE AND IMPOSING BERTHOLD PHOTOTYPESETTER MADE ITS DEBUT IN PRINTSHOPS...

...WITH FEATURES THAT WOULD SOON BECOME A FAMILIAR SIGHT:

A SCREEN AND A KEYBOARD.

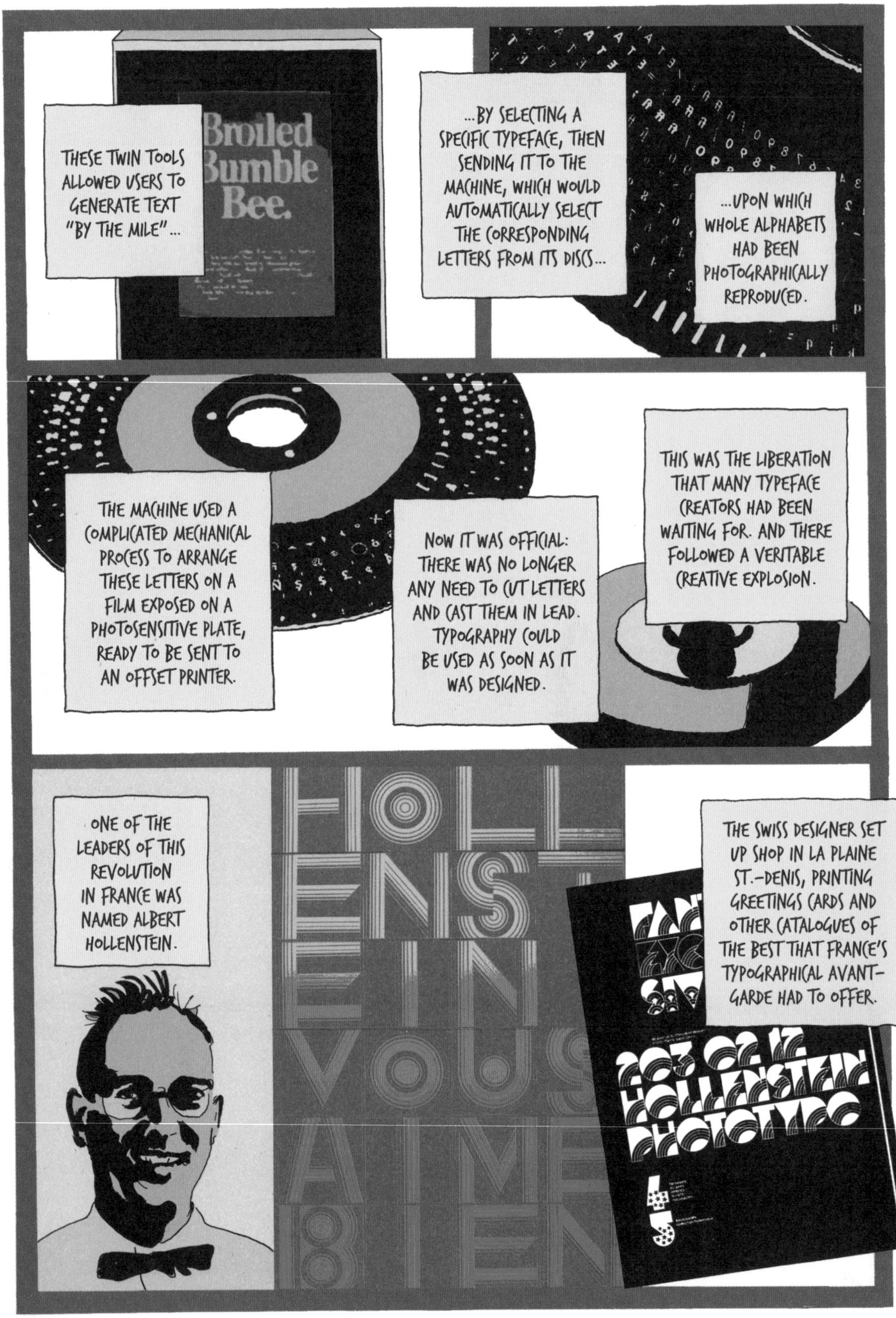
THESE TWIN TOOLS ALLOWED USERS TO GENERATE TEXT "BY THE MILE"...
Broiled Bumble Bee.
...BY SELECTING A SPECIFIC TYPEFACE, THEN SENDING IT TO THE MACHINE, WHICH WOULD AUTOMATICALLY SELECT THE CORRESPONDING LETTERS FROM ITS DISCS...
...UPON WHICH WHOLE ALPHABETS HAD BEEN PHOTOGRAPHICALLY REPRODUCED.
THE MACHINE USED A COMPLICATED MECHANICAL PROCESS TO ARRANGE THESE LETTERS ON A FILM EXPOSED ON A PHOTOSENSITIVE PLATE, READY TO BE SENT TO AN OFFSET PRINTER.
NOW IT WAS OFFICIAL: THERE WAS NO LONGER ANY NEED TO CUT LETTERS AND CAST THEM IN LEAD. TYPOGRAPHY COULD BE USED AS SOON AS IT WAS DESIGNED.
THIS WAS THE LIBERATION THAT MANY TYPEFACE CREATORS HAD BEEN WAITING FOR. AND THERE FOLLOWED A VERITABLE CREATIVE EXPLOSION.
ONE OF THE LEADERS OF THIS REVOLUTION IN FRANCE WAS NAMED ALBERT HOLLENSTEIN.
THE SWISS DESIGNER SET UP SHOP IN LA PLAINE ST.-DENIS, PRINTING GREETINGS CARDS AND OTHER CATALOGUES OF THE BEST THAT FRANCE'S TYPOGRAPHICAL AVANT-GARDE HAD TO OFFER.
HOLLENSTEIN PHOTOTYPO

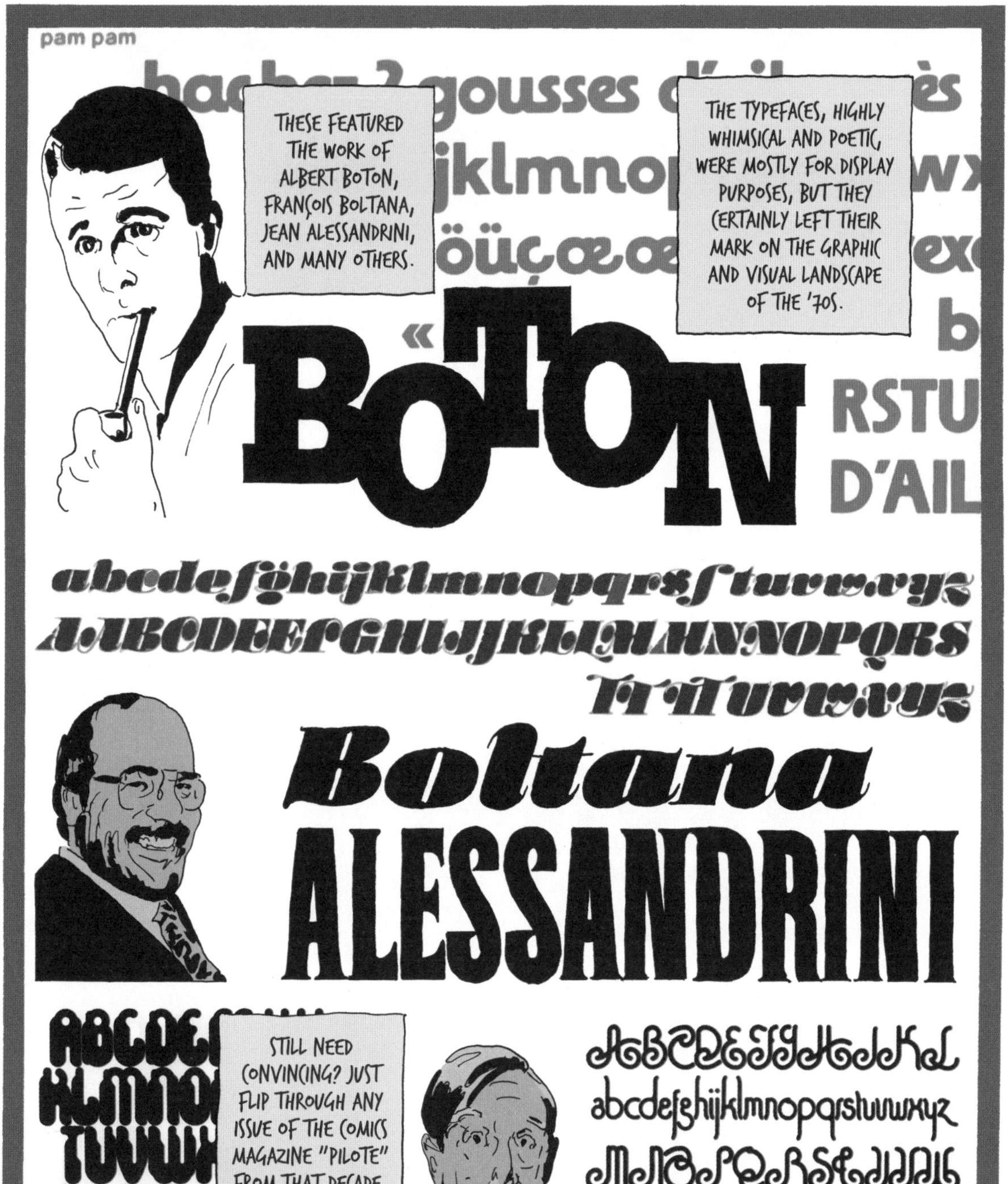
pam pam
THESE FEATURED THE WORK OF ALBERT BOTON, FRANÇOIS BOLTANA, JEAN ALESSANDRINI, AND MANY OTHERS.
THE TYPEFACES, HIGHLY WHIMSICAL AND POETIC, WERE MOSTLY FOR DISPLAY PURPOSES, BUT THEY CERTAINLY LEFT THEIR MARK ON THE GRAPHIC AND VISUAL LANDSCAPE OF THE '70S.
BOTON
Boltana
ALESSANDRINI
STILL NEED CONVINCING? JUST FLIP THROUGH ANY ISSUE OF THE COMICS MAGAZINE "PILOTE" FROM THAT DECADE.
1234567890
Pilote
SADLY, ALBERT HOLLENSTEIN DIED, FAR TOO YOUNG, IN A CAR ACCIDENT, IN 1974.
AND NOT UNTIL THE ARRIVAL OF THE INTERNET, TWO DECADES LATER, DID TYPOGRAPHY WITNESS A COMPARABLE EXPLOSION OF CREATIVITY.

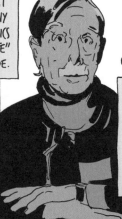

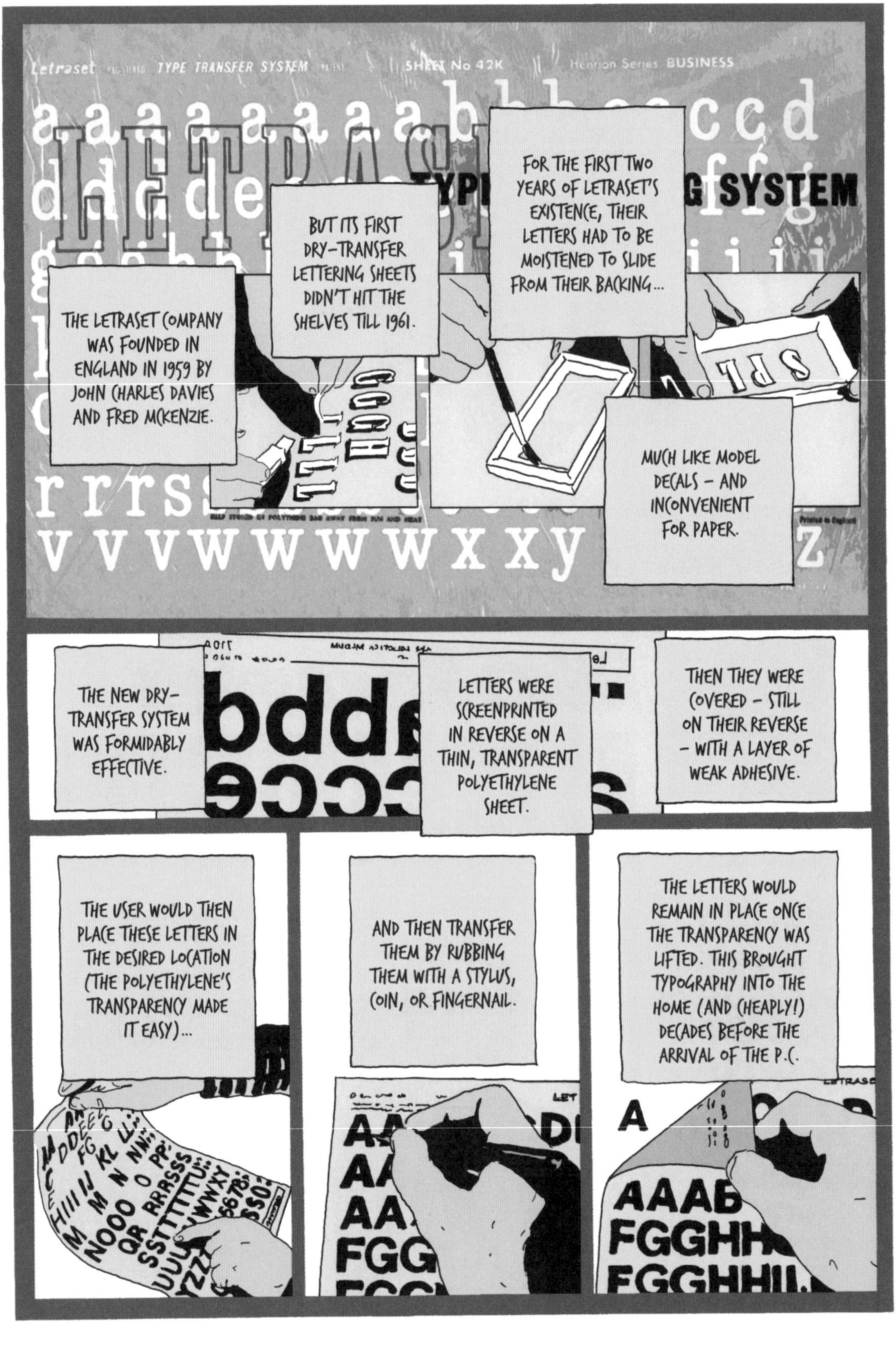
Letraset TYPE TRANSFER SYSTEM SHEET No 42K Henrion Series BUSINESS
THE LETRASET COMPANY WAS FOUNDED IN ENGLAND IN 1959 BY JOHN CHARLES DAVIES AND FRED MCKENZIE.
BUT ITS FIRST DRY-TRANSFER LETTERING SHEETS DIDN'T HIT THE SHELVES TILL 1961.
FOR THE FIRST TWO YEARS OF LETRASET'S EXISTENCE, THEIR LETTERS HAD TO BE MOISTENED TO SLIDE FROM THEIR BACKING...
MUCH LIKE MODEL DECALS – AND INCONVENIENT FOR PAPER.
THE NEW DRY-TRANSFER SYSTEM WAS FORMIDABLY EFFECTIVE.
LETTERS WERE SCREENPRINTED IN REVERSE ON A THIN, TRANSPARENT POLYETHYLENE SHEET.
THEN THEY WERE COVERED – STILL ON THEIR REVERSE – WITH A LAYER OF WEAK ADHESIVE.
THE USER WOULD THEN PLACE THESE LETTERS IN THE DESIRED LOCATION (THE POLYETHYLENE'S TRANSPARENCY MADE IT EASY)...
AND THEN TRANSFER THEM BY RUBBING THEM WITH A STYLUS, COIN, OR FINGERNAIL.
THE LETTERS WOULD REMAIN IN PLACE ONCE THE TRANSPARENCY WAS LIFTED. THIS BROUGHT TYPOGRAPHY INTO THE HOME (AND CHEAPLY!) DECADES BEFORE THE ARRIVAL OF THE P.C.

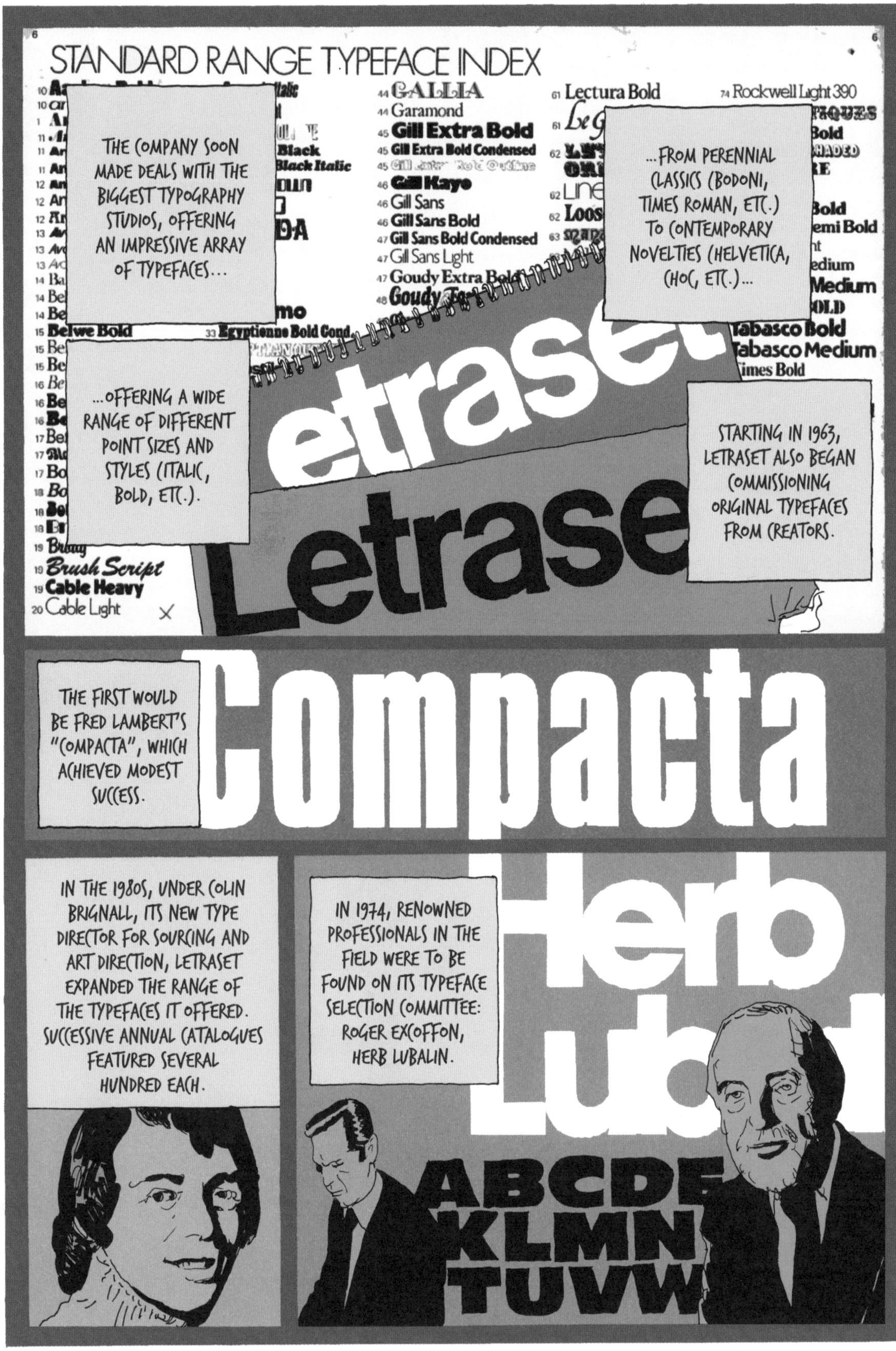
STANDARD RANGE TYPEFACE INDEX
THE COMPANY SOON MADE DEALS WITH THE BIGGEST TYPOGRAPHY STUDIOS, OFFERING AN IMPRESSIVE ARRAY OF TYPEFACES...
...FROM PERENNIAL CLASSICS (BODONI, TIMES ROMAN, ETC.) TO CONTEMPORARY NOVELTIES (HELVETICA, HOC, ETC.)...
...OFFERING A WIDE RANGE OF DIFFERENT POINT SIZES AND STYLES (ITALIC, BOLD, ETC.).
STARTING IN 1963, LETRASET ALSO BEGAN COMMISSIONING ORIGINAL TYPEFACES FROM CREATORS.
44 GALLIA
44 Garamond
45 Gill Extra Bold
45 Gill Extra Bold Condensed
46 Gill Kayo
46 Gill Sans
46 Gill Sans Bold
47 Gill Sans Bold Condensed
47 Gill Sans Light
47 Goudy Extra Bold
61 Lectura Bold
74 Rockwell Light 390
15 Belwe Bold
33 Egyptienne Bold Cond.
19 Brush Script
19 Cable Heavy
20 Cable Light
Tabasco Bold
Tabasco Medium
Letraset
Letraset
THE FIRST WOULD BE FRED LAMBERT'S "COMPACTA", WHICH ACHIEVED MODEST SUCCESS.
Compacta
IN THE 1980S, UNDER COLIN BRIGNALL, ITS NEW TYPE DIRECTOR FOR SOURCING AND ART DIRECTION, LETRASET EXPANDED THE RANGE OF THE TYPEFACES IT OFFERED. SUCCESSIVE ANNUAL CATALOGUES FEATURED SEVERAL HUNDRED EACH.
IN 1974, RENOWNED PROFESSIONALS IN THE FIELD WERE TO BE FOUND ON ITS TYPEFACE SELECTION COMMITTEE: ROGER EXCOFFON, HERB LUBALIN.
Herb
ABCDE
KLMN
TUVW

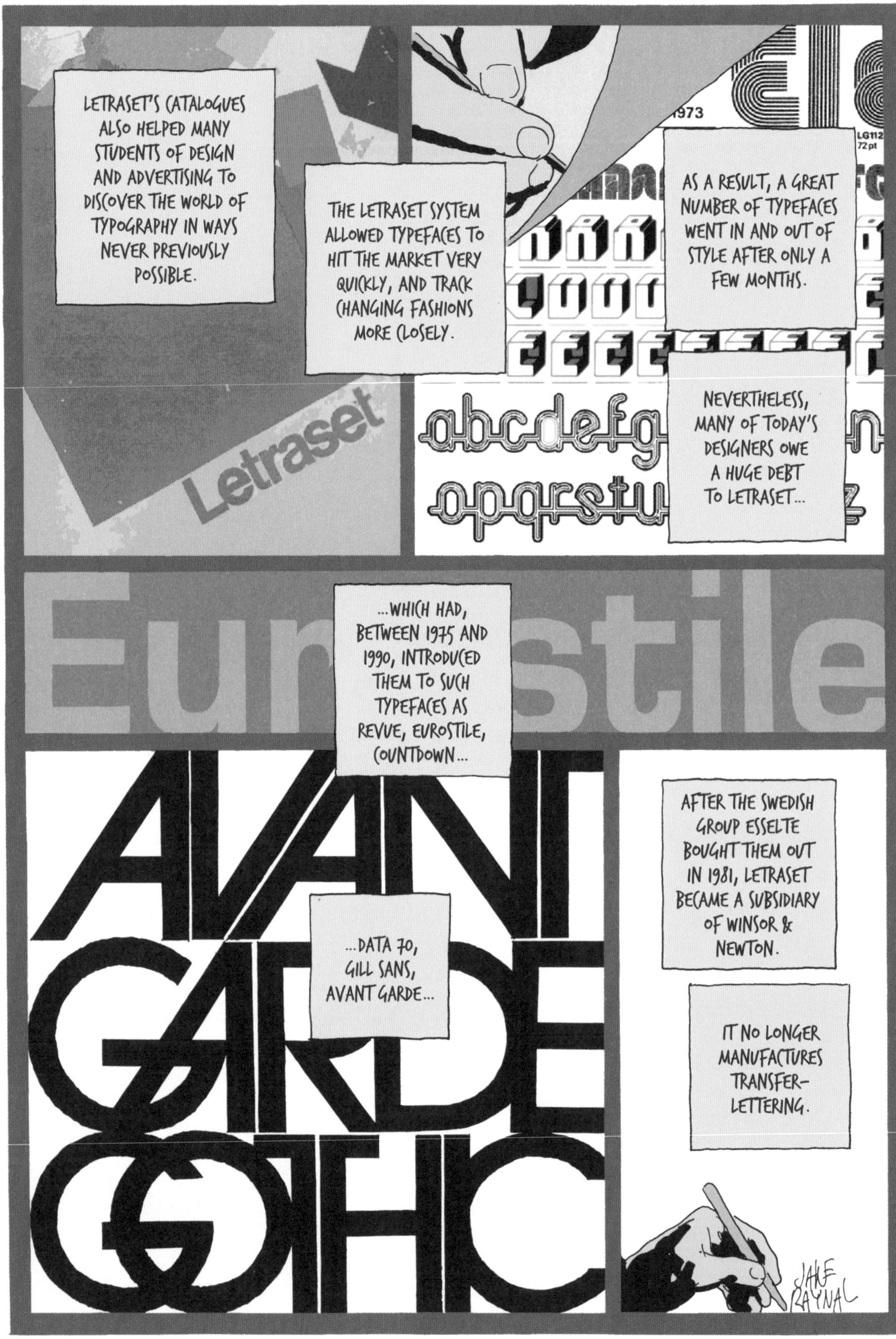
LETRASET'S CATALOGUES ALSO HELPED MANY STUDENTS OF DESIGN AND ADVERTISING TO DISCOVER THE WORLD OF TYPOGRAPHY IN WAYS NEVER PREVIOUSLY POSSIBLE.
Letraset
THE LETRASET SYSTEM ALLOWED TYPEFACES TO HIT THE MARKET VERY QUICKLY, AND TRACK CHANGING FASHIONS MORE CLOSELY.
1973
LG112
72pt
AS A RESULT, A GREAT NUMBER OF TYPEFACES WENT IN AND OUT OF STYLE AFTER ONLY A FEW MONTHS.
NEVERTHELESS, MANY OF TODAY'S DESIGNERS OWE A HUGE DEBT TO LETRASET...
...WHICH HAD, BETWEEN 1975 AND 1990, INTRODUCED THEM TO SUCH TYPEFACES AS REVUE, EUROSTILE, COUNTDOWN...
...DATA 70, GILL SANS, AVANT GARDE...
AFTER THE SWEDISH GROUP ESSELTE BOUGHT THEM OUT IN 1981, LETRASET BECAME A SUBSIDIARY OF WINSOR & NEWTON.
IT NO LONGER MANUFACTURES TRANSFER-LETTERING.

eoeçØ0I5242

BCDEFGHIJ!

LMNOPQR?

TUVWXYZa

bcdefghijklm

nopqrstuvwx

yz123456789;

0£$¢&%()/*

355.72 C
20 mm

355.4
13 mm

H

H

Optima black

ABCDEFGHIJ*

TYPOGRAPHY TODAY AND TOMORROW

FRANÇOIS AYROLES

From the 1990s onwards, typographical innovation was profoundly influenced by the rise of home computing.

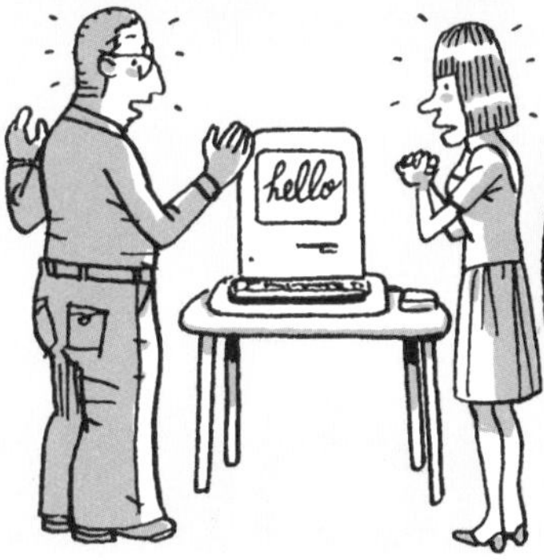
hello

Tools for manipulating graphics were now at everyone's disposal.

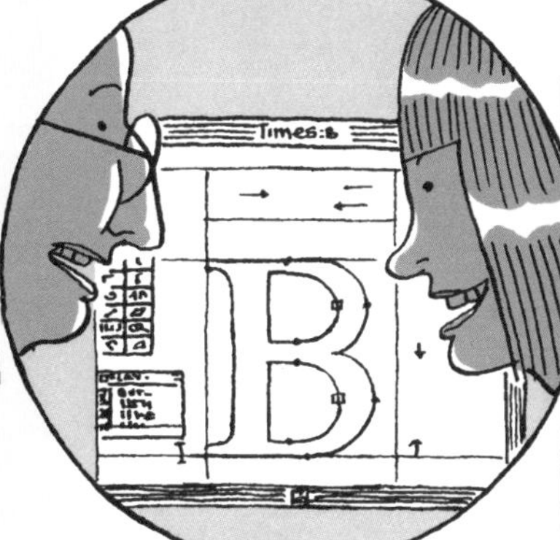
B

The arrival of the internet promoted the spread of typefaces.

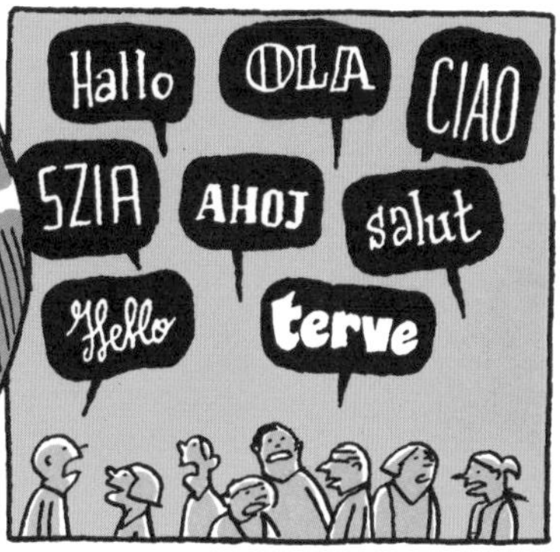
Hallo
OLA
CIAO
SZIA
AHOJ
salut
Hello
terve

The previous economic model for typographical creation was turned upside down. More and more young designers were creating their own typefaces and making them freely available.

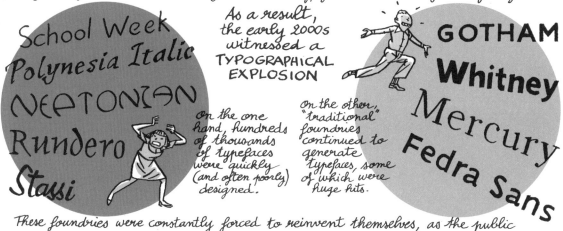

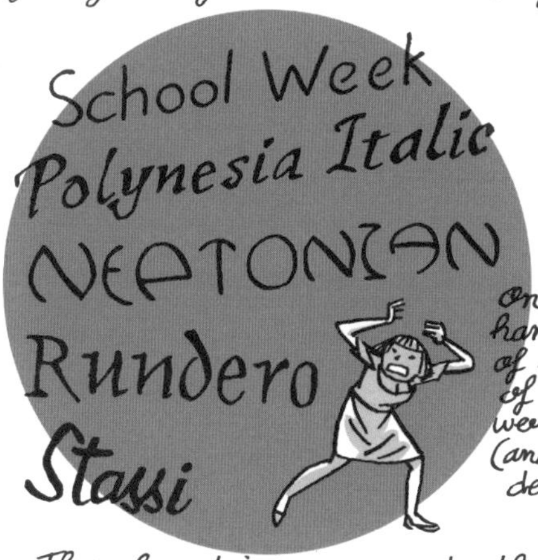
School Week
Polynesia Italic
NEETONIAN
Rundero
Stassi

As a result, the early 2000s witnessed a TYPOGRAPHICAL EXPLOSION

On the one hand, hundreds of thousands of typefaces were quickly (and often poorly) designed.

On the other, "traditional" foundries continued to generate typefaces, some of which were huge hits.

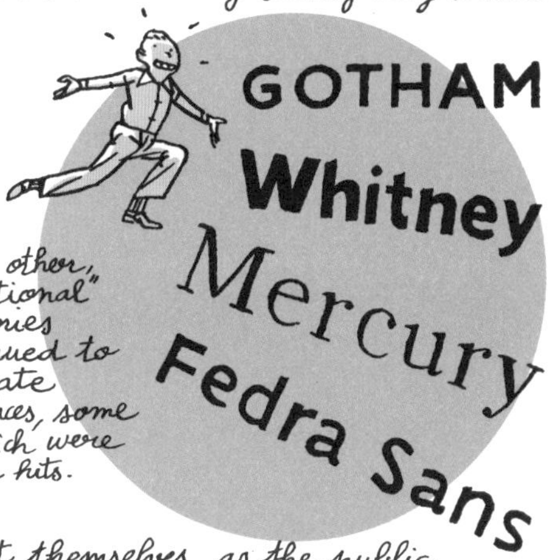
GOTHAM
Whitney
Mercury
Fedra Sans

These foundries were constantly forced to reinvent themselves, as the public could now so easily imitate and pirate the typefaces they made.

Since so many people think of these creations as freely available, they struggle with the idea of having to pay to use them.

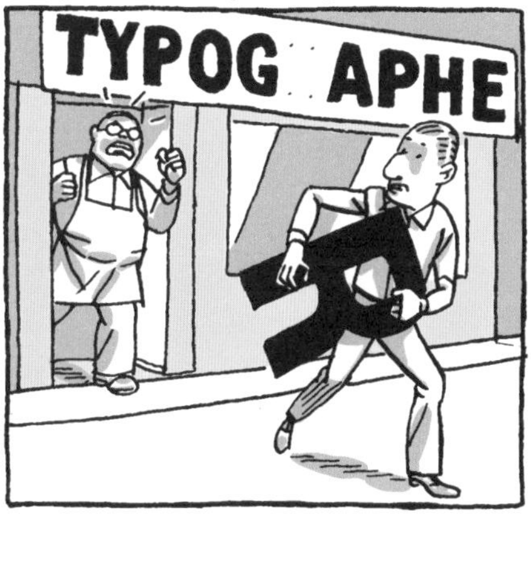
TYPOG APHE

Attempts are regularly made to address this problem, such as access to online font catalogues that involve complicated subscription rates.

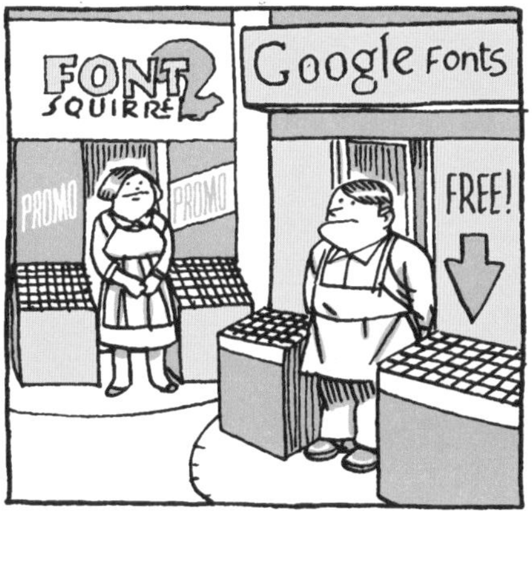
FONT SQUIRREL
Google Fonts
PROMO
PROMO
FREE!

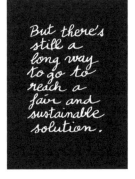

But there's still a long way to go to reach a fair and sustainable solution.

One of the most emblematic typefaces from the 1990s is **DIN**.

It first saw the light of day in Germany, when the Deutsches Institut für Normung (the German Institute for Standardization) first decided to establish speifications for civil and industrial engineering. The acronym DIN preceded all associated nomenclatures, including the typefaces designated for traffic signage: DIN mittelschrift 1451 and DIN engschrift 1451.

4 Berlin Eisenach
Frankfurt Würzburg 4
400 Herleshausen 5Km Wommen 1Km
Kassel 70km Eschwege 30Km 400

The structure of each letter was based on a coarse grid, so workers with little or no esperience in lettering could easily reproduise it.

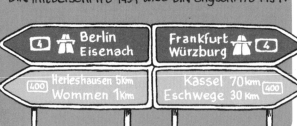

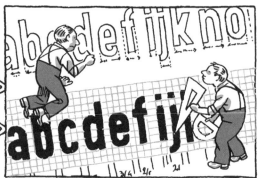

In 1994, typographer Albert-Jan Pool redesigned DIN 1451 for the Fontfont foundry.

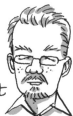

He improved it by adding more weights and modernizing it. The "new" FF DIN came out in 1995.

ABCDEFG

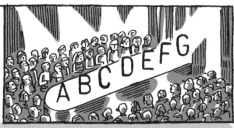

At the outset of the 2000s, it could mostly be seen:

In ads for cable internet.

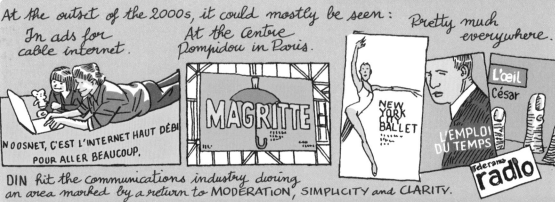

NOOSNET, C'EST L'INTERNET HAUT DÉBI
POUR ALLER BEAUCOUP.

At the Centre Pompidou in Paris.

MAGRITTE

Pretty much everywhere.

NEW YORK CITY BALLET
L'œil
César
L'EMPLOI DU TEMPS
Telerama
radio

DIN hit the communications industry during an area marked by a return to MODERATION, SIMPLICITY and CLARITY.

At the turn of the century, the internet was evolving faster than most consumers could absorb...

éseau
Proxy
modem
FTP
INTERNE
TCP/IP
HTLM
WWW
e-mail

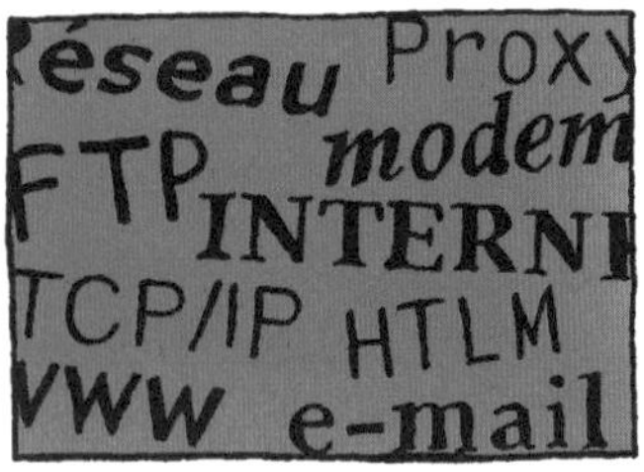

The times called for a typeface to ease the transition.

DIN

DIN's minimalist look – functional rather than aesthetic – and its lack of any obvious associations made it appear TRUE, PURE, HONEST and SIMPLE.

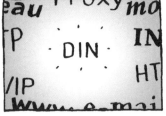

What it expressed was **SELF-EVIDENT** and **CLEAR**

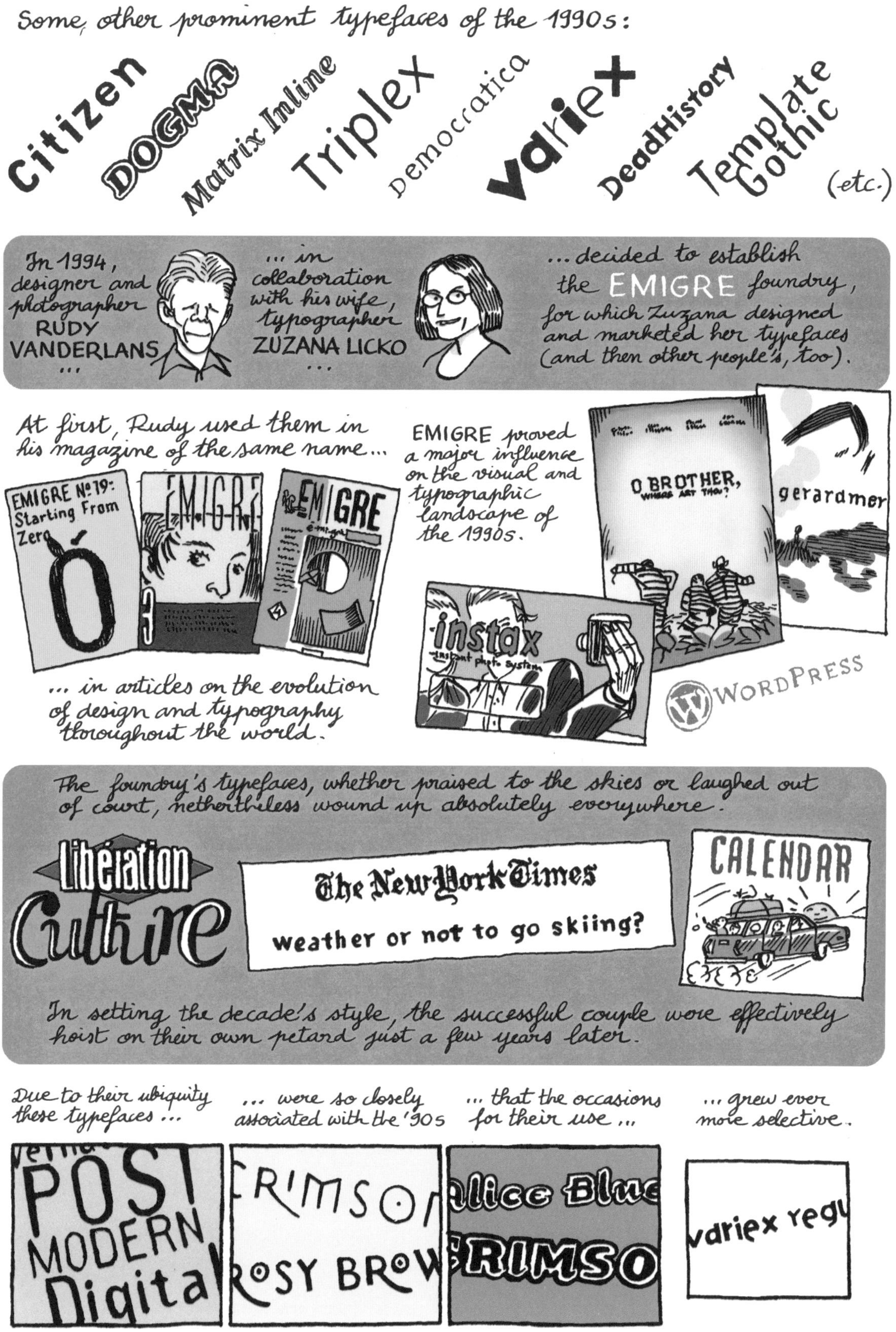
Some other prominent typefaces of the 1990s:
Citizen
DOGMA
Matrix Inline
Triplex
Democratica
Variex
DeadHistory
Template Gothic
(etc.)
In 1994, designer and photographer RUDY VANDERLANS ...
... in collaboration with his wife, typographer ZUZANA LICKO ...
... decided to establish the EMIGRE foundry, for which Zuzana designed and marketed her typefaces (and then other people's, too).
At first, Rudy used them in his magazine of the same name...
EMIGRE Nº 19: Starting From Zero
EMIGRE
EMIGRE
... in articles on the evolution of design and typography throughout the world.
EMIGRE proved a major influence on the visual and typographic landscape of the 1990s.
O BROTHER,
gerardmer
instax
instant photo system
WORDPRESS
The foundry's typefaces, whether praised to the skies or laughed out of court, netherthiless wound up absolutely everywhere.
Libération Culture
The New York Times
weather or not to go skiing?
CALENDAR
In setting the decade's style, the successful couple were effectively hoist on their own petard just a few years later.
Due to their ubiquity these typefaces ...
... were so closely associated with the '90s
... that the occasions for their use ...
... grew ever more selective.
POST MODERN Digital
RIMSO
ROSY BROW
lice Blue
RIMSO
variex regu

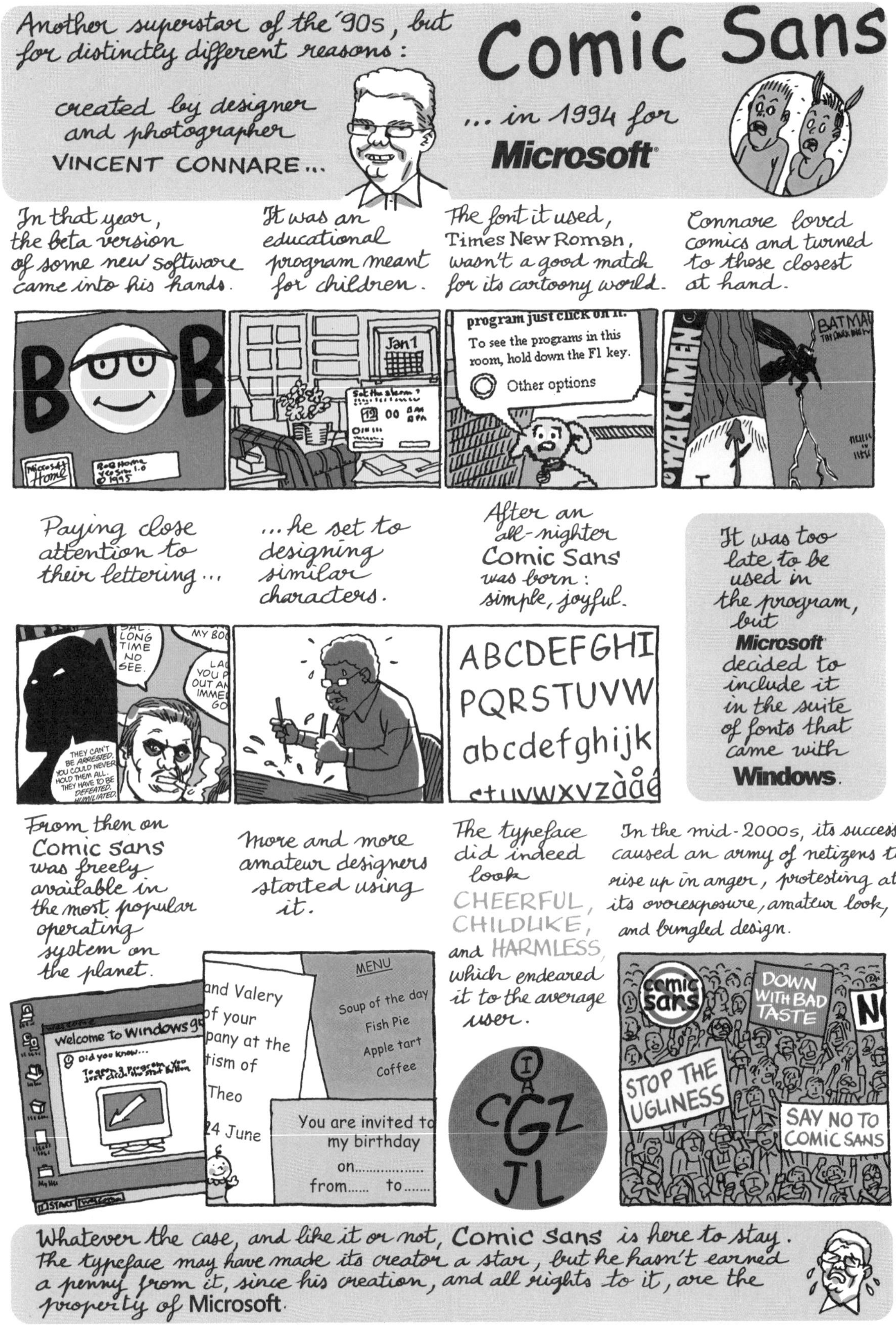
Another superstar of the '90s, but for distinctly different reasons:
Comic Sans
created by designer and photographer VINCENT CONNARE...
... in 1994 for Microsoft
In that year, the beta version of some new software came into his hands.
BOB
It was an educational program meant for children.
Jan 1
The font it used, Times New Roman, wasn't a good match for its cartoony world.
program just click on it.
To see the programs in this room, hold down the F1 key.
Other options
Connare loved comics and turned to those closest at hand.
WATCHMEN
BATMAN
Paying close attention to their lettering...
LONG TIME NO SEE.
MY BO
THEY CAN'T BE ARRESTED. YOU COULD NEVER HOLD THEM ALL. THEY HAVE TO BE DEFEATED. HUMILIATED.
...he set to designing similar characters.
After an all-nighter Comic Sans was born: simple, joyful.
ABCDEFGHI
PQRSTUVW
abcdefghijk
It was too late to be used in the program, but Microsoft decided to include it in the suite of fonts that came with Windows.
From then on Comic sans was freely available in the most popular operating system on the planet.
Welcome to Windows
Did you know...
More and more amateur designers started using it.
and Valery
of your
pany at the
tism of
Theo
24 June
MENU
Soup of the day
Fish Pie
Apple tart
Coffee
You are invited to my birthday
on..................
from...... to.......
The typeface did indeed look CHEERFUL, CHILDLIKE, and HARMLESS, which endeared it to the average user.
In the mid-2000s, its success caused an army of netizens to rise up in anger, protesting at its overexposure, amateur look, and bungled design.
comic sans
DOWN WITH BAD TASTE
STOP THE UGLINESS
SAY NO TO COMIC SANS
Whatever the case, and like it or not, Comic sans is here to stay. The typeface may have made its creator a star, but he hasn't earned a penny from it, since his creation, and all rights to it, are the property of Microsoft.

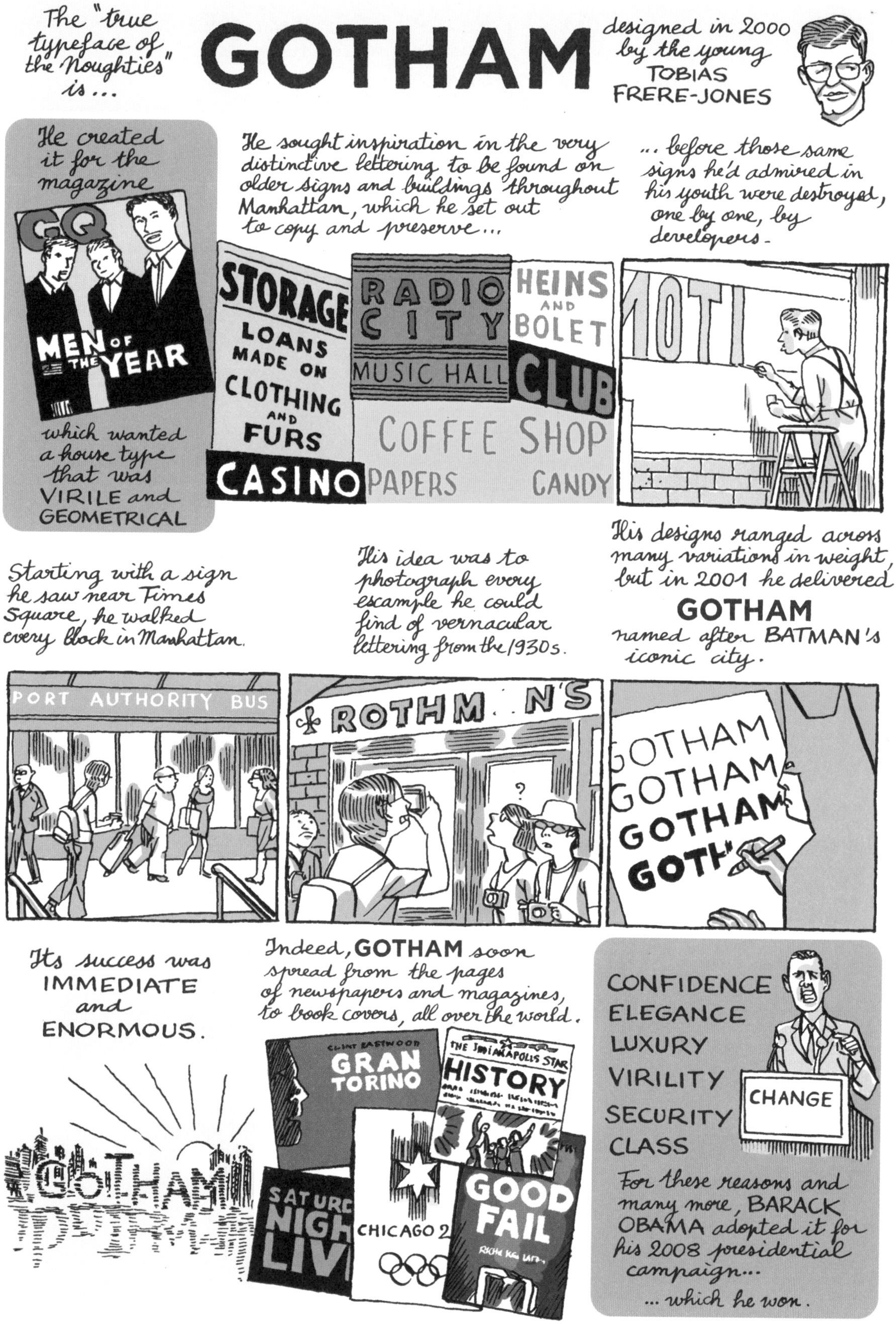

The "true typeface of the Noughties" is...
GOTHAM
designed in 2000 by the young TOBIAS FRERE-JONES
He created it for the magazine
GQ
MEN OF THE YEAR
which wanted a house type that was VIRILE and GEOMETRICAL
He sought inspiration in the very distinctive lettering to be found on older signs and buildings throughout Manhattan, which he set out to copy and preserve...
STORAGE
LOANS MADE ON CLOTHING AND FURS
CASINO
RADIO CITY MUSIC HALL
HEINS AND BOLET
CLUB
COFFEE SHOP
PAPERS
CANDY
... before those same signs he'd admired in his youth were destroyed, one by one, by developers.
MOTI
Starting with a sign he saw near Times Square, he walked every block in Manhattan.
His idea was to photograph every example he could find of vernacular lettering from the 1930s.
His designs ranged across many variations in weight, but in 2001 he delivered GOTHAM named after BATMAN's iconic city.
PORT AUTHORITY BUS
ROTHM N'S
?
GOTHAM
GOTHAM
GOTHAM
GOTH
Its success was IMMEDIATE and ENORMOUS.
GOTHAM
Indeed, GOTHAM soon spread from the pages of newspapers and magazines, to book covers, all over the world.
CLINT EASTWOOD
GRAN TORINO
THE INDIANAPOLIS STAR
HISTORY
SATURD NIGH LIVI
CHICAGO 2
GOOD FAIL
CONFIDENCE
ELEGANCE
LUXURY
VIRILITY
SECURITY
CLASS
CHANGE
For these reasons and many more, BARACK OBAMA adopted it for his 2008 presidential campaign...
... which he won.

These days, there aren't many creators of typefaces who can make a living from their craft: less than a dozen in France, and a few hundred throughout the world.

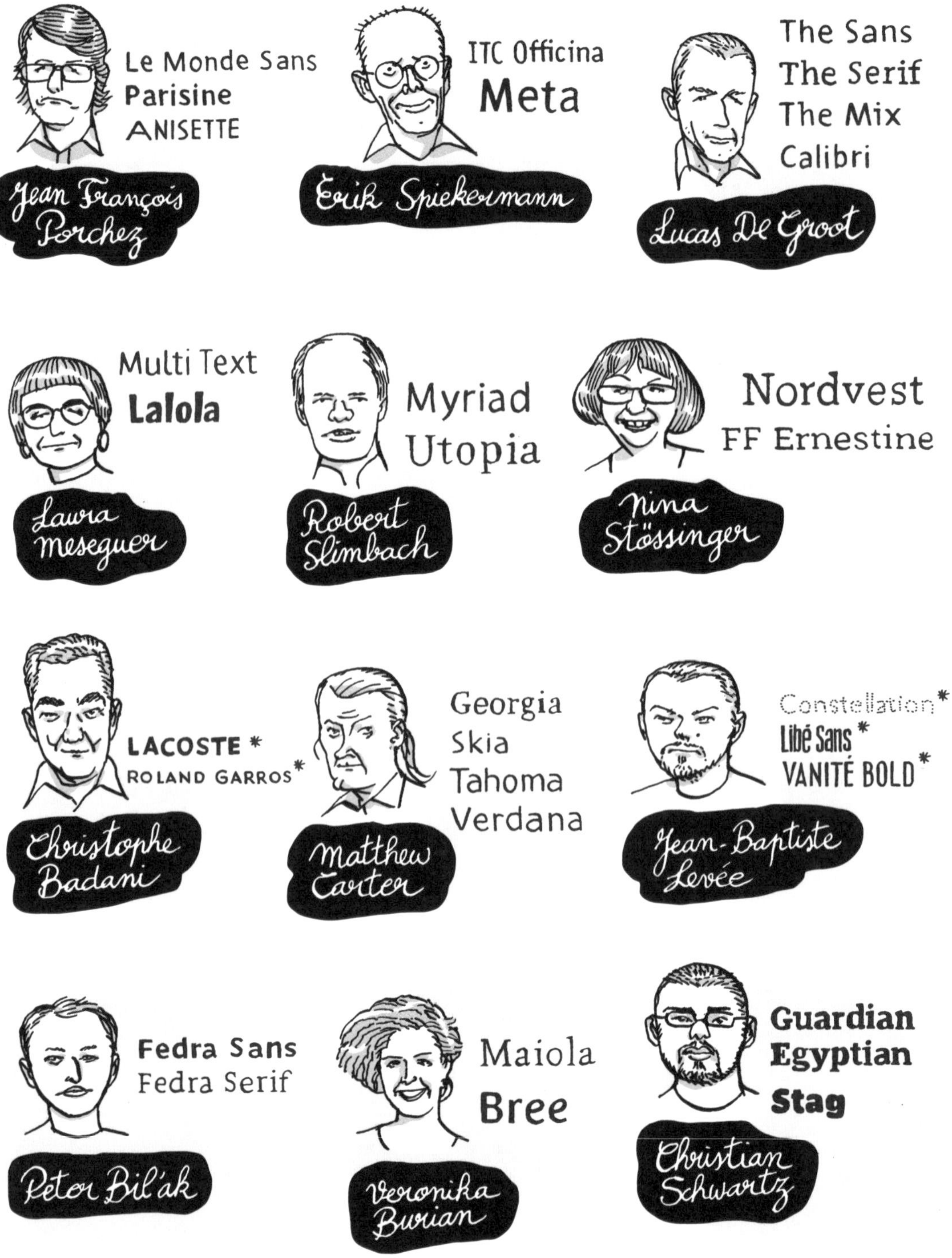
Le Monde Sans
Parisine
ANISETTE
Jean François Porchez
ITC Officina
Meta
Erik Spiekermann
The Sans
The Serif
The Mix
Calibri
Lucas De Groot
Multi Text
Lalola
Laura Meseguer
Myriad
Utopia
Robert Slimbach
Nordvest
FF Ernestine
Nina Stössinger
LACOSTE *
ROLAND GARROS*
Christophe Badani
Georgia
Skia
Tahoma
Verdana
Matthew Carter
Constellation*
Libé Sans *
VANITÉ BOLD*
Jean-Baptiste Levée
Fedra Sans
Fedra Serif
Peter Bil'ak
Maiola
Bree
Veronika Burian
Guardian
Egyptian
Stag
Christian Schwartz

* These typefaces are not available for public use, as they were created exclusively for the brands in question.

To be continued...

GOTH

Gotham is the nickname

Gotham is the nickname

Gotham is the nickname

Gotham is the nickname

Gotham is the nicknam

Gotham is the nicknam

Gotham is the nicknam

Gotham is the nicknam

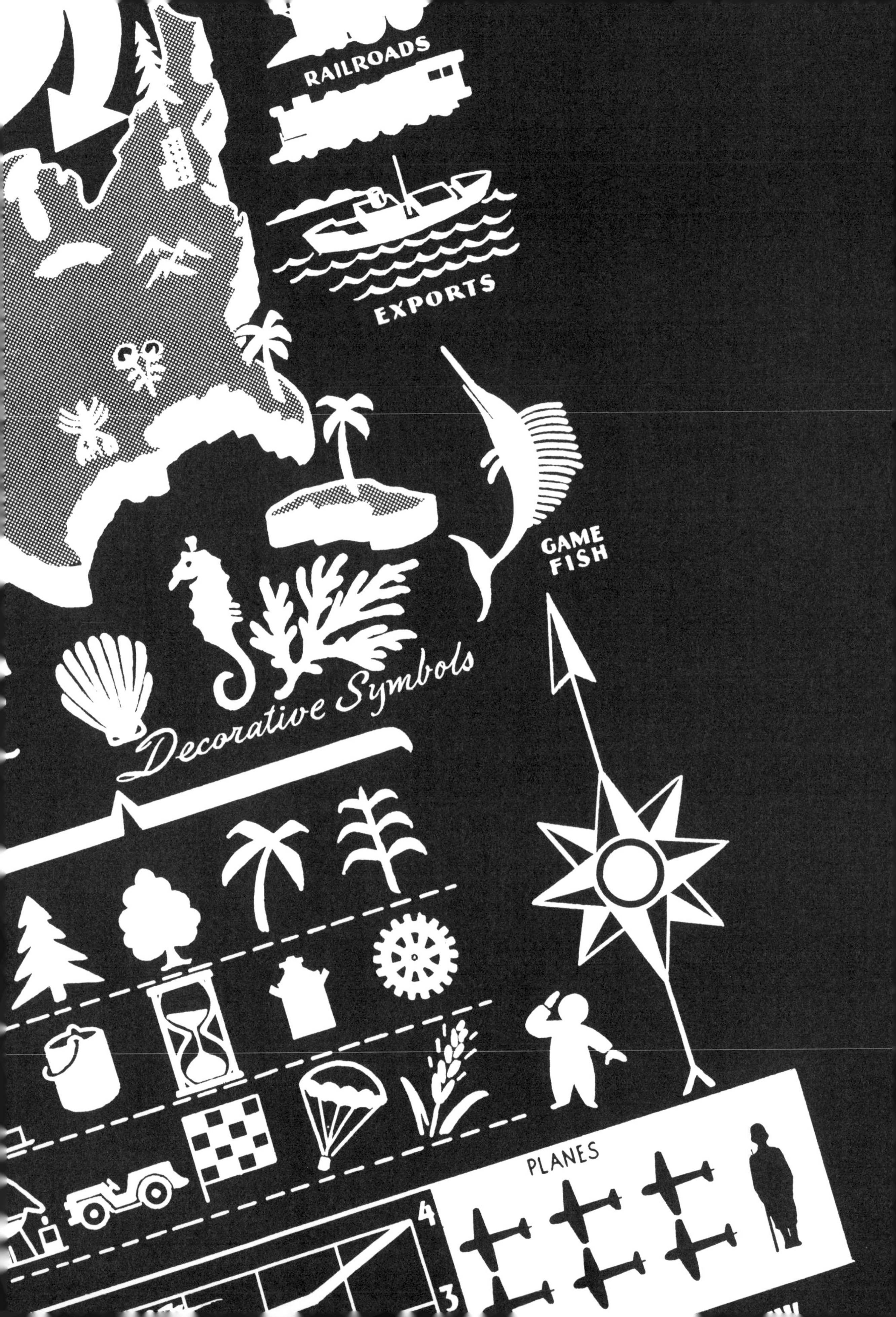
RAILROADS
EXPORTS
GAME FISH
Decorative Symbols
PLANES
4
3

GLOSSARY OF TYPOGRAPHICAL TERMS

Ascender: the part of a lower-case character (*b, d, f, h, k, l, t*) that extends above the x-height.

ATypI: Association Typographique Internationale, founded in 1957 by Charles Peignot and still active today. The ATypI adopted Maximilien Vox's typeface classification system in 1962.

Body height: the size of a typeface, or the complete vertical area covered by all of the characters in a font. Defined by the distance between the ascender and descender lines and measured in points—in other words, the top of the tallest letterform to the bottom of the lowest one.

Capitals: otherwise known as upper-case characters. The rules for use of capital letters tend to differ from language to language.

Crossbar: the horizontal stroke in a letterform. The (usually) horizontal stroke across the middle of uppercase "A" and "H" is a bar. The horizontal or sloping stroke enclosing the bottom of the eye of an "e" is also a bar. Although often used interchangeably, the bar differs from an arm and a cross stroke because each end connects to a stem or stroke and doesn't (usually) intersect/cross over the stem or stroke, as it might in a lower-case "t" or "f".

Descender: the downward stroke of a lower-case character (*g, j, p, q, y*) that descends below the baseline, or bottom line, of a piece of text.

Display (typeface): a typeface meant for short segments of text (titles, slogans, captions), as opposed to one meant for the body of a text.

Ductus: the direction and sequence of strokes in the formation of a letter.

Eye: in lower-case characters, a synonym for *bowl*, the generally round or elliptical forms of letters (such as *b, c, e, o, p*). Curved letters tend to exceed the x-height slightly, due to the visual compensation known as overshoot.

Font: a term derived from the earliest origins of typography, when it referred to a full set of lead type, each individually cast in a *foundry*, including an alphabet and all accessory characters, such as punctuation. In modern usage, with the advent of digital typography, "font" is frequently synonymous with "typeface".

Glyph: the graphical representation of a typographical character or letter. A typological character is an abstraction, but a glyph is a specific, concrete way of writing it.

Kerning: the spacing between individual letters in a line of type, and the process of adjusting it to achieve an elegant effect.

Letterform: a term used especially in typography, palaeography, calligraphy, and epigraphy to mean a letter's shape. Each letter is a unit in any writing system; but a letterform is a type of glyph. An alphabet is a collection of letters; but a typeface is a collection of letterforms.

Lettering: hand-lettered, as opposed to mechanically or digitally produced. A typeface can consist entirely of hand-drawn letters, but if lettering is mechanically produced, it's not lettering, it's typography. Many sources have confused the two terms, still do, and likely always will.

Ligature: two or more typographical characters joined in a single glyph to avoid visually inelegant juxtapositions. Some ligatures are widely used, like the ampersand (&—which elides the letters "E" and "t", for the Latin *et*, meaning "and"); or the @-sign (according to one theory, a monastic medieval abbreviation of the Latin word *ad*, meaning "at, toward, by, about"). An index of typographical quality in a given work is its handling of ligatures.

Long "s": the long, medial, or descending s (ſ) is an archaic form of the lower-case letter "s "in wide use till the 19th century. It replaced a single "s", or the first in a double "s", at the beginning or in the middle of a word, while the "s" we know today was only used at the ends of words, hence the modern letterform known as the short, terminal, or round "s". Its resemblance to the letter "f", the source of much inadvertent humour and confusion ("Where the bee sucks, there suck I"), led to its decline in use.

Lower-case: descended from minuscule characters, these derive their name from the fact that in the days of metal type, they were kept in the lower drawers of the compartmentalized wooden cabinet known as a type case or "job case".

Modulation: in calligraphy and typography alike, the strokes that make up letters usually vary cyclically and predictably in thickness or weight: thicker "stressed" strokes, and thinner "unstressed" strokes. Typefaces descended from or mimicking handwriting with a broad nib pen will feature a thinner cross or up-stroke (*délié*) and a thicker pull or down-stroke (*plein*).

Roman: in Latin script typography, one of the three main kinds of historical type, alongside blackletter and italic. Customarily lower-case ("roman") when referring to early Italian typefaces of the Renaissance period and most subsequent upright types based on them, but initial-capped when referring to "Roman" letters from antiquity.

Sans (or Sans Serif): a term derived from French *sans* (meaning "without") but popularized in English typography, referring to typefaces lacking those protruding features known as "serifs" at the end of strokes. Prior to its use, the term was (confusingly enough) "gothic".

Serif: a small line or stroke customarily attached to the end of a larger stroke in a letter or symbol within a particular font or family of (usually text) fonts. They are said to be of aid in reading-speed and legibility by creating a virtual line. The word can also be used to refer to a serif typeface. One theory as to its origin traces it to the Dutch noun *schreef*, meaning "line" or "pen-stroke", the past-tense of *schrijven*, "to write". (The Dutch word *Schreef* now also means "serif".)

Set width: the horizontal measure of a letter, consisting of the body of the letter plus the side-bearings, the slivers of space that protect it from other letters. Caution is advised when meddling with set width, as it affects proportions and hence readability.

Small caps: characters approximating lower-case size but upper-case appearance.

Squeezing: anamorphically narrowing the horizontal scale of a letter. A practice to be avoided, as the results are never pretty. Instead choose a typeface with the desired proportions to start with, such as a condensed or compressed font style.

Stem: the main vertical stroke of a letter.

Stylus: a small tool for writing or some other form of marking. Early reed styli with bevelled tips were used to impress characters into wet clay tablets, resulting in the unique "wedge" shapes of cuneiform. Later, sharpened or split nib reed pens dipped in ink were used to write on papyrus.

Text (typeface): a typeface meant for bodies of text (e.g. novels, newspaper articles) as opposed to titles or signage.

53224 D

Weight: the darkness of a typeface as an effect of thickness of character outlines relative to height, ranging from "Ultra-light" to "Extra-Black".

X-height: the distance the baseline and mean line as measured by the height of lower-case letters (specifically the lower-case "x") not including ascenders and descenders.

BIBLIOGRAPHY

Yves Perrousseaux
RÈGLES DE L'ÉCRITURE TYPOGRAPHIQUE DU FRANÇAIS
[The Rules of French Typography]
Atelier Perrousseaux

A clear, instructive account of the rules for typographical usage in France, preceded by a concise and pleasant survey of the histories of writing and printing. A reference manual that anyone interested in the field should have on their desk or, better yet, in hand.

Simon Loxley
TYPE: THE SECRET HISTORY OF LETTERS
I.B.Tauris

Biographies of famous typographers punctuated with anecdotes of varying degrees of interest. Light in tone but often enlightening and scholarly in content.

**Collectif,
sous la direction
de Jacques André & Yves Perrousseaux**
HISTOIRE DE L'ÉCRITURE TYPOGRAPHIQUE
[The History of Typography]
Atelier Perrousseaux
[History of Typography, multiple authors, under the direction of Jacques André & Yves Perrousseaux]

The hefty and definitive sum total, in 7 volumes, of typographical knowledge previously scattered to the winds. Educational and well-researched, an exciting, richly illustrated read. Every professional, school, and student of the graphic arts should own this collection.

Lars Müller & Victor Malsy
HELVETICA FOREVER: STORY OF A TYPEFACE
Lars Müller publisher

Without a doubt, the most widely used typeface in the world, and paradoxically, the least well-known, Max Miedinger's Helvetica now has its own reference manual: incredibly well researched and splendidly laid out, this book is a must.

Michel Wlassikoff & Alexandre Dumas de Rauly
FUTURA, UNE GLOIRE TYPOGRAPHIQUE
Éditions Norma

Another reference manual, this time devoted to Paul Renner's Futura and prefaced by designer and publisher Étienne Robial. Documents, layouts, information: all impeccable. Not much to add—or delete.

Simon Garfield
JUST MY TYPE: A BOOK ABOUT FONTS
Gotham Books

A playful and accessible little book about the history of typography, its connotations, etc. A few inaccuracies and errors that will only infuriate purists; others (for whom this book is intended) will be delighted. An excellent place to start exploring the occasionally dry and abstract world of typography.

Gary Hustwit
HELVETICA
Plexifilms

To date, the only documentary film about a typeface. Garlanded with praise and (well-deserved) awards, Gary Hustwit's film is both intriguing and a pleasure to watch. Obviously essential for any lover of typography in general—and Helvetica in particular.

David Rault
GUIDE PRATIQUE DE CHOIX TYPOGRAPHIQUE
[A Practical Guide to Typographical Choices]
Atelier Perrousseaux

As it would be indecent to promote one of my own books, I'll let Gaël Poupard of ffoodd.fr do the talking: "After reading David Rault's book, I must confess that there's no other book like it. The author's goal is to help readers understand the impact a typeface can have and, when the time comes, to choose wisely. He manages to do so in a remarkably simple fashion. I wholeheartedly recommend it!"

CONTRIBUTORS' BIOGRAPHIES

David Rault

Author of *Comicscope* (L'Apocalypse, 2013), *Guide pratique de choix typographique* (2009, new edition revised and enlarged in 2015), *Roger Excoffon, le gentleman de la Typography* (2011), *Jean Alessandrini, le poète de la lettre* (2013), and *Jean François Porchez, l'excellence typographique* (2015, multiple authors), all published by Atelier Perrousseaux. David Rault also contributed to the Rencontres de Lure in August 2011 and leads the annual typography seminar Typex in Bordeaux. He lives and works in Nuremberg, Germany.

Aseyn

Born in 1980, Aseyn studied illustration at the École Estienne, Paris's academy for the printing arts. For the last decade, he has created comics. He is a regular contributor to the series *Les Autres Gens* as well as the magazines *Pandora* and *Topo*, with short strips. He has also authored books including *Le Palais de Glace* and *Nungesser* (with Fred Bernard). His latest work, *Bolchoi Arena* (with Boulet), came out in September 2018 (Éditions Delcourt).

Singeon

After studying graphic design, Singeon attended the Beaux-Arts academy in Paris, where he published his first comics/fanzines. On graduation, he went into comics full-time, learning to place speech balloons while living in garrets (*Bienvenue*, 3 vols. with Marguerite Abouet, Gallimard BD), fry knights in fiery dragon breath (*Tristan & Yseult*, with Agnès Maupré, Gallimard BD), and tell the stories of 2nd-generation Algerian immigrants (*Vacances au bled*, based on a thesis by Jennifer Bidet, Casterman). On his own, he developed oneiric wanderings where his drawings, instead of serving a story, instead supply its impetus.

Libon

Libon was first and foremost a graphic designer of several video games before turning to comics. He published his first full-length story, *Jacques le petit lézard géant*, in *Spirou*; the first volume was published by Dupuis in 2008. Dupuis then put out another series of his, *Les Cavaliers de l'Apocadispe*, about three children and their zany, madcap adventures, as well as *Animal lecteur* written by Sergio Salma. He is also the author of *Tralaland* in *J'aime lire Max* since 2005, and *Hector Kanon* in *Fluide Glacial.*

Seyhan Argun

Seyhan Argun is an illustrator and comics artist based in Istanbul, Turkey, where he was born in 1984. A graduate of the École Saint-Michel in Istanbul, he studied graphic arts at the University of Marmara, and began working as a graphic designer. As an independent illustrator, he published his first strips in several Turkish magazines. His work has been published in France by Éditions Perrousseaux and Éditions Désiris, and in Turkey by Iletisim Yayinlari.

Delphine Panique

Delphine Panique was born in 1981 in the south of France. After years of studying modern literature and much professional tergiversation, she discovered Éditions Misma by accident, and in 2013, they published her first comic: *Orlando*, a very free adaptation of Virginia Woolf's novel, then *En temps de guerre*, a historical chronicle of doubtful accuracy about the First World War. In 2016, she joined the ranks of BD Cul, publisher Requins Marteaux's porn imprint, with the outerspace *Odyssée du vice. Le Vol nocturne*, a fantastical essay about witches, appeared in January 2018 from Éditions Cornélius. Since 2016, she has cartooned about great literary classics in the pages of *Topo*. She lives in Toulouse with her daughter and her cat.

Olivier Deloye

Olivier Deloye was born in Saint-Malo in 1979. He spent his childhood in Senegal, Djibouti, and La Réunion, before heading to Paris. With his science baccalaureate, he started out in creative advertising at a visual communications school. He then worked in children's illustration and corporate communications for a few years. He wrote scripts and fairy tales for children's magazines, and worked on short stories for *J'aime lire*, but his first comics series was *Oliver Twist* (5 vols, Éditions Delcourt, translated into several dozen languages). He now teaches graphic design and typography in Bordeaux.

Hervé Bourhis

Hervé Bourhis was born in Touraine in 1974 and now lives in Bordeaux. Best-known for his books on music, such as *Le Petit Livre Rock* and *Le Petit Livre Black Music*, he is also the author of over thirty graphic novels since 2002, both as writer and writer-artist (*Le Teckel, Naguère les étoiles...*). In addition to his work for the press (*Libération, Télérama*, lemonde.fr, *Spirou, La Revue dessinée...*), Hervé also writes and illustrates for a range of audiovisual media. He received the Prix Goscinny in 2002, the Prix Jacques Lob in 2010, and the Prix Landerneau in 2014.

Alexandre Clérisse

After studies in visual communication, Alexandre Clérisse attended the European School of Visual Arts in Angoulême. There, he finished his first comic, *Jazz Club*, initially published online and then by Dargaud. He was selected for a residency at the Maison des Auteurs in Angoulême, where he wrote and drew *The Bugle Boy* (Dargaud, 2009). At the same time, he contributed to various magazines for children and adults, freelanced in publishing, and designed festival posters. In 2013, he teamed up with Thierry Smolderen for the graphic novel *Atomic Empire* (Dargaud), which received several prizes. In 2016, Dargaud published *Diabolical Summer*, again with Thierry Smolderen. Clérisse also authored a "find the hidden objects" book about movies: *Alfred, Quentin et Pedro sont sur un plateau* (Milan et Demi, 2017).

Anne Simon

Born in 1980 in Deux-Sèvres, Anne Simon lives and works in Paris. In 2004, she won the Prix Jeunes Talents at the Angoulême International Comics Festival, and Éditions Michel Lagarde published her first comic, *Perséphone aux enfers*, in 2006. She published three graphic biographies with Dargaud (*Freud, Marx*, and *Einstein*) in collaboration with writer Corinne Maier. For the last decade, she has been creating the series *Contes du Marylène* for Éditions Misma (3 vols and counting: *La Geste d'Aglaé, Cixtite Impératrice* and *Boris l'enfant patate*). She also works as an illustrator for children's magazines and publishers.

Jake Raynal

After studying applied arts at Paris's printing academy, the École Estienne, Jake Raynal has been making comics since 1994. In *Fluide Glacial*, he published a series of fantastical chronicles that were turned into three books: *Combustion spontanée, Esprit frappeur*, and in 2015, *Les Nouveaux Mystères*. At the same time, he collaborated with Claire Bouilhac on the series *Melody Bondage* and

especially *Francis Blaireau farceur* (7 vols, Éditions Cornélius). *Cambrioleurs*, his first foray into adventure comics, came out in 2013 (Casterman), followed in 2017 by a volume of the Little Comics Library of Knowledge devoted to the Situationists (with Christophe Bourseiller, Éditions du Lombard). With David Servenay, he created *La Septième Arme* (Éditions La Découverte, 2018).

François Ayroles

François Ayroles was born in Paris in 1969. A graduate of the European School of Visual Arts in Angoulême, he has worked with the independent publisher L'Association since 1994, and joined their editorial board in 2011. He has also published comics with mainstream publishers (Casterman, Dargaud, Delcourt, Dupuis) and alternative imprints (Alain Beaulet, Denoël Graphic, L'An 2...), alone and in collaboration (Ted Benoit, Anne Baraou). He also does illustrations for children's and adult magazines. He is a member of the Workshop for Potential Comics, OuBaPo (Ouvroir de Bande Dessinée Potentielle), an experimental comics group.

Jean Alessandrini

Illustrator, typographer, and author (of over forty books), Jean Alessandrini began an apprenticeship in design at the Corvisart High School for Graphic Arts in Paris before joining Raymond Gid's studio, which he soon left to strike out on his own. He has designed many logos and illustrations for *Elle, Lui, Paris Match, Pilote, J'aime lire*, and publishers Gallimard and Marabout. In 1980 he created Codex, a system for classifying typefaces, and has designed highly successful several typefaces distributed by the Hollenstein foundry in the 1970s. He lives and works in Strasbourg.

ACKNOWLEDGMENTS

A big thank-you to all the creatives who came along with me on this wonderful adventure
(I hope they know I am immensely and sincerely grateful to them),
as well as Jean Alessandrini for his beautiful preface.

Thank you to Jean-Christophe Menu for bringing his illuminating talents
as a graphic and book designer to the project.

Thanks, too, to Gallimard, and especially to Nicolas Leroy and Thierry Laroche
for believing in this project and supporting it, come wind and weather
(and storms sometimes more violent than anticipated).

Thank you to Emma Hayley, Guillaume Rater, Sam Humphrey
and everyone at SelfMadeHero for so beautifully bringing
this book to English-speaking readers.

More generally, thank you to all the men and women who supported this book
in one way or another, from the beginning. They know who they are.

My deepest gratitude goes to Michel Mirale and the late Yves Perrousseaux,
without whom I wouldn't be where I am today.

And thank you, it goes without saying, to Özge and Anton.
This book is for you.

DAVID RAULT